CRIMINAL LEGAL DOCTRINE

Criminal Legal Doctrine

Edited by

PETER RUSH
SHAUN MCVEIGH
ALISON YOUNG

Ashgate

DARTMOUTH
Aldershot • Brookfield USA • Singapore • Sydney

Published by
Dartmouth Publishing Company Limited
Ashgate Publishing Limited
Gower House
Croft Road
Aldershot
Hants GU11 3HR
England

Ashgate Publishing Company
Old Post Road
Brookfield
Vermont 05036
USA

British Library Cataloguing in Publication Data
Criminal legal doctrine
  1.Criminal law
  I.Rush, Peter II.McVeigh, Shaun, 1947- III. Young, Alison
  345

Library of Congress Cataloging-in-Publication Data
Criminal legal doctrine / edited by Peter Rush, Shaun McVeigh, Alison
  Young.
     p. cm.
  Includes bibliographical references.
  ISBN 1-85521-969-7
  1. Criminal law--Philosophy. 2. Law and ethics. I. Rush, Peter.
II. McVeigh, Shaun, 1947- . III. Young, Alison, 1962- .
  K5018.C76 1997
  345'.001--dc21   97-19615
                                                                       CIP
ISBN 1 85521 969 7

Printed in Great Britain by Galliard (Printers) Ltd, Great Yarmouth

Contents

List of Contributors

Lindsay Farmer is a Lecturer in the Department of Law, Birkbeck College, England. He is the author of a monograph on criminal law and tradition (Cambridge University Press, 1996) as well as articles on the jurisprudence of criminal law. His current research is on the history of codification.

Yifat Hachamovitch has taught at several universities in the United States. Her published work includes articles on philosophy and legal theory, and she is a co-editor of *Politics, Postmodernity and Critical Legal Studies* (Routledge, 1994). She is currently completing a book on psychoanalysis and the law.

Piyel Haldar is a Lecturer in the Department of Law, Birkbeck College, University of London. He is the author of articles on the aesthetics of law, legal history and legal theory, as well as a forthcoming monograph on evidence and the semiosis of the legal institution.

Gerry Johnstone is a Lecturer in the Department of Law, University of Hull, England. He is the author of *Medical Concepts and Penal Policy* (Cavendish, 1996) as well as articles on the therapeutic interventions of criminal justice. His current research interest is in social control and popular justice.

Shaun McVeigh is a Senior Lecturer in the Faculty of Law, Griffith University, Brisbane. He is the co-author of *Postmodern Jurisprudence* (Routledge, 1991), co-editor of *Law, Health and Medical Regulation* (Dartmouth, 1992), and is currently working on issues of medico-legal ethics.

Leslie J. Moran is a Senior Lecturer in the Department of Law, University of Lancaster, England. His published work includes articles on company law and gay legal politics. He is the author of *The Homosexual(ity) of Law* (Routledge, 1996) and co-editor of a forthcoming collection on legal perversions.

Alan Norrie is a Professor in Queen Mary and Westfield College, University of London. He is the author of several books on criminal law, the philosophy of punishment and legal theory, including *Crime, Reason and History* (Weidenfeld & Nicolson, 1993).

Peter Rush is a Senior Lecturer in the School of Law, Deakin University, Australia. He is the author of *Beyond the Edge* (George Allen & Unwin, 1985), *Criminal Law* (Butterworths, 1997) and *Trials of Sex* (Routledge, forthcoming) as well as articles on legal education, legal theory and indigenous law. His current thinking concerns questions of criminal jurisdiction, architecture and aboriginal legal politics.

Alison Young is a Senior Lecturer in the Department of Criminology, University of Melbourne, Australia. She is the author of *Femininity in Dissent* (Routledge, 1990) and most recently *Imagining Crime* (Sage, 1995); she has also written numerous articles on the intersections of law and feminist theory. Her current research concerns the reproductive technologies of law, and art as a mode of criminal aesthetics.

Editorial Introduction

PETER RUSH, SHAUN MCVEIGH & ALISON YOUNG

It could be argued that the central concern of criminal law is that it wants and lacks a corpus, a teaching, a subject. One of the most persistent moves of legal thought has been to associate criminal law with the loss of order and the restoration of law. In thinking about this association and its thematics, a useful entry-point is to elaborate the problematic of loss and restoration as a question of the status of doctrine in contemporary legal thought. In general terms, the several essays of this collection address the peculiar and uncanny commonplace that doctrine is the subject of law. Their theme is the various and varied relations between law, doctrine and crime. The problem, as we see it, is that there is a recurrent or structural tendency to collapse or compress each of these instances into a single identity. Law, doctrine, crime: all seemingly occupy the place of the subject of law. At the same time it seems that something has been misplaced, so to speak, in the advent of criminal law. It appears that the struggle to place the teachings and arguments of law within a legal order has been lost — and with this, the possibility of interrogating the structural site of the enunciation of law, the power and authority to speak in the name of the law. Such is the predicament that is addressed here in a number of different contexts and in a variety of ways.

The essays collected here fall roughly into three parts, corresponding to the general elements of the dogmatic tradition of law: namely, the questioning of address, of institution, of judgment.

Under the question of address, Alan Norrie reconsiders the issue of community in the context of the moral debate over responsibility. Taking the responsibility of and for James Bulger as a starting point for a series of more general reflections on the relations between law and community, Norrie argues that there has been a hardening or sclerosis of the legal narrative of moral responsibility and intentional agency. His essay ends by suggesting possible ways of reformulating the persistence of community within law. On the other hand, Yifat Hachamovitch investigates the places of intention in law, by following the phantasmatic resonances of intention and murder over the *longue durée* of law. What is recovered in her essay is the address of malice as a doctrinal mode of communication and, in a phenomenological turn, the attachment of that order of fiction to the corporeality of law.

The essays by Lindsay Farmer, Gerry Johnstone and Piyel Haldar are primarily concerned with the questioning of institution. Farmer takes his cue from Blackstone's cartographic metaphor of law, and investigates the forgotten substrate of criminal law in terms of the institution of jurisdiction in both its physical and metaphysical aspects. The elements of this jurisdiction emerge, for Farmer, in the transformation of criminal procedure over the course of the nineteenth century. The institution of criminal law is thus returned to its fundamental adhesion with procedure. Gerry Johnstone's essay also returns to the nineteenth century but this time to reconsider the contemporary relations between penality and psychiatry. These relations involve not only professional and administrative boundaries but also the conceptual representations or rhetorical processes which institute those boundaries. What emerges is a complex of connections and rapprochements between law and psychiatry, but also and just as importantly the mutual misrecognition of both law and psychiatry. By way of this thick description, Johnstone reformulates the possibilities of exchange between criminal law and the psy-disciplines. One context for the essay by Haldar is the relationship of criminal law with medicine and its order of symptomatology. In his investigation of the institutional and adjudicative logics of criminal law, Haldar explores the sacrifices upon which are predicated the various types of criminal legal processes and, specifically, trial by jury and its precursors. Finally, he follows that order of sacrifice as it is thrown within the modern legal forensics of *mens rea*.

The essays by Alison Young and Leslie Moran are concerned primarily with the questioning of judgment. Young's essay pursues the manner of the juridical reconstruction of the event as the facts of legal judgment. It provides a case study of the imbrication of the victims of conjugal violence and the victims of legal order. What is investigated is the differential affect of judgment, so as to exhibit the narration of sexual difference and the violence that inhabits law. Young ends by engaging in a questioning of the mode and manner of judicial responsibility in and for judgment. The essay by Moran is concerned with judgment as a structure of representation. Its particular focus is the issue of corporate capacity as the subject-matter of both criminal and civil law. Putting to one side the recurrent formulation of law as an administrative exercise directed at the corporate legal subject, Moran pursues the modern history of the grammar and symbolic form of corporate responsibility in law. Moran argues that the incorporation of the corporation in law is governed by an anthropomorphic order of speech, a metaphorical fiction which both creates the corporate legal entity and the difficulties or unintelligibility of corporate criminal responsibility for law.

As a conclusion and exergue to the collection, the last two essays by McVeigh and Rush, and Rush return to the formal structuring of the idiom of doctrine and its rewriting by law and jurisprudence. What is investigated is the division of modern criminal law into a theory of moral responsibility and a theory of action — and its consequences for the subject of law. The final essay by Rush restages the life of criminal law in terms of its transmission and, specifically, the biography of inheritance. Taking James Fitzjames Stephen as exemplary, the essays retrace the return of doctrine as the repressed grounds of law, not so much to refound law but to rewrite the predicament in which criminal law is found.

* * *

This is also the predicament of the apostrophe. Over the time of putting together this collection, we have incurred debts of gratitude and friendship: the contributors, the students in the criminal law and evidence courses at Lancaster University (1988–1995), Costas Douzinas, Danielle Go, Peter Goodrich, Niki Lacey, Elena Loizidou and C-A Bois. We take this chance to remember Ronnie Warrington.

Melbourne, Australia

1 Legal and Moral Judgment in the 'General Part'

ALAN NORRIE

[I]ntentional agency provides the paradigm of responsible agency. This is why intention is the central or paradigm determinant of moral culpability.... As with morality, so with law. (Duff, 1990, 102)

We possess indeed simulacra of morality, we continue to use many of the key expressions. But we have — very largely, if not entirely — lost our comprehension, both theoretical and practical, of morality. (MacIntyre, 1985, 2)

Introduction[1]

In the dominant view, criminal law contains a 'general part' containing principles and rules which reflect a philosophical understanding of the relationship between the individual, law and the state. This liberal and Kantian understanding is elegantly expressed by Andrew Ashworth (Ashworth, 1991) in the idea of respect for individual autonomy, from which stems desert for punishment. Criminal law is, or should be, reflective of the idea of individual choice, and penal sanction should only follow a freely chosen act. From these premises is born the subjective approach to criminal law principles affirming the need for intention, foresight, knowledge and belief concerning actions and their consequences. These constitute, in Ashworth's terminology, the 'positive fault requirements' which have to be established in order to prove an offence (Ashworth, 1991, ch. 6). Beyond these, however, there exist certain 'negative fault requirements' which operate to supplement and qualify judgments of responsibility that might otherwise be made on the basis of the positive requirements (Ashworth, 1991, ch. 6). Into this category, there fall the various 'defences' — 'excuses' and (on some analyses)[2] 'justifications' — which may negate responsibility otherwise established on the basis of the positive criteria.

It is this relatively simple picture of a general part consisting of acts and mental elements, qualified by justificatory and excusatory defences, and based

1

upon principles of individual autonomy, that I wish ultimately to examine. This picture does however have one complication worth mentioning, for Ashworth notes 'how individualistic, even atomistic, are the assumptions implicit in the liberal theory which underlies the subjective principles' (Ashworth, 1991, 132). No person is an island, and the subjective approach must sometimes be restricted in the light of the demands of social defence 'which one can expect to suffer in a society based on mutual co-operation' (Ashworth, 1991, 132). Restrictions of this kind in the criminal law directly affect the 'general part', for example in the law of recklessness, where obviousness of risk supplements foresight as a ground of liability.

This approach is attractive both for its image of a society resting on individual autonomy and social cooperation, and for its simplicity. It seems to provide a relatively straightforward basis for organising the criminal law, and it is also compelling because of the relationship it posits between legal and moral judgment. At one level it is an axiom of liberal theory that there is a division between law and morals, so that legal and moral justice are essentially different. Max Weber expressed this in terms of the distinction between law's formal rationality (decisions deduced from existing rules) and substantive rationality (decisions based upon substantive ethical ideas). But it is important to note that the separation of 'legal form' and 'moral content' does not mean that legal judgments of responsibility are in this view lacking in moral significance. On the contrary, legal justice, though separated from morals and politics, is still regarded as morally legitimate and legitimating because it is based upon respect for individual autonomy in a world based upon social cooperation. There is therefore, as the prefatory quotation from Duff proposes, a homology between the principles of the general part and broader principles of moral justice. The spirit of Kantianism within the criminal law informs this overlap between judgments in law and in morality. Legal judgment is understood as a form of moral judgment — a morality of form — in the liberal tradition.

I want to question the adequacy of the liberal tradition in relation to those aspects that I have said make it attractive. I will argue that the image of individual and social life that it produces is indeed partial; that the simplicity of its schema is ultimately simplistic; and that a key problem stems from the Kantian nexus between legal and moral judgment. I shall make three arguments against the idea that legal judgment shadows or reflects moral judgment. The first is that legal judgments based upon the responsibility of the subject fundamentally fail to capture the nature of moral judgments about responsibility for wrongdoing; indeed, they act as barriers to such judgments.

The argument here (which is in the spirit of the prefatory quotation from MacIntyre) starts from the same critical observation as Ashworth, that liberal theory is too individualistic and atomistic in its conception of human subjectivity, but it takes it in a different direction. Rather than moving to social policy ideas as an alternative justificatory basis for legal judgment, I ask how these notions of individualism and atomism structure legal judgments of guilt (section 2). I argue that they lead to a hardening and narrowing, a sclerosis, of judgment that drives a wedge between legal and moral judgment and, in the extreme case, paralyses society's ability to judge crime. I illustrate this by discussing the recent trial of two small boys for the killing of James Bulger.

My second argument is that the legal sclerosis of moral judgment is the result of a historical and political process of suppression of alternative moral and political judgments to those that ushered in our modern world of private property and crime (section 2). The modern legal combination of formalism and individualism (the 'atomism' to which Ashworth refers) involves a complex separation *and* identification between legal and moral judgment. This is based on the figure of the responsible individual deserving punishment under formal law. Despite the division between law and morals, the form of the abstract responsible individual permits a morality of form to be built on the back of the law. The abstract legal individual, deserving punishment under formal law, appears to 'rise above' morals and politics understood substantively, and therefore to constitute a formalistic legitimating basis for the judgment (and punishment) of conduct.[3] I will argue that the legal individual is not morally and politically neutral. It is the site of inclusion of certain moral and political views and exclusion of others. The moral and political neutrality of the legal subject, on which is based the formal morality and legi-timacy of modern legal judgment, is only an appearance, although an appearance which has important practical effects. I will illustrate this in the second section by focusing on a primary separation that occurred in the crimi-nal law at the end of the eighteenth and beginning of the nineteenth centuries, a separation of motive and intention, which helped induce the sclerosis within legal judgment.

My third argument is that the division between legal and moral judgment, whose practical effects and historical roots have already been examined, informs and undermines the logical structure of the law's general part, and especially the particular combination of mental element, justification and excuse (section 3). This conceptual trinity, which is central to law's 'architectonic of judgment', is a historically specific combination of elements which operates to suppress deeper moral and political issues within the law, and to maintain a morality of form. These deeper issues, however, are only artificially repressed and therefore continue to irrupt within sophisticated analyses of the logic of the general part. In this section I consider in particular Antony Duff's work on intention, justification and excuse (Duff, 1990), which I see as an attempt to rationalise and defend legal judgment, but one which exposes in the process its fragile, irrational and repressive character.

Finally, in a concluding section, I will relate the discussion of the nature of legal and moral judgment to broader questions of the possibility of judgment in modern society with reference to themes in the work of Alasdair MacIntyre (MacIntyre, 1985). I begin, however, with a case which illustrates more practically the difference between legal and moral judgment, and the significance of legal judgment in our society.

1. The Guilt of Children and the Sins of their Fathers

Sentencing two 11-year-olds found guilty of the murder of two-year-old James Bulger, Mr Justice Moreland described their crime as 'a cunning and wicked act of "unparalleled evil and barbarity"'.[4] Echoing this condemnation of the boys, a senior policeman stated that 'These two were freaks who just found each other. You should not compare these two boys with other boys — they were evil'. As they were driven from the courtroom, their departure was accompanied by shouts of 'kill them' and 'hang them' from an awaiting crowd. In a rare show of moral and social solidarity, a discourse of individual wickedness and evil had united the bench, the police and the crowd in judgment against two boys who, at the age of 10, had committed so terrible a crime. Such a judgment is not incidental to the law, it is sanctioned by it. The law itself allows a 10-year-old to be found criminally responsible, and normal rules of *mens rea* may apply.[5] Such a person can be as guilty in the eyes of the law as any adult of the most serious offence. England has a low age of crimi-nal responsibility compared with France (13), Germany (14), Norway (15) or Spain (16) (though not with Scotland where the age is 8), yet there was some concern expressed after the trial that the age of responsibility might not be low enough, for, had the boys been eight months younger at the time of the killing, they could have escaped punishment altogether.

These categorical judgments of guilt and wickedness were undercut as soon as they were uttered. Mr Justice Moreland undermined his own view of the boys' wickedness with his accompanying evaluation (presented as a non-judgment) of their families. 'It is not for me to pass judgment on their upbringing, but I suspect exposure to violent video films may be part of an explanation.' Similarly the Detective Superintendent in charge of the investigation could say both that the boys 'had a high degree of cunning and evil' and that why the boys committed the killing 'will not be known for some time'. Yet, if believed, the former view can be a complete answer to the latter question: the boys killed precisely because they were 'cunning and evil'. Another policeman contrasted what he saw as the chilling coldness of one of the boys in the police station with the evening he went with three other burly officers to pick him up, and found only a small boy in pyjamas coming down the stairs. In order to interview and 'take instructions' from this boy, his solicitor had to sit and play a Gameboy with him for hours.

The legal attitude evinced in these judgments permits a narrow, essentially unreflective attitude to the question of individual responsibility and guilt. It does not look beyond the individual and his or her act. When a person viewed in this way does something terrible, there is no need for recourse to anything other than an abstract metaphysical conception of wickedness to explain what happened. A disembodied concept of responsibility for crime calls forth an equally disembodied explanation of its genesis. In the legal gaze, the boys in this case can be 'evil', yet their childishness evokes a sense of their innocence as victims themselves. They are constructed as juvenile Jekyll and Hydes — unconnected embodiments of good (as children) and evil (as killers).

Of course, other judgments abound in this case. There are the judgments of the child care experts who see 'disordered and emotionally inadequate families' and educational problems, problems of inadequate parents breeding inadequate children in a cycle of deprivation. There are the judgments of the environmentalists who see inner city living, social deprivation and poverty as the root causes. Yet none of these judgments seems entirely adequate either: many families would be classified under the headings of the child care experts, and an increasing number of children live in deprived inner city conditions, yet few commit the kind of crime that these boys did in Liverpool. Somehow, a convincing account evades us. In these circumstances, it is tempting to follow the line argued by some in the government and the media[6] that this was an isolated event from which there is nothing to be learnt. Yet this is surely unsatisfactory too. The problem is that all these judgments try to understand an event that can only be judged in terms of its synthetic combination of social levels and individual factors united in one incident. It is a 'one-off case' that paradoxically is not a one-off case because it mixes social, educational and familial circumstances with individual chemistry in a way that turns two not uncommon boys into killers. In the words of another 10-year-old Walton kid, 'They were just your average scruff — like the rest of us'. Sometimes 'your average scruff' do cruel, violent things, which is to say neither that most do, nor that those who do are in some way fundamentally different from the rest.

The situation calls for a form of judgment that can unite appreciation of social and political environment with individual agency. Such a form is extremely hard for the representatives of our various institutions — the government, the media, the law, the caring professions, the police — to arrive at. The scale of the tragedy of the death of this child, and the way it happened, sits uneasily with the simplistic judgments that have been made as to the causes and who was to blame. Yet the trial of the boys who killed James Bulger highlights a general issue of judgment about crime and punishment, one that is more starkly seen in this case because of the age and vulnerability of the killers,[7] as well as their victim. I suggest that the failure to find adequate judgments in such a case is in substantial measure a result of the primacy that society gives to law and legal judgment in the way that it looks at these matters. Law is the organising discourse for a process of judgment that ramifies far beyond the courtroom. Its easy accounts of guilt and innocence and good and bad, echoed by judges and police, and broadcast through the media, constitute society's starting point. Thus *The Guardian* front page on the day following the convictions headlines its reportage with the moment of criminal guilt ('Boys Guilty of Bulger Murder'), and then, at the foot of the page, begins the analysis which, potentially, subverts the banner headline ('Two Youngsters Who Found a New Rule to Break'). *The Guardian* is known for its attention to social issues and does at least give these other accounts some significance, but they are afforded a secondary position to that founded upon the law.

In any case, because of law's hegemony, such accounts tend to accommodate themselves to the law. Psychiatrists, who could provide an alternative account of crime in such cases, have testified to the law's (recently abandoned) 'knowledge of wrongdoing' test, and, with other behavioural experts, accept the law's standard of normal responsible conduct from which they construct an image of the abnormal individual as the exception to the law's rule. On the other hand, social environmentalists, focusing on the conditions of crime, hardly address the question of why *this* person committed the crime, leaving the field of individual responsibility unchallenged by default. Politically, this may lead to a dualistic affirmation of the need both for a system of law that is hard on criminals, and a policy to address the criminogenic environment ('tough on crime, tough on the causes of crime'). Legal judgments, in other words, still set the agenda, and structure the field in which other discourses have their play. What they produce, routinely, is a kind of 'rush to judgment' in which precious few are able to catch their breath and look beyond the easy answers. We only notice this in a case like that of the two boys in the James Bulger case, for the combination of their age and the horror of their acts challenges the narrow and bounded categories of responsibility we employ.

Taking all the views that have been proffered, it is not that the prime candidates for moral judgment are wrongly identified; it is rather the methodology by which they are judged, and the resultant quality of the judgments, that is at fault. The process of judgment must take in the broader environment, social policy and conditions, because these establish the circumstances under which family life occurs and children grow up. It also includes the parents of the children, the surrounding neighbourhood, and ultimately the broader society. These are not easy judgments, they are multi-sided *and* particularistic, recognising circumstance *in the moment of* individual agency (or omission). They must also, I suggest, include the two boys because they were actors in their own 10-year-old way, and, treated with compassion, they will have to come to terms with what they did. Their crime has, as Hegel put it, a 'positive existence' for them (Hegel, 1952, 69).[8]

Such a complex process of judgment, which involves all sections of the community, cannot be encapsulated in the finding of a criminal court on the basis of black and white categories of guilt and innocence or good and evil. The law's wigs and gowns lend only a spurious *gravitas* because the legal categories hypostatise rather than contextualise. They separate event from structure and history, and fragment moments of socially produced agency. This is convenient administratively, for it identifies processable individual subjects, and politically, since it produces ready scapegoats and easy 'law and order' solutions for complex social phenomena, but the judgments it produces are facile and backward looking.

If this criticism appears abstract and hypothetical, I suggest that one very concrete indication of the inadequacy of a legal discourse of judgment is the failure of a social control system imbued with it to come up with any plausible view of how one might avoid a repetition of so horrid an event as the killing of James Bulger, hence the 'wisdom' that there is nothing to be learnt. In reality, there is nothing that *can* be learned because the discursive categories organise out the possibility. It is true that the legal process does have its immediate effects, both psychological and political, and some of these, for the victim's family for example, are positive. A public record of wrong done seems to help the process of mourning. But in the long run, for society at large, one effect is to trivialise the issues, to provide easy solutions by means of an individualistic and momentary focus upon a complex social phenomenon embodied in individual agency.[9] Like others before, the social memory of James Bulger and his killers will fade, but only until the next time, when we again witness the demonisation of lost innocents in a world they cannot comprehend.

2. Law's Sclerosis of Judgment: The Separation of Motive and Intention

The argument of the previous section suggests the failure of law to reflect a deeper moral sense of judgment which *synthesises* contextual social particularity with the normative appraisal of individual agency. The James Bulger case is not exceptional, only stark in its exemplification of the point because of the age of the killers. The legal judgment simply fails to reflect a broader moral judgment of the wrongdoing in this case.

The general problem is witnessed in the murder cases of recent years where there is an important gap between the legal concepts mobilised to judge deaths, and the moral quality of the killings. The main legal concept is that of an intention to kill or cause grievous bodily harm (the *mens rea* of murder), yet the haphazard progress from *DPP v Smith* ([1961] AC 290) and *Hyam v DPP* ([1974] 2 All ER 41) through to *R v Moloney* ([1985] 1 All ER 1025), *R v Hancock & Shankland* ([1986] AC 455) and *R v Nedrick* ([1986] 1 WLR 1025) suggests a deeper normative agenda that is unsatisfied by the law of intention. As Lacey, Wells and Meure put it, the legal categories of judgment operate, inadequately, in the place of proper moral judgments:

> Although often obscured by the conceptual apparatus of the law with its use of mental elements as a means of delineation, a moral judgment is also being made.... [T]here is an ever more desperate search for a magic formula whereby the murderer can be distinguished from the man-slaughterer through the use of the notion of intention.
>
> (Lacey et al., 1990, 268)[10]

In the law of murder, the legal definition does not distinguish actions that are substantially dissimilar from a moral point of view, for example the difference between a contract killer and a mercy killer. The legal categories have to be teased and twisted to reflect the moral quality of killings in particular cases. A man who shoots his beloved stepfather in a drunken race to load a gun after a family party (*Moloney*) is not morally the same as a woman who puts petrol through a letter box and kills two young girls in order to frighten (*Hyam*), or two striking miners who drop a concrete block off a bridge to obstruct a motor convoy and kill a taxi driver (*Hancock & Shankland*). All three are cases in which the law of oblique intention is manipulated to produce a legal judgment that in some ways matches a sense of moral culpability. This is not possible without substantial conceptual discomfort within the law.

What is lacking in all these cases, and within the law, is consideration of the different contexts and motivations that gave rise to these deaths. There is a moral decontextualisation at work, which we can approach by examining the division between motive and intention within legal judgment. This division, I will argue, is one root source of law's moral problems, and is central to its general conceptual organisation, its architectonic, of judgment.

I begin by examining two alternative discourses which historically threatened the discourse of the responsible subject within the criminal law.[11] The first is a discourse of need, the second a discourse of competing (counter) right. The former states that a person broke the law because of acute personal or familial need. The latter claims that the breaking of the law was not wrong in the first place, but was legitimate in itself. If the social world was one of economic plenty and broad political and moral consensus, the law might dismiss such claims as impertinent or cranky. Where, however, processed criminality was (and is) structurally linked to social differentiation, economic inequality, and to the protection of a particular socio-political order, this is not always so easy. The problems of need and counter-right were confronted by criminal lawyers from the late seventeenth through to the early nineteenth century when capitalism was developing and consolidating its hold upon social relations, and when the liberal ideology of individual subjectivity was dominant. That ideology could not immediately rule out disruptive discourses of need and counter-right. The legal task at hand was to draw the boundaries of the legal subject-citizen in a way that 'respected' his or her liberty and freedom, but not too much.

One central element in the lawyers' strategy was the division of motive and intention. A modern conception of mentality conceived of the individual as a purposive actor acting in the context of his or her environment, reacting to the opportunities and constraints which surround him or her. This was represented as a modern subjectivity of intention and motive. Both could be, and were, taken as universal features of subjectivity: everyone forms intentions to act regardless of who they are, whence they come, what they experience; everyone experiences the force of desires and fears, and is motivated by them to action. But motive could go further: it could contextualise the subject in his or her social and political environment. The poor and dispossessed could say that their motive was need, or could claim that they acted on right. Motive represented a threat to the law, and was therefore excised from legal subjectivity, from the juridical attributes of responsible citizenship. Abstract mental states of intention, recklessness and agency were constructed as *the* moments of liberal legal subjectivity, to the exclusion of motive.

Theft occasioned by hunger was known as the 'common excuse' in eighteenth-century England. Writing in the seventeenth century, Hale noted the significance of motive only once in his criminal law treatise, and that was in order to reject it. Larceny born out of hunger or lack of clothing remained 'a felony and a crime by the laws of England punishable with death' where there existed the *intention* to steal (Hale, 1736, 54). At the beginning of the modern period of development of a systematic criminal law, the early Victorian Criminal Law Commissioners quoted with approval the judicial comment that '[w]e must not steal leather to make poor men's shoes' and the 'compassionate' words of the Scots criminal lawyer Hume:

> Whatsoever be the cause which impels a person to the doing of those things, which are destructive of the interest or bonds of society, his will is not on that account the less vicious or his nature the less depraved.
>
> (Criminal Law Commissioners, 1843, 29)

Hume constructs the issue in terms of the breach of a universal social interest (the 'bonds of society'), but universality was proclaimed in opposition to the interests of the poor, for whom poverty was endemic. As an excuse, however, it cut little ice.

The second cause of the rule concerns not the denial of motive out of compassion, where compassion threatened to undermine private property, but the squashing of alternative definitions of right and wrong. The poor might not just claim an absence of malice but the positive existence of rightful or good motive on their side. E.P. Thompson made the point well:

> Viewed from [the commoners'] standpoint, the communal forms expressed an alternative notion of possession, in the petty and particular rights and usages which were transmitted in custom as the *properties* of the poor. Common right ... was *local*

right, and hence was also a power to exclude strangers. Enclosure, in taking the commons away from the poor, made them strangers in their own land.

(Thompson, 1991, 184)

A new universal definition of right and wrong was sought that could legitimate property expropriation within new relations of production. It was the political success of these classes in forcing their interest and will that ensured that the legal reformers could express legal rules, which were the product of sharp social conflicts, in terms of consensus, good common sense and opposition to anarchy. The rule of private property became the 'rule of law', so that attacks on the former could be condemned as attacks on a universal social good. Instrumental in this process was the creation of an abstract and formal definition of human subjectivity that would cut off reference to substantive moral argument. This abstract and formal conception of human subjectivity was central to both the philosophy and criminal law of the period:

The motive by which an offender was influenced, as distinguished from his intention, is never material to an offence. If the prohibited act be done, and be done with the intention by law essential to the offence, it is complete, without reference either to any ulterior intention or to the motive which gave birth to the intention.

To allow any man to substitute for law his own notions of right, would be in effect to subvert the law ... [A] man's private opinion could not possibly be allowed to weigh against the authority of the law ... though he (the offender) thought that the act was innocent, or even meritorious. (Criminal Law Commissioners, 1843, 29)[12]

But legal formalism cut both ways. In choking off alternative moral and political voices and social arrangements, legal formalism also constricted its own potential for moral judgment. It is that constriction that lies at the heart of the criminal law today. We see it, as I have shown, in the law of murder, where a reliance simply on intention to kill or cause grievous bodily harm provides an ineffective basis for the judgment of the moral quality of killings. James Bulger's killers, under the law's definition — its formal moral arrangements — are as guilty as anyone who intends to kill or do grievous bodily harm. This is juridically simple, but morally simplistic. What is lacking is a synthetic view of the relationship between mental state, social context and criminal act, but the possibility of synthesising different aspects of responsibility and judgment was consciously suppressed in the foundation of the modern criminal law.[13] The apparent neutrality of the criminal law's individualist concepts of responsibility was achieved at the cost of neutering the process of judgment.[14] Law represents a simulacrum, a pale and ambiguous *doppel-ganger*, of moral judgment. However, in the dominant view, represented in the prefatory quote from Duff, moral and legal judgment are homologous. In the next section, I explore the way in which this relationship is presented in legal theory, and the flaws within it.

3. Law's Architectonic of Judgment

In the standard view, the structure of criminal law involves a 'general part' which applies *ceteris paribus* to the specific offences. The general part is composed of *actus reus* and *mens rea*, which occupy the central position.[15] While acts and intentions are central to the establishment of criminal responsibility, general defences incorporating ideas of justification and excuse may operate where *actus reus* and *mens rea* have already been established in order to exonerate the accused according to the nature of the defence he or she has invoked. It is this conception of a general part in which *mens rea* is central to legal judgment, while defences of justification and excuse are regarded as secondary and exceptional, that I describe as the architectonic of legal judgment. It is presented in orthodox accounts as commonsensical and rational (if problematic in its detail), but I will argue that this particular shape of the categories of judgment is the result of the process of scleroticisation described above.

According to Antony Duff, intention is integral to human action, and intended and intentional agency form the central paradigms of responsible agency. This is true in both law and morality, so that Duff affirms this homology:

> The underlying assumption here is that criminal liability should, in principle, be ascribed in accordance with moral responsibility. A defendant should be criminally liable only for conduct for which she can properly be held morally responsible or culpable.... That is why *mens rea* should be required for criminal liability, and why intention should be the most serious kind of criminal fault.
>
> (Duff, 1990, 103)

Duff's analysis is however ambivalent in its effect. On the one hand, intention in his account is central to both legal and moral responsibility, so that he seeks to rationalise the morality of form that legal judgment entails. On the other hand, because of the rigour of his exposition and his commitment to an interpretivist approach to judgment, Duff ends up by showing the irrational and morally suppressive character of judgment within law's architectonic. I deal with this in relation to three aspects of Duff's work. The first concerns Duff's account of the relationship between intention, justification and excuse; the second involves Duff's account of the nature of intentional agency; and the third relates to Duff's critique of what he describes as the orthodox consequentialist and dualist account of criminal responsibility. My argument will be that in all three areas, Duff's discussion reveals the impossibility of maintaining a separation of questions of intention (form) from the broader context of normative judgment (content) in which they are constructed. The morality of form, with intention as its anchor concept, is shown to be irredeemably infected with, and unsustainable apart from, the broader normative context within which perforce it operates.

Intention, Justification and Excuse

A central question for any explanation of law's architectonic of judgment is why *mens rea* has pole position ahead of questions of justification and excuse. There is a *prima facie* problem, as Duff notes. Questions of *mens rea* may not be sufficient to establish criminal guilt, for an act may be intended, yet be justified or excused. This raises the question whether intended agency is truly the central question for criminal responsibility as contended, or whether matters of justification and excuse have overriding importance. As regards justification, Duff argues that this *prima facie* case can be countered:

> One who justifies her action is prepared to *answer* for it, by showing it to be right: the possibility of avoiding blame or criminal liability by justifying our intended or intentional actions, therefore, does not undermine the claim that intended and intentional actions are paradigms of responsible agency.
>
> (Duff, 1990, 100)

As regards the latter, excuses operate with, not against, intentional agency, for they 'at least qualify, even if they do not wholly rebut, the ascription of intended or intentional agency' (Duff, 1990, 100). Justification and excuse issues are therefore compatible with the centrality of intended and intentional agency to moral and legal culpability. The relationship is complementary rather than contradictory.

Dealing first with justification, Duff's analysis of the relationship between justification and intention hinges upon his understanding of responsibility, which is cast in terms of answering for one's actions:

> To act with the intention of bringing a result about is to make myself fully
> responsible for that result — I must be ready to answer for (to explain, to justify,
> to accept criticism for) my action of bringing it about; and I bring about intentionally
> those effects for which I am held responsible. (Duff, 1990, 99)

Hart has shown, however, that there are a number of different meanings of the word 'responsibility' (Hart, 1968, ch. 9), and although he does not identify Duff's conception of 'being called to respond' as one of them, it is doubtful whether this idea fits with either legal or moral notions of responsibility. What Duff, I think, is looking for (or at least needs) is something like Hart's account of 'moral liability-responsibility'. For Hart too, there is substantial homology between legal and moral responsibility. Differences, he says, 'are due to substantive differences between the content of legal and moral rules and principles rather than to any variation in meaning of responsibility' (Hart, 1968, 225–6). But Hart explains such responsibility not in terms of being 'called to respond', but in terms of being 'morally blameworthy, or morally obliged to make amends for the harm' (Hart, 1968, 225). Duff's account by comparison appears to describe a preliminary situation prior to that of ascribing blame, in which the issue of blameworthiness has yet to be settled. To be 'called to answer' is, put simply, not the same as to 'have one's answers found wanting'.

Because the concept of responsibility-as-answerability does not settle the issue of responsibility-as-blameworthiness, it cannot settle the proper relationship between intention and justification with regard to culpability. At best, it gives rise to a kind of prima facie culpability,[16] but even this is questionable, for even such culpability depends on a proper allocation of matters of justification alongside intention. Yet this is Duff's chosen means of reconciling justification with intention.

As regards excuse, I will focus on Duff's treatment of the twin excuses of duress and necessity, which present problems for his analysis of the centrality of intention. Duff argues that intentional actions are done for reasons; this means that intention is linked to rationality. Duress and necessity claims:

> serve to rebut the presumption of rational competence which ascriptions of
> intentional agency normally involve. Duress or necessity should excuse if the
> pressure to which the agent is subjected is so severe that it impairs her capacity to
> grasp, to weigh or to act on good reasons for action — to realise that and why she
> should resist the pressure, or to carry through a resolution to resist it.
> (Duff, 1990, 102)

Note first that this 'irrationalist' analysis is at odds with the standard analysis of the way in which duress and necessity operate in relation to intention. According to this approach, it may be perfectly rational to intend to commit an act under duress because of the threat that has been made. There is no assumption that the agent cannot grasp, weigh or act on good reasons for action. She may perfectly well realise why she should resist the pressure, yet submit to the duress.

Duff's account, I think, recognises as much in that he introduces the idea of *good* reasons for action, but the significance of this goes against rather than for his argument. In introducing in effect a notion of morally substantive rational agency *into* his conception of intention, he reveals that it is not simply the issue of intention that grounds a notion of responsibility, but intention related to a particular, morally substantive context. Thus duress as excuse forces Duff into a position on responsibility in which a substantive moral position is needed to supplement his analysis of intention. This, however, is a 'dangerous supplement'[17] because it reveals that the matter of normative content is a central and constitutive component of responsibility *alongside* the ability to form intentions and act intentionally.

To put this another way, duress and necessity are defences which operate to deny responsibility notwithstanding the existence of intended or intentional agency, and therefore they undermine the claim that intention and intentionality are the central moral features of judgment. It transpires, in these cases, that excuses invoke broader issues of normative judgment as the basis for settling matters of responsibility, and that questions of intention and intentionality are relevant only within this broader context. While it is true that law's architectonic of judgment, of which Duff's analysis is a very good representation, focuses on intention and intentionality, the extreme cases of duress and necessity reveal that the normally hidden substratum of these categories is moral and political. Duress and necessity force this normative basis into the open, revealing that intention and intentionality are only the primary categories of responsibility so long as this deeper normative element remains hidden.

The legal conception of responsibility normally seeks to suppress this contextually synthetic account of judgment in favour of a morality of form, in which apparently neutral categories like intention are given primacy. Potentially threatening normative issues such as those of justification and excuse are portrayed as contained and secondary exceptions. Yet a sophisticated attempt to rationalise this position such as Duff's only shows the act of suppression and denial that goes into law's architectonic. Moving to Duff's conception of intention itself, we will see the continuing juridical need to suppress content in favour of a morality of form, and a vivid example of the logic of legal practice in this regard.

The Normative Foundation of Intentional Agency

Intention in Duff's account includes both direct and oblique forms. One either acts with the intention of bringing something about, or one brings something about not as one's intention, but as a foreseen by-product of one's actions. In the latter instance, one does not intend, but one still acts intentionally. With regard to oblique intention a question arises as to whether we ascribe responsibility with regard to all or only some unintended but foreseen consequences. But Duff observes that we cannot ascribe every foreseen consequence to an agent because there is a moral dimension involved: 'Ascriptions of intentional agency do not describe neutral facts: they express normative judgments of responsibility, in which we may disagree' (Duff, 1990, 84).[18]

Such normative judgments involve a potential conflict of view as to what an agent *ought* to recognise and take into account as a foreseen effect of action. If an examiner fails a student to the student's serious detriment, the examiner, Duff argues, is not responsible even where the consequences are foreseen, for it is part of the normative role of an examiner to judge a student on her performance and not on the consequences of that performance. Similarly, whether a doctor is criminally liable for aiding and abetting unlawful sexual intercourse by prescribing contraceptives to an underage girl depends upon how one views the role of the doctor: morally, is a doctor's duty only to the patient, or to the patient and the law? If one adopts the former or latter normative view of the doctor's role, one will come up with a different conclusion to the question whether the doctor intentionally aided and abetted the offence.

This issue of normativity has emerged in a number of cases, including those of *R v Steane* ([1947] KB 997) and *R v Ahlers* ([1915] 1 KB 616). Both were cases involving charges of intending to assist the enemy in time of war. In the former case, Steane was acquitted because he broadcast for the Germans under threat of death to his wife and children; in the latter, Ahlers, a German Consul, was held not to assist the enemy by helping Germans to return home because he was only doing his duty as a Consul. Both cases involve a normative judgment about the scope of what was intended, since to broadcast and to assist repatriation were both actions that *ceteris paribus* would have the effect of assisting the enemy.

Normative questions involve matters of moral and political judgment and raise centrally the question of what justifies a person in acting in a particular way. Thus Duff's analysis of intentional agency undermines his account of intention and intentionality as the simple paradigms of responsible agency. Justification is a central and constitutive component of judgment, part, as it were, of its 'molecular structure'. Judgment is like a chemical compound, not a mixture of separate atomic elements of intention, justification and excuse. But this is what the law has to deny, for the historical reasons given in the previous section, and it is this denial that drives a wedge between legal and moral judgment. While Duff shows that oblique intention involves potential normative disagreement, he also notes that such disagreement is 'more typically found outside the law than within it':

> Outside the law our different normative standards (our different moral values, for instance) will generate conflicting criteria of responsibility, of relevance, and of intentional agency: but the law provides authoritative criteria which determine our legal responsibilities, the legal relevance of expected side-effects, and thus the scope (in law) of our intentional agency. (Duff, 1990, 84)

An individual swimming naked in public view might have no oblique intention to indecently expose herself, and might insist that she is entitled so to swim. Still the law may hold that the conduct is intentionally disgusting, and, no matter what the person thinks, she 'will not be heard to deny that [she] cause[s] it intentionally'. In such a circumstance the law forecloses the issue of normative disagreement by insisting that the oblique intention is present whatever the individual's own normative view. The issue of judgment is settled by the court according to its view of what is acceptable. The normative issue of what is justifiable is finessed by the law's unilateral declaration of what the 'authoritative criteria' are to be. As with the distinction between motive and intention, or the sidelining of justification and excuse, so in relation to intentionality we see the way in which matters of normative justification and judgment are suppressed within the law's base categories. Once that is done, and these categories have been 'secured' against moral infection, issues of justification and excuse are permitted as 'subsidiary' categories within law's architectonic. Law does not run with morality, it cuts against it.

A good example of this opposition is seen in Duff's discussion of the potential duress case, *Steane*.[19] Taking this to be a case of intentional rather than intended assistance of the enemy, there arises on Duff's account a substantive normative question that is a source of potential disagreement and argument. There must be room, on his analysis, for moral dispute as to whether Steane's assisting the enemy was *normatively* intentional. Rather than arguing the case on moral terms, however, Duff does what I argue the law does: he finesses the potential normative disagreement by positing a utilitarian argument as to why Steane should not be allowed to claim his assistance was unintentional:

> If we deny that he intended to assist the enemy, because he intended to save his family, we must likewise deny that one who broadcasts for the enemy in order to earn money intends to assist the enemy: but it would be outrageous to acquit such a person of 'doing acts likely to assist the enemy, with intent to assist the enemy'. Mr Steane's defence should have been duress, not lack of intent; his intention to assist the enemy was excused by the threats under which he acted. (Duff, 1990, 93)

There is however a world of moral difference between Steane and a mercenary that should, on Duff's own analysis, be reflected in his consideration as to whether Steane acted intentionally. This can be seen if we compare Duff's treatment of *Steane* with that of *Ahlers*, where he argues on the moral issue. Ahlers' intention 'was simply to do his legal duty as consul, which required him to help enemy aliens return home when war began' (Duff, 1990, 93). The difference between Ahlers and Steane is that the former was not a 'private citizen' and his role and duties as a Consul constitute a moral threshold over which the known side-effect of assisting the enemy cannot pass. This is, however, no more than a normative judgment that the role and duties of a Consul are somehow more valid than those of a husband and father. In both there can be moral disagreement on Duff's account, and in neither can the matter be avoided (though it can be evaded) by a utilitarian argument. In foreclosing on the moral question of intentionality in *Steane*, and sidelining it to the excuse of duress, Duff does precisely what the law does in order to avoid contestable moral issues around its paradigm categories of intention and intentionality.

Consequentialism Versus Interpretivism

Law's architectonic of judgment thus privileges an apparently de-normativised (or de-politicised, de-moralised) concept of intention and intentionality, relegating the 'difficult' moral and political issues to what is constructed as a subsidiary category of justification and excuse. There, in the back alleys of legal judgment, they become relatively unimportant 'exceptions to a rule' rather than what they really are: inherently constitutive elements.

If Duff's work can be seen as seeking to defend and rationalise law's architectonic, he also provides us with an important theoretical tool for its critique. The most radical part of *Intention, Agency and Criminal Liability* sketches a critique of the individualism, dualism and consequentialism at the heart of the criminal law's categories. Duff argues that legal judgment entails a number of dualisms, the most important of which is the subjective/objective dichotomy within a consequentialist account of harm and blame. For the consequentialist, harm is defined 'objectively' according to principles of political utility, and separately from questions of fault which operate as a side-constraint. Fault in turn stresses practical issues concerning subjective individual knowledge and control over the occurrence of harm, and it is for this reason that questions of intention are central to the consequentialist theory of criminal responsibility. Consequentialism therefore depoliticises or demoralises the question of criminal harm by establishing the bounds of harm 'objectively', and by identifying subjective responsibility for harm in terms of apparently 'factual' categories of knowledge and control.

Duff's critique in his 'non-consequentialist' account of responsibility correctly points out that this separation of subjective and objective components misses the *synthetic* nature of the moral judgment of harm. Such a judgment attributes responsibility for murder, for example, in terms of the quality of the mental state that *combines with* a particular resultant death.

> Both the murder victim and the victim of natural causes suffer death: but the character of the harm that they suffer surely also depends on the way in which they die. One who tries to kill me ... *attacks* my life and my most basic rights; and the harm which I suffer in being murdered ... essentially involves this wrongful attack on me.... The 'harm' at which the law of murder is aimed is thus not just the *consequential* harm of death, but the harm which is *intrinsic* to an attack on another's life. (Duff, 1990, 112–13)[20]

Criminal law, with its separation of *mens rea* (fault) and *actus reus* (harm), reflects the dualist position which Duff regards as inadequate. His argument is that the essence of murder is not the consequence of death but the intrinsic harm in the attack on another's life. That intrinsic harm is paradigmatically present in a wilful killing, and therefore paradigmatically present when there is an intention to kill. Duff still insists on the centrality of intention, but it is a morally substantive conception that he invokes in his discussion of the intention *to kill*. It is not the factual issue of control over one's conduct that is important, but the moral badness revealed by one's intention:

> Human actions are purposive: they are done for reasons, in order to bring something about; their direction and their basic structure is formed by the intentions with which their agents act. It is through the intentions with which I act that I engage in the world as an agent, and relate myself most closely to the actual and potential effects of my actions; and the central or fundamental kind of wrong-doing is to *direct* my actions towards evil — to *intend* and to *try* to do what is evil. (Duff, 1990, 113)[21]

Duff's emphasis on the intrinsic connection between the subjective and objective elements in murder opens the door to a recognition that there is an element of interpretation and normative evaluation in the establishment of any death as murder that goes beyond the combination of result and mental state, narrowly conceived in terms of intention. His interpretive analysis of judgment, with its unification of moral form and content, still makes intention a central part of the judgment of wrong-doing but it at the same time decentres it. It is the 'moral colour' of the intention that is now crucial, and on which the judgment is based. It is impossible to judge intention separately from the quality of the act that is being done. If we return to the example of Steane, it is clear that his (indirect) intention to assist the enemy in no way matches that of the mercenary. The moral colour of his oblique intention is provided by his direct intention to save his family. Steane, quite simply, does not seek in moral terms, 'to do what is evil', while the mercenary does. The interpretive account takes this into account in a way that the consequentialist cannot.

In making these points, I would argue that Duff quite rightly takes us beyond the narrow understanding of judgment contained within the traditional consequentialist view. However, so doing, he also takes us beyond the law's demoralised architectonic of judgment. The radical and critical thrust of Duff's interpretivism takes us beyond law and Bentham. The question then becomes: beyond law to what?

4.   Beyond Legal Judgment

I have argued that the creation of a legal architectonic as a morality of form involved an attempt to demarcate a legal sphere that was immune from overt normative — moral and political — questions. The separation of motive from intention was one central element in legal practice that was directly linked to the establishment of an apparently apolitical and amoral sphere of judgment. The prioritisation of *mens rea* over justification and excuse in the 'general part' is a corollary of this, for it was indeed matters of justification (motive of right) and excuse (motive of need) which were suppressed by the central reliance placed upon intention in the primary act of separation.[22] Yet scrutiny of the logic of this architectonic of separation and suppression reveals that questions of moral and political context are inseparable from questions of act and intention. Legal judgment seeks to differentiate itself from moral judgment, but ultimately it fails. In this section, I seek to locate this return of a repressed connection to broader questions about the nature and possibility of judgment in modern society.

I draw substantial support from the work of Alasdair MacIntyre who has written of an impasse in modern thought resulting from the incommensurability of ethical claims:

> [W]hen claims invoking rights are matched against claims appealing to utility or when either or both are matched against claims based on some traditional concept of justice, it is not surprising that there is no rational way of deciding which type of claim is to be given priority.... Moral incommensurability is itself the product of a particular historical conjunction. (MacIntyre, 1985, 70)

The problem stems from the invention of an autonomous moral individual as the source of morality in the modern world. The price paid for this 'homuncular' morality (Norrie, 1991, ch. 9) is a failure to establish any sense of moral bonds beyond the individual. Utilitarianism, as MacIntyre puts it, is an inadequate attempt to replace traditional moralities with a principle with which to 'contextualise' individual acts. It fails to do anything other than create an opposition between the collective interest and individual autonomy.

I agree with MacIntyre about this sense of incommensurability at the heart of the discontents of modernity,[23] and I also agree that the problem can be diagnosed as an historical one, as a result of the way that Western societies have been constructed in modern times. This essay can be read as supporting MacIntyre's project by showing the way in which one aspect of how we live — through the law and its judgments — crucially contributes to, as well as reflecting, the broader moral impasse. Thus Ashworth's presentation of liberal criminal law[24] can be seen to reflect the rights/utility antinomy, and the discussion of the failure to achieve a synthetic and contextual judgment in the James Bulger case, and more broadly in the law of murder generally, stems from the structuring of judgment around the law's individualist motif.

The historical dimension is as important to the analysis presented here as it is to MacIntyre, perhaps more so. Indeed, I think it is possible, through a reading of the law's individualism as a social and historical process of exclusion, to see a way of at least beginning to address one central failing of the moral analysis in *After Virtue* (MacIntyre, 1985). MacIntyre seeks to re-establish a moral conception of the good life for man in the face of the individualism of the modern world and the moral fragmentation that flows from it. His approach is to argue for a sense of community and tradition, implicit in all moral discourse, which we take forward into our conceptions of what is morally good. But this leads MacIntyre into his own moral impasse because he has already argued that it is precisely the failing of the modern sense of community that has caused the loss of coherent moral vision. In grounding his analysis of the morality of individualism in the historical development of the modern community, he fails to establish the existence of an 'other' community that can found a sense of moral order. The basis for an alternative sense of community to modernity is denied by his historical method, and MacIntyre is ultimately forced into a leap of faith that somehow it will be possible to construct, out of nothing, a new community. From somewhere, we must find 'men and women of good will' who can construct 'local forms of community within which civility and the intellectual and moral life can be sustained through the new dark ages which are already upon us' (MacIntyre, 1985, 263). How these mysterious 'men and women of goodwill' (at once a highly abstract and a very 'modern' construction) can appear is not explained, and nor can it be, given his description of the moral failings of the modern individualist community.

Yet MacIntyre's quest appears legitimate. The very ability to feel and reveal the failures of the morality of modernity which informs his work suggests a sense of morality that *could* exist, even if he fails to adumbrate it.[25] My suggestion is that through looking at the historical way in which modern law and politics scleroticised moral judgment, we are able to posit a sense of morality beyond the law's individualism, within our already existing communities.

My method has not been to elaborate an alternative morality to that of the law, and thence to criticise the law for its failures. I have worked out of the failures of the law adequately to capture an immanent sense of moral judgment in both practical and theoretical settings. Thus I have suggested the failure of a law-dominated universe of judgment to reflect a more profound sense of the complexity of wrong evoked by the James Bulger case, and I have argued that the law's analysis of intention, justification and excuse unsuccessfully represses a more synthetic methodology of judgment. The creation of our modern categories of judgment is based upon a suppression of deeper moral possibilities which remain sensible and serious even if (and because) they appear legally impossible or impractical. Duff's conception of an interpretivist moral strategy shows the inadequacy of legal judgment, even as his rationalisation of the law evokes a morality choked off by homuncular forms of responsibility. Individualist legal forms *repress* deeper, more complex architectonics of judgment which do not go away: they lurk behind and within the contradictions of law.

Part of MacIntyre's problem lies in his version of history, which represents the character of modern society in vague cultural terms. His main premise is cultural change in Northern Europe in the seventeenth and eighteenth centuries from which individual autonomy and the separation of morals, religion, law and aesthetics emerged (MacIntyre, 1985, 36–9). Later in his analysis, he recognises as a central characteristic of modernity the existence of social conflict in modern society, acknowledging that we are 'fundamentally right in seeing conflict and not consensus at the heart of modern social structure'. Modern liberal conceptions of morality, he argues, 'furnish us with a pluralist political rhetoric whose function is to conceal the depth of our conflicts' (MacIntyre, 1985, 253). But MacIntyre forges no instrumental connection between individualism and social conflict.

On my analysis, the relationship between ideological form and structural context is stronger and more explicit. Legal individualism operates as a mode of exclusion and repression of alternative substantive views of right and wrong, and the moral absences of modernity and law are based on that repression. The forms of law scleroticise our sense of judgment not only because they stand apart from moral judgment but also because they stand in the way of alternative, immanent formulations. We are not talking only, *pace* MacIntyre, of a concealment of social conflict, but of a repression of moral and political alternatives in a structurally conflictual environment. This is achieved by virtue of the abstract individualist forms of law and morality, while the moral contents that are excluded within law's formal architectonic of judgment keep forcing themselves back to our attention as felt 'lacks' to which we try to give names. Much of the time we are unable to articulate what these alternative moralities are, but this is exactly what we should expect given the historical experience of repression of which our own cultural imaginations are the victims.

In this context, it makes sense for us to look to alternative processes of judgment to try to understand what is lacking in our own legal and moral processes. On a personal level, we may reflect on the processes of judgment that we are familiar with friends, in families, or sometimes in the workplace.[26] As legal actors, we may look to systems of 'alternative' or 'popular' justice that exist in the interstices of, or in opposition to, Western style systems such as described here. This is not the place to do other than indicate in very broad terms what we find in these other places of judgment.[27] Frequently categories of judgment are nuanced and more reflective than those of the state and the law. Judgments recognise the context of agency and measure knowledge of background and competence against action. There is not an abstract standard, but a graded sense of what a family member, a friend, a colleague, a member of the community could have done, as well as what he or she did do, and there is also a reflexive sense of the judger's own role in relationships and the outcomes that they generate. There is also a sense that the result of judgments should be constructive and developmental, not punitive and regressive. There is an emphasis on particularisation in the application of norms to individuals, and a correlative sense of the need to act flexibly with regard to the selection of norms.

I can do no more than gesture at this discussion, but I think it is clear that the rough sketch I have outlined is closer to the alternative sense of judgment evoked by the James Bulger case than the abstract conception of judgment that is generated by law, and that was predominantly and publicly applied in that case. Thus my suggestion against MacIntyre is that a more critical historical methodology can help us to see that the alternative sources of moral judgment do not require a complete rupture with the present as a social and political reality in order to search out a community 'beyond' what exists. How would such a community ever exist? The other community that MacIntyre seeks beyond our own is an illusion and an impossibility, but this should invoke relief not desperation. The resources to work morally and politically against the 'new dark ages' in which we live already exist in the here and now.

It is the sense of alternatives suppressed in the past and the present that burns in the late E.P. Thompson's recent work, *Customs in Common*:

> As capitalism (or 'the market') made over human nature and human need, so political economy ... came to suppose that this economic man was for all time. We stand at the end of a century when this must now be called in doubt. We shall not ever return to pre-capitalist human nature, yet a reminder of its alternative needs, expectations and codes may renew our sense of our nature's range of possibilities. (Criminal Law Commissioners, 1843, 15)

Thompson reminds us, *pace* MacIntyre, that we need not go back to aristocratic Athens for a sense of moral community and tradition, for eighteenth-century plebeian England will do just as well. Ordinary people, not extraordinary 'men and women of goodwill', sharing 'experiences in labour and social relations' generate their own moral judgments *alongside* 'the necessary conformity with the *status quo*' (Criminal Law Commissioners, 1843, 11). As in the past, such judgments can constitute the basis for alternative counter-legalities in the present. Whether they will do so was something about which Thompson expressed pessimism, and caution,[28] and it is indeed hard to feel anything else in the present Western social and political climate. But we should understand that alternatives exist as part of 'our nature's range of possibilities', and not as a vague and mystical ideal for an 'other' community, operating somewhere beyond the social world in which we live.

With MacIntyre, we may agree that the dominant intellectual structures of our social (and legal) world are not necessarily immanent in human existence, but are the politically achieved artefacts of a particular kind of historical society. It is this historical and political location of law's architectonic of judgment, represented as a 'general part' of intention (and recklessness), justification and excuse, that ultimately guarantees its strength and longevity, rather than either its intellectual coherence or its ability to match the presumed essential moral characteristics of judgment and responsibility in social life.

Notes

1. This paper was originally presented in two different forms at seminars at the Universities of Warwick, Edinburgh and Hull. I would like to thank those who participated in discussions, and Shaun McVeigh and Nicola Lacey for their written comments. It is part of an ongoing attempt to develop one argument in my *Crime Reason and History* (1993), and to build a bridge to themes in both legal theory about the nature of judgment in Western societies ('modernity'), and also in the sociology of law about alternative forms of judgment. I should make it clear that it represents the further exploration of *one* of the central themes of *Crime Reason and History*, that of legal individualism as a negative and repressive mediation, and it does not pursue the other theme, of law as an affirmative political force. My overall view (Norrie, 1993, 221–5) reflects the complexity and contradictory moral and political values of modern law. The conclusion to this paper, about the possibilities of popular forms of judgment counter to those of the law, is not to be taken as an endorsement of 'popular justice' as opposed to 'law'. I would take such a view to entail a false opposition. See also note 28 below.

2. Ashworth in fact treats justifications separately from the negative fault requirements, though he notes the provisional character of his, and others', schemata (Ashworth, 1991, 78–9).

3. It is the presentation in liberal criminal law theory of a separation between (a) law as the embodiment of a formal morality and politics, based on the abstract individual subject, and (b) substantive moral and political concerns, together with the impossibility of that separation, that constitutes my main object of investigation here. Law's 'trick' through this separation is to present itself as a form of politics that is apolitical, as a morality purely of form. So liberal criminal law theory both acknowledges and denies its politicality. Kramer (1994, 118–19) misunderstands this crucial point in his criticism of an earlier paper of mine on the law of recklessness (Norrie, 1992).

4. All reports are drawn from *The Guardian*, 25 November 1993, and *The Observer*, 28

November 1993. For important discussions of the case, see D.J. Smith (1995); Sereny (1995, 273–333); and Young (1996, ch. 5).

5.   The requirement that a child between the ages of 10 and 14 knows that he or she has done something seriously wrong was removed by a Divisional Court ruling (*C v DPP* [1994] 3 WLR 888), but then restored by the House of Lords (*C (a Minor) v DPP*, [1995] 2 WLR 383). This judicial activity was in part a result of the Bulger case.

6.   For example, the then Minister of State David Hunt, and the BBC's Home Affairs correspondent Polly Toynbee.

7.   My argument is that the issue in this case goes beyond the question of the age of the defendants, and how children *qua* children should be judged, though the fact that the killers in this case were children brings out more starkly the abstract and narrow character of legal judgment. This is not to deny that Western systems can and do differentiate child from adult killers on occasion, as the recent French treatment of three boys who killed a tramp shows. The magistrate withheld the case from the press until the Bulger case was finished to avoid comparisons. The boys were allowed to return to their families without period of confinement. Rather than demanding more severe treatment *à l'anglais*, it might be noted, French newspapers 'generally preferred to question the wisdom of submitting Jon Venables and Robert Thompson to a full blown trial' (*The Guardian*, 23 March 1994).

8.   Gitta Sereny makes this point in different language (Sereny, 1995, xv, 331). While her vindication of punishment in a morally bankrupt social context replicates some of the problems raised by the killing of James Bulger (cf x, xii, 331), her emphasis on the children's common brutality is of central importance (cf D.J. Smith, 1995, 243).

9.   Geoff Dyer has made the following point: 'Since Conrad it has become a cliche to talk of a journey to the heart of a narrative darkness, but this was the path the Bulger trial followed.... [At the end we were still] left with the tantalising question "why?" Like this, with no one knowing why two unidentified children had committed such a crime, the nation would have felt thwarted. Justice may have been done but the hunger for a closure of the narrative which brought us right to the brink of some terrible insight would not have been assuaged. This is why — although he too refused to disclose his motives — the trial judge had no choice but to allow publication of the boys' names; this is why *The Guardian* ... carried a huge picture of Bobby Thompson on the front page. Narrative must not only be resolved, it must be seen to be resolved' (*The Guardian*, 12 March 1993). My argument is that legal judgment seeks to establish the closure that moral narrative requires, but it is always an inadequate closure, and this becomes apparent in the Bulger case. Superficially, the finding of guilt brings things to an end, but the deeper questions remain unanswered. The inadequacy of the conviction to close the case necessitates a further attempt at closure in terms of a demonisation of the two children — by publishing their names and photographs, and by labelling them as evil. This goes beyond the law's own judgments, but it relies on the law's initial conferral of guilt to set the ball rolling. Symbiotically, it both thrives on, and compensates for, the law's failure. This demonisation is in my view negative and damaging for all concerned, the convicted boys, the family of the victim, and the broader society. It permits a continuing climate of hate to pervade the debate and the lives of those involved. A parallel example, and illustration as to where this may lead, is provided by the case of Myra Hindley which remains in the headlines thirty years after her convictions for murder. It seems that she must remain in prison for no reason connected with standard principles of penal administration, but only to assuage the sense of her evil, constructed in similar circumstances so long ago, and never allowed to dissipate.

10.   See also Lacey, 1993, 624–6.

11.   The argument in the rest of this section follows Norrie, 1993, 39–40.

12.   The last sentence in quotation marks is from Hume.

13.   On the nature of this suppression in the law of recklessness, see Norrie, 1993, ch. 5.

14.   On the ambiguous role of sentencing as a symbiotic, yet contradictory mode of judgment

to that provided by the categories of legal responsibility, see Norrie, 1993, 45–6. Of course, mitigation is not available on a murder conviction, a contingency which serves to point up the failure of the legal categories to reflect a moral sense of wrongdoing.

15. Cf J.C. Smith, 1989.

16. Cf Gardner and Jung, 1991, 587.

17. Cf: 'To supplement jurisprudence, then, could be just a matter of making sure that valuable things are kept on board. The supplement provides what is lacking. It serves to complement and complete that which is supplemented.... But, as Derrida has it, the supplement is also 'dangerous'. The supplement is not fully assimilable. It remains outside, challenging the completeness and the adequacy of that which is within' (Fitzpatrick, 1991, 2).

18. Cf Williams, 1987, and Norrie, 1989.

19. *Steane* was in fact decided as an intention case, though for reasons that are not entirely clear.

20. Emphasis in original.

21. Emphasis in original.

22. This is the point of direct contact between the historical analysis of section 2, and the conceptual analysis of section 3.

23. Cf Norrie, 1991, ch. 9.

24. See above, Introduction.

25. In his subsequent work (MacIntyre, 1988 and 1990), MacIntyre appears to slacken the historical and contextual strictures of *After Virtue* (MacIntyre, 1985) in order to argue for the possibility of reconstituting older moral traditions in the present. But it has recently been rightly noted that if he is to attach importance to the 'social embeddedness of thought and enquiry, [then] his largely negative view of modernity continually threatens to undermine any attempt to root his positive proposals in the contemporary world of advanced industrial societies' (Horton and Mendus, 1994, 13–14).

26. This is not to deny that these too are structured and conflictual environments, but they are not so clearly or so closely constructed around a legal architectonic of judgment.

27. Important discussions in a voluminous literature can be found in the following: Allison, 1990, 409–28; Burman and Scharf, 1990; Fitzpatrick, 1987; Fitzpatrick, 1992a; Gundersen, 1992; Merry and Milner, 1993; Sachs and Welch, 1990; Scharf and Ngcokoto, 1990; and Spitzer, 1982.

28. See Thompson's comments about 'rough music', a form of law that 'belongs to the people, and is not alienated, or delegated', but which is not 'necessarily more "nice" and tolerant'. Rough music was 'only as nice and as tolerant as the prejudices and norms of the folk allow' and Thompson comments that '[l]aw and a bureaucratised police must have been felt as a liberation from the tyranny of one's "own"' (Thompson, 1991, 530–1). These comments are important in Britain today, where forms of 'popular justice' have begun to emerge as a result of the perceived failures of the police and the courts to contain some forms of criminality. The value of producing an analysis of the particular architectonic of Western law is to formulate a clear analysis of the strengths and limitations of such law. This can then form the basis for comparison with other architectonics of judgment in different times and places. The argument of this final section makes it clear that it is possible to conceive morally and historically of the possibility of such alternative architectonics of judgment. This is a prelude to considering what role law-like regulation might play under alternative moral, social and political arrangements. See also my comments in note 1 above.

2 The Dummy: An Essay on Malice Prepensed

YIFAT HACHAMOVITCH

> The subject of the Cartesian *cogito* does not think, he has only the possibility of thinking, and remains stupid at the heart of this possibility.
>
> (Deleuze, 1968, 354)

Murder [1]

It is impossible to blow open the top of a man's head, says the judge in *R v Moloney* ([1985] 1 All ER 1025), a case about a man who blows open the top of a man's head, — to unshell it, as it were, so as to examine his thinking like an oyster, or a watch-spring, or a nut.

For there to be murder, and not manslaughter, there must be thought, but the difference of what is called thinking is sealed inside the history of murder itself — it is an internal difference, a difference which remains inclusive. In *R v Mawgridge*, Chief Justice Holt reconsiders this problematic, insensible difference, a difference of statutes which have been 'the occasion of many nice speculations' (*R v Mawgridge* (1707) Kelyng 199 at 120).

A Danish King thought a murder to be the killing of a Dane by an Englishman. '*Murdru quidem inventa fuerunt indiebus Canuti Regis, qui post acquisitam Angliam & pacificatum, rogatu baronum Anglioe remisit in Daciam exercitum suum.*' Thereupon a law was made:

> that if any Englishman should kill any of the Danes that he has left behind, if he were apprehended, he should be bound to undergo the ordeal trial to clear himself; and if the murderer were not found within eight days, and after that a month was given, then if he could not be found, the ville should pay forty-six marks, which if not able to pay, it should be levied upon the hundred. [2]

The thought of a murder is from the very start out of joint: it is the thought of a King who affixed the imperative of thought to every killing of a King who affixed the imperative of thought to every killing of a Dane by an Englishman, by conferring upon the English a common fine called 'murdro' for every such slaying. The name of 'murdro' was then attached to the death of a Norman by William the Conqueror, and again to the killing of a Frenchman by Henry 1.³

The imperative of thought was addressed to the English and only to them, since for every offender not found it is the village which must pay; and for every murder left unthought or every *ville* which would not think, and could not pay, the imperative to think on the murder carried over to the hundred like a debt.

The scene of the murder is the scene of a thought that comes before thought, a foreign and partial and incomplete thought that comes from without and takes thought from within, as it were, leaving it disarmed, unable to think and thus defend itself as thought; unable to call a murder a murder, an Englishman an Englishman, or a Dane a Dane.

One supposes that the thoughtless killing of a Dane or a Norman or a Frank would have been prohibitive by virtue of the accompanying fine of *murdrum*:

> [F]or as the law stood, or was interpreted before [the Statute of Marlebridge], if a man was found to be slain, it was always intended: 1. That he was a Frenchman. 2. That he was killed by an Englishman. 3. That killing was murder.⁴

Thought only ever happened to a country, and every thought was a charge.

One should imagine an old thinker at an even older village scene: 'What part or partial thoughts, what fragments or fractions of thought, what thoughts not fully formed, what *petit* or petty thoughts, have taken here the place of thought: *par malice devant pourpense*?' The *pourpensed* belies not thought but its sombre precursor, not thought but what forces thought to think, or think badly.

(One should already begin to conceive of stupidity as a revolutionary act, an ambush.)

What was at stake in the debt of a nocturnal killing, and what was at play in the notion of the *prepensed* which followed upon it, and cancelled the debt like the dawn, was the minimal possible thinkable difference between an essentially private reality and a public one.

It should not surprise us that by the time of the Bractons a murder denoted a killing at night, or in stealth, a secret or hidden killing. *That a murder was not and would not be seen was the effect of its own nature and not that of the night.* There is something *aliquot* in thought that lies in wait for thought, something in thought that ambushes thought, that forces thought to think, or think *badly*, and this something is not the object of recognition. To call a death a murder was to mark it as that which *must not* be seen, which *would not* be seen, which *ought not* to be seen; to register a recognition which *must have* remained unrecognisable, a thought which *must have* remained unthought. For centuries, the unknown knowledge of the murder sanctioned a conformity to law without law; for centuries, what must have been thought must have remained unconscious.

A slow moving history of what is called murder uncovers a thought that comes before thought, a not-yet thought, a becoming-thought, a part or partial thought, a thought in process and on trial. It is said that for there to be murder, there must be thought but what is called thought is not at all obvious: malice prepensed or precogitata, malice devant pourpensed, malice devant pretence, and malice precedent? *What is this malice prepense or pourpensed or precedent?* Is it to think in advance, to map out or preconnoitre a reality which does not yet exist, or is it some prohibited but fantasmatic equivalent of thought, some 'wild' side of thought whose anteriority is 'older' than the *a priori*?

The following essay suggests that it is by way of the murder that English Law confronts what remains incidental to it; what never registered in any register of any beginning, because it was not English, specifically, because it was French.

Waiting

> For 'Socrates is mortal' the stoics would substitute 'Socrates takes a walk'.
> (Duhot, 1989, 139)

One must imagine thought, waiting. One must imagine thoughts moving like trees.

Consider the inchoate thought of the fourteenth century — the thought of those who lay in ambush, or who rode about in armed bands looking for victims, but had not yet actually committed felonies.

The problematic of *mens rea* in fourteenth-century law is precisely this not-yet felon[5] — this wild, impersonal, incidental, itinerant thought that cannot be recognised or represented, that travels in gangs or packs, that lies in wait for a murder but cannot be made out from the bushes and the weeds.

It is this problem of recognition which makes it impossible or almost impossible to capture, to captivate, *to get the animal off the King's road.*[6] It is this problem of recognition which prompts the Statute of Winchester to demand the trees and hedges be trimmed and cut back from the highway, so as to reduce the number of lurking places.[7]

It is this problem of recognition which calls for a back-up for what is called thinking; a *night-watch*[8] to sit up and look out for thought *before it is thought.*[9]

It is the Statute of 1390 (King's Presentation to Benefice (1390) 13 Rich. II c. 1)[10] which first recognises the sombre precursor of what is called thinking: the occasional thought = x. No pardon of the King, it decreed, would excuse '*Murdre, Mort d'ome occis par agait, assaut, ou malice pupense, Treson ou*[11] *Rap*'.

Statutory recognition[12] fragments the murder into absolutely identical Things — that is to say, *causes [choses]*. The virtuality of the murder-effect displaced the stake of death from the scene of the killing and assigned to thought the work of death as such: from the fourteenth century onwards, the law institutes thinking as a form of waiting,[13] and attaches to the murder the rigour of a *cause*.[14]

But there is always something which escapes recognition, some vagabond of the night [*vagabundus de nocte*] who does nothing as yet but lurks about in a menacing way, disturbing the peace [*communis perturbator pacis*], and eavesdropping.[15] There is always some empirical element of thought that remains in itself a contingency with a perpetual line of flight, that cannot be captured or captivated by any occasional, sensible or proximate cause.

Causality must be felt, rather than conceived (Hume, 1888, 627). Thus it is also possible to read the statute as depicting four separate disguises and deferrals of thought: some unseen, unformed, insensible fatality; some thought that sits and waits, that takes up a position, or puts into a position to be taken; some thought taking thought from behind, as it were, leaving it disarmed, unable to use defences normally turned toward the outside: *murdre*; *assaut purpensed*; *agait purpensed*; *malice purpensed*. The *pourpensed* belies not thought but its sombre precursor, not thought but what forces thought to think, or think *badly*.

What is called *prepensed* is the smallest possible unit of thought, the shortest possible thought, the minimal possible thinkable distance between a *here* and a *there*: a distance which remains completely indescribable, like the difference between a straight line and an intended line or the distance between:

Nichol de C, ke cy est, [who was] 'in the peace of God and in the peace of the King the day of St Peter and Vincula in the first year of our present King's coronation at the houre of my *relevee* in a certain place called C on the King's highway[16]

lying between the township of E and the township of C as he was making his way
towards the fair of St Botolf to attend to the needs of his Lord and himself' [and]
'*Adam de C, ke la est*', [who came] felonnessement com felon et en assaut purpense
et le assailli devileynes paroles et felones ein ke il unkes le aprocha [feloniously
as a felon and assailed him with wicked and felonious words before he even drew
near to him]. (Kaye, 1966, 10)

or the distance between two neighbours who are at the same time so far apart
that it would take centuries to conjoin them.

The juridical fantasy of pinning down an essentially frayed[17] part of murder
— at a distance of centuries — is completely determined by this unthinkable,
irreducible *impasse*.

Consider in this regard the decision of Catlin CJ 'and other erudites in
law' in the case of *Stowell* (10 Eliz):

If two by *malice prepensed* ambush each other and one kills the other, it is murder,
and it doesn't matter who struck the first blow, because even if the first blow is
that of the victim, the other one is still guilty of murder. *(Quaere: how could the
combat arise in such a case?)*[18]

The problematic of simultaneity[19] *demobs an entire dialectic of rivals
and suitors,*[20] a rivalry wherein what is at stake is not the determination of a
precedent, but the recovery of a *lineage*. The law does not really care when
thought comes as long as it comes before the law (does) — that is, as long as
it stands accused (*ca prevenu*) (Lacan, 1986, 56-7fn).

For there to be murder, there must be a movement from a 'here' to a
'there'[21] — and yet it would be wrong to define a felon by his movement.
The felon, on the contrary, should rather be conceived as 'he who does not
move': he clings to the thorns and the bushes at the side of the highway
where the King's Peace advances *and never lets ago*.[22] The King invents an
itinerant Bench as a response to this clinging; a Bench which, in some sense,
carries its place with it so that, in each Sitting [*assize*], the place itself changes
place.[23]

For centuries, there is something in thought that lies in wait for thought,
something in thought that ambushes thought, that forces thought to think, or
think badly, and this something cannot be figured, only *demonstrated*.[824] In
the fourteenth century, the road to Colchester is full of demonstrations.

Insidious the thought of John Worme and others *iacerunt latitando et
insidiando populum domini regis in viis de Freston ... malitia praecogitata*

insidiaerunt Adam Smyth *et eum felonice interfecerunt,* that comes on the scene already multiplying and dividing, *interfecerunt* not merely to slay but to interpolate, to make something be between the parts of a thing so as to separate and break it up. In fact, thought interrupts nothing. It is rather an integral element of interruption: under order to intercept, and so impossible to intercept; too divided to distinguish, too intermittent to arrest, too fast, too sudden, too charged to discharge [*intendo*] or accuse [*intentio* hence fr. *intention*] or to threaten [*intento*]; too diffuse, too dispersed, to map out; a rebel as old as the old *Pax Romana* of an even older Roman and its threefold formula of '*Restitutio, Renovatio, Reparatio*', then when *rebellare* meant only — to start the war all over again (Ladner, 1983, 780-1).[25]

Insidiavit ... et felonice interfecit. Insidious the thought that lies low ... *in insidio latitantes* and awaits *et iacentes* ... John Barker, coming from a session of the King's Justices at Lincoln, ... and persuades him with false befriending words *per dictas falsas confederaciones* and *malitia praecogitatae* to ride with it, and in a quiet place, *eum felonice interfecerunt* (Kaye, 1967, 390) — assassinates.[26]

Insidious the thought of Simon de Lund of Hull *iacuit in insidiis* that comes *sua sponte* spontaneously as if of itself too suddenly *cum uno gladio ad interficioendum Thomas Potter ... et sic insidiando,* to turn an instrument against itself.

Insidious the universal inquietude of the animal on the watch (*guet-apens*) and so impossible to watch, to preconnoitre, or to hear one's own thinking (*entendre*).[27] It is impossible to relieve a thought on the watch by means of one's own thought. Impossible to sit and wait for a thought that sits and waits, impossible to hear a thought, that comes 'before' the blow comes, *as if* from itself, '*sua sponte*' (spontaneously), to pledge [*sponte*] the soul to pain.

Yet how, after all, can one say that a thought is spontaneous, in the soul of the felon who lies in wait, seeking the imperceptible signs of what would change his pleasure into pain, his chase into *flight,*[28] his rest into movement? To the ellipse there belongs not one thought, but a series of inquietudes — *points de suspension* — a series of petty messengers, a choir or a chorus. The tension preceding the killing betrays the total legibility of a body not yet acting, the rhetoric of a completely animated posture or position of emotion approaching its limit, without ever becoming an action, without ever becoming an extended thing.

Against this moving grove of thought, a dogged Peace Commission sets off doggedly in 1380 to grasp a thought impossible to recognise by any other means. It is *this* problem of recognition which prompts the Statute of Winchester to demand that trees and hedges be trimmed and cut back from the highway, where a thought that lies in wait for justice approaches a justice that lies in wait for thought. Indeed, it is a problem of recognition all around. It is impossible to recognise a thought in a country where murders were scattered like so many accidents.[29] It is impossible to think such a thought by means of one's own thought, when every thought starts the war *all over again*.[30]

The Big Sit[31]

It seems an unaccountable thing how one soothsayer can refrain from laughing when he sees another. (Cicero, 1972, 25)

To lie in wait for justice, or for a death that moves as quickly as justice — it is the same thing. The object of thought does not really matter. What matters is the place where one is sitting; what matters is to have a place: to sit, to wait, *perchance* ...

... *to think* is first of all to conjure, to make an image of what will have come about and what is already in the process of coming about and never stops coming about because it is always already there[32] — the murder itself is always somehow *on the road and on its way, an eternally yet to come*, an ordeal of reason which is no less mystic, no less mantic, no less mystagogic than the ordeal of fire and water.

To think, in the country — to think, for the jury [*le pays*], is to speak the 'truth' that is known about the defendant, a truth — according to conscience — a truth, Green argues, *fundamentally opposed to the letter of the law*.[33] It is written, for example, in Edmund de Ovyng's coroner's roll that:

William came upon his brother Thomas, and Richard as they quarrelled. William drew his knife and stabbed Richard in the back. The King's coroner termed the homicide a felony. The trial jury's reworking of the facts provided ample evidence of last resort and asserted that Godmanchester had died of a wound in the stomach — a rather more reasonable place for a self-defender to stab his adversary.

(Green, 1985, 4)

The entire machinery of the *prepensed* is invented by way of fixing or mending the 'fact' with a fantasmatically preferable substitute: an *image of truth* broad enough to cover 'misreadings of evidence and verdicts rendered knowingly against the evidence but inspired by mercy' (Green, 1985, 27). Indeed, an image which dissimulates the murder, by attaching to the dead man the thought of the accused.

It is the malice of the dead man which is alleged to put the accused into a position of self-defence. It is the intention of the dead man that turns the accused into the passive, affective, objectal 'me' of a defendant. The very thing that bars the pre-subject subject , the '*moi*' of the accused from the grammatical position of a subject is where it finds its defence, and its relief.[34] The reversal or turning[835] of the subject on itself must be a disarticulation or a distention of the murder, a reversion of the mood, the tense, the position of the accused *to the dead man's place*.

Consider the plea of 'A Man Taken for a Killing Done in Self-Defence' in the *Placita Corone*:

Sire, si vous plest, Je ne fu unkes felon.... Sir if you please, I have never been a felon and never did mischief to any living man ... and so I have done nothing wrong against the man whose name you ask: who, feloniously as a felon and en assaut purpense tried to kill me on such a day at such an hour, in such a year, in my own house in such a township, for no fault on my part and solely on account of his own malice. (Kaye, 1966, 19)

It was always the dead man who started it. The 'me' of the accused only ever drew the knife or sword to defend himself, 'holding it steady as a bar to further assault', while the dead man of his own accord plunged himself *sua sponte* — as if by himself — into the defendant's weapon (Green, 1985, 90). The trial roll tells us that:

The deceased had thrown the defendant into a ditch and had fallen accidentally on the latter's knife; the court asked whether the defendant had out of any malice — held the knife upward toward the deceased.... The defendant had held a sword between himself and his assailant without moving it.... After the deceased had struck the defendant and gravely wounded him, he ran after the defendant who held a pitchfork between himself and his attacker; the deceased then stupidly ran upon the pitchfork. (Green, 1985, 91)

The subject of thought comes on the scene not only dead but a dummy — *le mort* — a *pseudo*, to relieve, to protect, to facilitate a social and emotional subject of truth.[36]

The jury divines or devises a false *grammatical* subject who reflects, as if in a mirror, the positions or postures of the accused. It is this *reflection* which triggers the subject's recognition. The jury's interpolation of the dead man's thought makes the 'me' see itself, makes it see the image it bears for the other as thought.

The dummy is not merely a folly of law, a juridical construction which comes from the outside but a *crisis*, a *breaching*, a *facilitation* interior to thinking itself, the instrument and effect of an ordeal[37] which had become *non-localisable*, taking thought from within, as it were, forcing recognition from the subject, from out of the subject.

> [When] the tenant (that is, the party attacked by the Writ of Right) ... puts himself on the grand assize of our lord the king, the action is removed out of the lord's court and is brought before the king's justices, four knights of the neighbourhood are summoned to choose twelve other knights who are sworn to say, to 'recognise' (*recognoscere*) whether the demandant or the tenant has the greater right to the land. (Maitland, 1989, 21)

The subject of recognition is first of all a tenant: a settled, seated, sitting duck. One cannot get around it: the thesis which *holds the place of the dead man*, is no more and no less than the horizontal and dative dimension of a *seat*.

From out of his place, the 'jury',[38] the *recognition* must divine what the trial leaves still unknown, what the dead man cannot *convey*,[39] but what could have been heard if such hearing was, at the same time, an *overhearing*:[40] a rendering, a resounding, a wringing of truth from the dead man's place,[41] that is, *an accuser*.

> When it is a question of knowing who shall be given the task of presenting the accusation and when two or more people volunteer for this office, the judgment by which the tribunal names the accuser is called divination.... This word comes from the fact that since the accuser and the accused are two correlative terms which cannot continue to exist without each other and since the type of judgment in question here presents an accused without an accuser, it is necessary to have recourse to divination in order to find what the trial does not provide, what it leaves still unknown, that is to say, the accuser.[42]

There is no lifting of the royal repression of thought, no arrival of thought, no *accusation*, until what is heard in the accusation is *entended* — is heard as one's own thinking: the 'me' must hear the accusation as its own thought, must hear the 'me' address the 'me' in the form of an accusation — *you!*[43]

The entire *mise en scene* of a juridical conscience revolves around this second origin of sense, of common sense, of good sense, this accuser who is at once a register and a foil of the law: *you!*[44]

Moi? From out of the resonance of a 'me' in defence, a 'me' on trial and in process, the reflexivity of the *cogito* is conjured: a thinking thing which *resonates* legitimacy.

It is by eavesdropping on the thought of the dead man, by identifying *with* the thought of the dead man, that the subject of thought comes into being: *feloniously as a felon, thievishly as a thief, the felon lifts the truth of his thought from the dead man's place, from a dummy.*

The art of the jury was to *demonstrate* thought, to make thought *entend* itself as thought: to turn thinking into a *phenomenon*.

> Typically, jury verdicts were conclusions based on assessment of facts gathered before the defendant went on trial. Although juries were probably influenced by the defendant's hearing in court, their reactions to that drama must have been played back against what they had already [heard]. (Green, 1985, 27)

The task of the jury is to *oyer and terminer*: to hear and determine — to hear, to *over*hear what was already heard in such a way that the fantasy of overhearing, the fantasy of being overheard produces in fact an other scene of thought, an other scene of the murder — *the appeal*.

The jury's image of truth sets up a false memory or memory-screen[45] which registers as thought the very one who would not have been thinking, the dead man, a dummy. What is archived is the thought of a dead man, a dead fold of thought, an impassible setting of thought — a preconscious screen of re-pression or censorship,[46] what Lacan calls the Imaginary. This is because a thought that stays awhile,[47] that remains a thought for long enough, becomes a part or partial thought, a thought too old, too obvious to recognise *or to think*, a thought already thought, a *prethought*: something like a custom, something like a precedent, something like *malice prepensed* or *malice devant pourpensed*.

The frayage or fraying or [ap]pealing of the laws from within — the perpetual collapse of the letter into fact, of evidence into *rumour, hearsay*, and *news* is not accidental. It is rather a deliberate interruption of the juridical machinery, its *a posteriori*, its unregistered tail, its spur. It was not simply that the 'facts' — the pretrial incarceration, the unhappy remand before pardon, the automatic forfeiture of chattel by the accused if excusable slayer —

'interacted with the law of sanctions to produce a substantial distortion in the legal process' (Green, 1985, 99),[48] but that the appeal was made *off the record*.[49]

The unofficial nature of this mechanism explains the failure of the murder as an appellate process. The law institutes felony as a betrayal of thought and reduces the multiple fealties of thought to the figure of felony.[50] But for the jury (*le pays*) thought was only ever a political insurrection which denied the law the power to legislate over the right to wander (*ius spatiandi*).[51] *A mind which wanders off the record cannot be instituted by it.* As Milsom points out in relation to the failure of the writ of error, 'law which exists off the record cannot be corrected on it' (Milsom, 1985b, 188–9).

This is because what is thinking is always a jury, a collection of local 'mes' and their emotional postures and positions and positionings; their excuses, their defences, their nocturnal councils, their misreadings, their erasures, their forfeitures, their errors, their opinions — the misadventures and misfortunes of the rumours, the posters, the news[52] — all handed down as indefeasible and received as immemorial.[53] How, after all, can one say that the jury *erred* when the entire proceedings were represented by two lines saying that afterwards, *postea*, the jurors came and said that the defendant was or was not guilty? How, still yet, could a voiding of law be found out, when the law was sealed inside the facts themselves, and the facts were locked up in the jury room? By what means could an omission of thought be made out when *thinking itself is always omitted from the record, when the dummy takes the record with it*?[54]

The dummy (which is to say, the wandering mind) was always already there in the grammar: an adverb of manner that functions as a substantive or subject, a *communis ascultator sub tecta* and *agent provocateur* implanted by the country in the letter of the law.[55] It is this *agency of the heard* that will make impassivity, mischance, *chaudemellee*, accident, forgetfulness, and all the defences possible. A sudden chance medley, *throw suddande chaudemellay* or *chaudemellee*,[56] do not archive a failure of thought, a misadventure of thought, an error of thought. Thinking is just this incidence, this crisis or mixture of bodies, this clashing of sense, a subordinate or accessory effect, an essentially frayed part of a juridical event. It is this juridical agency[57] of a time out of joint, a time out of mind, that it will make it possible to foil thought with its own instrument (*com un gladio*), to kill thought with its own weapon, to know the places where thought will be in advance,[58] to map out thought according to its own plan, to see thought as it would see itself, to lie in wait for a King on the road and on his way, reflecting what is called thought to itself as its own denegation, its own blind.

To think, then, is to follow a line or a sorcery — that is, to fly in the face of the symbolic for the sake of that which is unassimilable within it, *the real*.[59] It is to hear the phantom of the undecideable which 'remains caught, lodged ... in every decision, in every event of decision' (Derrida, 1990, 965), so as to keep up a certain essential relation with the murder's original truth: a murder was *still* a nocutural or hidden or unexplained killing, a killing whose perpetrator would remain unknown.

Malice prepensed was used from the very start as a lure, a decoy, a *fantasmatic juridical dummy* to capture the malice of justices cruising[60] for what is called thought.[61]

It would be wrong to castigate the ploy as just the sort of thing one might expect in godforsaken country villages from dotards, farmhands and oafs. Thievishly as thieves, the justices lifted their image of thought from the dead man's place, from a dummy; what is called malice prepensed tricked out the felons like foxes.

A Bedside Science

> Was it that the king's judges found their lists silting up with cases adjourned for thought, or that they did not like thinking? (Milsom, 1985b, 182–3)

It all takes place offstage, as it were, in some dark interior tribunal, some night-court of the soul, where some nocturnal 'my', some pleonastic 'not' of me, or some mistaken moiety of me bars me from [half of] myself. This misplaced me, this displaced me, obsesses me with a reflection of myself,[62] or what is at stake in the self — the 'not' again, mistaken for a half. The 'my' is seized of something it has never had, an old French 'not', a *'ne'*: *'Biaux chires (beaux sires) loupes n'écoutez mie. Femme qui tasse son enfant qui crie.'* (*Daniel v Camplin* (1845) 7 Man. & G. 172; Blackstone, 1979, vol. 2, 182). It is a fantasmatic little *'mie'* or *ne* — the 'not' of *me* mistaken for a *mi*[63] — that labours in law — French under the English, that lapses into French under the English, to undermine not merely sensibility, but sense.[64]

This problem of a missed or missing sense at the bottom of a slow moving history of sense, of common sense, of good sense, has always been a problem at common law. It is a question of what is at stake *chez* common law or what is at home there when law is at home — if there is someone at home in the precedent. It is impossible to tell.

This is the problematic situation of the justices, the situation of a *-ment* (a mind) that is merely an accessory, an appendage, a difference of manner; indeed, the problem of a mind in the grammar: a mind full of faults, not illegible but irreadable, fractions and fragments of sense, mute particles, forgotten sounds no longer pronounced or pronouncable, words buried alive, defunct, fossilised words, dead letters, obsolete punishments no longer enforced or enforceable (Derrida, 1986, xxxv–vi), arcane procedures, misguided notions of trial by battle as a normal method of settling appeals, although the proof by ordeal had almost entirely disappeared by 1250,[65] ancient customs, mistaken references, erroneous usages, old torts, rituals no longer understood but noted, legends reported — old rumours, old posters, old news; not so much pleas of the Crown as formulas for the fantasy of a peaceful Crown, remedies for the King's broken peace — dreams to mend the King's broken sleep [*en coupe ment de la Corone*]: 'The policy of the judges was to leave the facade of ancient rules standing while demolishing the structure behind it', Kaye writes of the *coup* (Kaye, 1966, xvii).

Here lies the mind, with knobs on: not *ici*, but *ci git*.[66] Here is where the mind is as-if lying. But it is the head, and only the head [*caput*], that founds a tradition of precedent, because it is the head that generates the image and it is from its image that the law is recognised: *caput, cuius, imago fit, inde cognoscimur*.[67]

Every precedent, every plea is a placebo, a dummy. It either pleases or it doesn't, and when it does, *there is absolutely no method by which you can demonstrate to the dummy that it is wrong*.[68]

All law is a process of internal scaffolding, supposing technicians (Legendre, 1988, 314), masons, scaffolders, mortarers — mediterranean types — hammering, grammering, emptying, mending the breach, filling the dovecots of old rumours, old posters, old news. If it is impossible to see this filling work [*coulisses*], it is because it is the letter itself by means of which what has never been written is constantly being revised.

The unwritten letter can say almost anything: it only speaks when the judges do and it only says what they tell it to. The entire social imaginary and its machinery of sense, of common sense, of good sense, is generated from this not-being-at-home of the letter, this being away, *en vacance*[69] and on the road of the French.

Can you hear what is said in the cooing of the letter, in the precedents that fell at the feet of the letter? Along came Adam ...:

la vint memes celi Adam, Ke la est, felonessement com felon et en assaut purpense et le assailli devileynes paroles et felones einz ke il unkes le aprocha ... there came this Adam, who is *there*, feloniously as a felon and en assaut purpense and assailed him with wicked and felonious words before he even drew near to him.

(Kaye, 1966, 10)

Before any relation or possible contact, the letter is *there*.[70] Before being read, the letter assails me. It falls without any warning, spontaneously, all of a sudden and before even signifying, the grammar *is* proximity. Before being English, the force of the law, the spur of the letter, is French.

In the old Norman French of the *Placita Corone* or *La corone pledée devant justices*, thought only ever appears as an adverb of manner, a '*mind*' in the grammar — further inside the felon than any judge can ever be, judging by contact without the mediation of skin.

Feloniously as a felon, felonnessement com felon — is a scale in the grammar. The *com* puts a manner or mannerism on a par with a substance at law.[71] The trial is a counting (and each count, a charge) which registers a repeated adjustment of substance to manner: an arithmetic response to the inaudible but indubitable *how?* and *how much?* — not only *comme* but *comment* — of a scale devised to capture, perchance to *captivate* the double necessity of being *this much* felon, this much *like a* felon.[72]

Felonessement com felon, laronessement com laron: The mind of the felon is there in the grammar, in the scale made of grammars, indeed only there — a *mens* carved out of the felon himself, dovetailing the felon by mending his grammar, by fixing his gendre, by seizing his letter; a pacification-effect that only makes itself felt as an internal difference — a difference which is constantly being denied: the felon does not breach, *he takes the breach with him* (Milsom, 1981, 287).

The pleas of the crown convoke, summon, call together personnages which reconstitute the breach by way of internal modifications: moods, tenses, inflections, elisions, contractions, 'internal accusatives'[73] and 'postures which defend the Body' (Lamy, 1986, 226), *essements* or ease*ments* of grammar: the smallest possible units of thought which would separate only to put on a par, a *here* — and a *there*. The grammar is made to resemble the breach in the peace, and through this resemblance, *to fix it*.[74]

The Peace of the King is a temporal-emotional matter; the felon only ever made out by means of his manners, the felony always being internal.[75]

What is the plea if not a dream which mends the narcissistic wound in the plaintiff, by filling his mouth with a dummy, a representation — what

Freud calls the *Vorstellungsrepresentatanz*? *Pleading changes nothing in the object which is pleaded but it changes something in the spirit which pleads* (Deleuze, 1991, 66-9). The peace is constituted *inside* the plaintiff; it is from the start a placebo-effect.

This repairing, restoring, renewing of Peace is, one might say, the infinite task of the plea or placebo, the infinite task of the dream — an assembling, an enjoining, a conjuring of justice by fantasmatic means, an internal carpentry which doubles, redoubles what is called thought by means of contagions, attachments, accessories, appositions, contiguities, series of incidentalities, allosemes (Abraham and Torok, 1986, 81): *purpensed, prepensed, pretenced, propensed, devant pourpensed* — thus a prethought which defers and disguises[76] itself as if by itself, a precedent which mends and conserves itself as if by itself (*sua sponte*), an autoplastic law[77] in which grammar functions as a knife, as the instrument and sentence of castration, where castration is understood as the possibility that a subject identify what he is for the other and identify what the other demands of him (Legendre, 1982, 113).

To think.

'*Ein kind wird geschlagen*': A Child Is Being Beaten

> At dawn I found myself looking out the window at the neon lights and the traffic, which made me think of *Dasein*, that is, the intermittent and blurred spectacle of 'thought thinking itself without knowing it'. The most synthetic image I can give you of the unconscious is Baltimore in the very early morning.
>
> (Lacan, 1990, 412)

The sovereign subject is stupid,[78] and it is this stupidity that dictates the infinite task of the Law: to solicit the forces of thought from a melancholy and watchful animality, to organise its encounter with reason, to institute a specific memory, a precedent, a fantasy of an original Conquest as a juridical norm.

The emotional conditions for the possibility of thought would lie in an evermore remote or hypothetical past, *which could only be postulated on the distant horizon of a fantasy. So soon as the serjeants begin to reason — and institute reason — they fall into the subjunctive:*[79]

> *And if* he is convicted [*atteint*] by the country [*par le pays*] of having been accessory or principal in doing the deed he will be deemed just as guilty *as if* he had been beaten into submission on the place of battle with shield and club,[80] and he will

suffer judgment at the appellor's hands: that is to say he will be blinded or castrated at the discretion of the justices, depending on the nature of the wrong.

(Kaye, 1966, 3)

The imaginary scene of a conquest put into play a stage with multiple entries in which the felon was to find his part — the 'me' might attach to any term in the sentence, it might have become the beater, the beaten, the beating.

The logic of the as-if[81] locked into place the position of thought, closing the gap between the *praecogitata* (what might have been thought, what could have been thought, the unformulated forces of thought) and the *cogitanda* — what must be thought, what ought to be thought, what thought is forced to think to prove a fantasy:[82] *Ein kind wird geschlagen*, a child is being beaten.[83]

Consider comment la justice parle aux prisoners:

Beal amy ... my good friend, the country has indicted you for homicide: how do you wish to acquit yourself? ...

'Sir, I am an honest man, and no thief, and had no part in such a theft or homicide; and if there is anyone who dares or wishes to speak against me I am ready to defend myself by my body against the accusation.' And then the justice will say: 'The king does not wish to do battle: how do you want to prove that you are good and honest?' And the other will reply in the same words as before. And then the justice will say: ' My good friend, no man makes suit against you except the king, and you cannot defend yourself against the king *by your body*,[84] or in any manner other than by the country. Consequently you are bound to pursue this course, if you think it fitting.'

And the prisoner, being doubtful of the jury, will say, if he is sensible [*si il est sages*] that 'pur unte de son linage' he would rather die in prison than be hanged. And if the justice should ask: 'My good friend, but how do you want to prove that you are good and honest?', the other will give the same reply as before, and each time he is asked. And the justice will reply, again and again, 'My good friend, you cannot do that: as I said before the king will not do battle, and no more will I...' And finally he will be ordered back to prison until another day. (Kaye, 1966, 23)

Having been taken for a thief, to empty the country of thieves, the felon became '*le enfant le Roy*' — the King's child — and 'he will have each day from the King three half pence to sustain him' (Kaye 1966, 24).

The unhappy encounter (*tuche*) — the non-encounter (*dustuchia*)[85] — with the King demonstrates the *fantasy* of the accused, the *thought* of the accused, the *truth* of the *accused*, not the truth of the *act*. Laplanche and Pontalis have given us the name of this fantasy: not so much *a child is being beaten* but rather *a father seducing a daughter*.[86]

For there to be murder, the science of the common law must be a science of the rare and not the general in nature, a science of the uncommon, the exceptional, the remarkable, a clinical science — from the Greek *cline* meaning bed — a science of the bedside,[87] of the nocturnal scene, a science of fantasies, a science of dreams.

To make a being think was first of all to *conjure*: to fascinate and convert a pathological volume, to make it move with the fates, with the *logos*, the *gunas*, and thence, with reason; to make it resonate with some inner demon, to make *this demon speak* — the speech of destiny, the speech with which Oedipus addresses himself in uncovering his parricide (Legendre, 1989, 29).[88]

(*But it is not only necessary to imagine Oedipus as innocent, but as full of zeal and good intentions.*) (Deleuze, 1990, 202)

A catastrophic situation must be brought about by words[89] for thought to appear — as a Thing — and the '-ment' to stand accused as if by itself, as *reus* or *rei-jos*:[90] the mind which is possessed by the Thing, the guilty mind, *mens rea*.

The lure of a battle would lock into place the position of thought, closing the gap between what the *praecogitata* — and the *cogitanda*, what should have been thought, what must have been thought, what will have been thought, what thought is forced to think to prove a fanatsy: that the appellor in a murder *should only be a dead man* — or a dummy [*le mort*].[91] The unconscious demonstrates itself by *happening* — as if chance, by coming on the scene *live*, that is to say *unconscious*.

What is called *malice prepensed* is an *impasse of thought*, a denegation of the impossibility of fighting a *symbol*, a *letter*, a dummy, R. *The Inquisition is the Proof* — all the while it appears to deny, to negate, to foreclose it.[92] The dummy, the letter R, the 'dead' King, phantom and father, takes thought from behind as it were, leaving it disarmed, locking into place a conformity to thought *before* thought.

We thus see how a fixed point — R — becomes a *point of view*,[93] simulating a central perspective while imposing on it an apparently incidental origin. The king's pardon serves not as a shield against the king but as a shield against future proceedings of third persons who might want to question him on the same fact, which is now restricted to the original appellor. R takes the place of the Third, he stands at the gate and blocks entry (Legendre, 1988, 356).[94] R is the *Third* who seems to have always *just now* appeared on the scene, not a *you* but a *he* who comes to oversee or overhear,[95] so as to recover *for his own account*,[96] and for the first time, the 'but for' or 'for what?' (Duhot, 1989, 145), the absent cause of law.

When he made the prisoner a grant of three half pence a day, the King was not just playing the role of a benefactor — he was securing for himself a man (Milsom, 1985a, 233; Bloch, 1993, 202).[97] Not *'un homme de bouche et mains'*, a vassal, but a man *without a mouth*; a minor or ward whose person and property were held by his lord *in custodia*; a son, but a son with the juridical status and unsecured fate of a *daughter*.[98] Here too the lord keeps land and daughter in custody [*custodia*] — *but this custodia is not going to end when she attains some age, and he is never going to make livery to her* (Milsom, 1985a, 234).

The daughter, the subject, *lives* in the *pre-thought*, in the smallest possible distance of law from nature, from Reason, from fate, moving with the angle of deviation of thought, like a common law judge, establishing the smallest possible distance between equilibrium and inclination, between what is given and what ought to be given, effecting the smallest possible disturbance to the soul of the judge, the minimum ado, making images of what she is for the Other and what the other demands of her: *to* kill *in the name of* the law, to *kill* — in the name of the *other* Father.

To think, then, is to follow a line or sorcery; in Lacanian terms — to encounter the real 'in the form of that which is *unassimilable* in it — in the form of the *trauma*' (Lacan, 1986, 55). In terms of doctrine, it is to encounter the immemorial *origin* of English law, and thence the immemorial *Englishness* of English Law, that is to say, the very *Proof* of its *Englishry* — in the murder of the French.

A thought, then, is only some friend of the friendless — a mitra, a Robin Hood, a mercenary; a lover of causes *as such*; bound to no particular army, no particular force-keeping-force; fighting *en assaut purpense*, killing *en agait purpense* and *en malice devant pourpensed*, moving through the streets like a dummy, that is to say — *Britishly as a Brit*.

Notes

1. Thanks to Peter Rush for his conjuration of the language. Thanks also to Jeremy Horder, Jeffrey Hackney, Ronnie Warrington, Niki Lacey, Rory Hachamovitch, Harvey Rabbin, Vikram Sachadeva and Antonio de Nicholas.
2. Holt CJ in *Mawgridge* at 1108.
3. It is always the Third, (Equity's) Darling, the arriviste on the scene, who establishes himself as the limit point, the law, and the 'reason' for the murder.

4. 'If any one was apprehended to be the murderer, he was to be tried by fire and water, though he killed him by misfortune; which was extended beyond reason and justice in favour of the Normans: but if an Englishman was killed by misfortune, he that killed him was not in danger of death, because it was not a felony' (*R v Mawgridge* (1707) Kelyng 119 at 1109).

5. Kaye (1967) tells us that it is impossible or almost impossible to 'visit with adequate punishment persons who lay in ambush, or who rode about in armed bands looking for victims, before they had actually committed felonies. As the law stood there was little opportunity to nip such conduct in the bud or to instil fear of consequences into potential offenders. A man who ambushed another with intent to kill, attacked him and left him for dead, had committed only a trespass for which he might be amerced'.

6. 'A laconic report, in the *Liber Assisarum*, leads one to suppose that under the pressure of circumstances the Council, if not a majority of common lawyers, were prepared to create a severe law of inchoate crimes: a man is there said to have been hanged for an unsuccessful attempt to rob, but this was anomalous, and no trace of such a rule is found in enrolments of proceedings before justices of the peace or itinerant justices. Later, the rule, though evidently acceptable to certain judges in the reign of Henry IV was repudiated by the common lawyers, though it was no doubt remembered by the Council, in Star Chamber days, and used as a basis of their creation of a general law of attempts. Similarly a desperate attempt to invoke the law of High Treason to deal with homicides committed by armed bands on the highways, riding in "warlike array", had to be terminated in 1351 because, probably, of the political dangers thought to be inherent in such an experiment: the remedy was likely to have proved worse than the disease' (Kaye, 1967, 382).

7. 'The battle over oversized gardens at a Dade public housing development has ended in compromise.... The height was a safety hazard, officials said. *Criminals could hide from police*' (*Miami Herald*, 11–14 September 1994, emphasis added).

8. The old problem of the archive, of where thought lies before it is thought, has always been a babysitter's problem: a problem of sitting up at night, of watching by night, of what remains at rest and that does not remain at rest, a problem of the nightwatch.

9. 'In 1380, the commons asked that the justices of the peace be given power to try and punish two named trespasses: item, *denquere & terminer de touz ceuz qi chivachent ove grantz routes en effrai del pees pur malfaire, & ensement touz ceuz qi gisent en agait pur gentz tuer, robber, ou mayhemer*' (Kaye, 1967, 379).

10. What *was* the word Murder *doing*, Kaye asks, 'between 1340 when, with the abolition of the murder fine, it temporarily ceased to appear in enrolments, and 1390 when, according to Stephen and Maitland, it re-emerged clad in the mantle of malice aforethought'? (Kaye, 1967, 368). One clue might be the famous 1352 statute of treasons whose definitions of Treason prefigure the coupling of murder and thought. 'The statute [25 Edw. III] makes treason to consist in *compassing or imagining* the death of the king, his consort, or his eldest son; violating his consort or eldest unmarried daughter, or the wife of his eldest son; levying war against the king in his realm, or adhering to his enemies in his realm, giving them aid and comfort in the realm or elsewhere; forging the great seal or the coinage, and knowing importing or uttering false coin; slaying the treasurer, chancellor judges while sitting in court; all of which involved forfeiture of lands and goods to the crown' (Plucknett, 1956, 393).

11. This *ou* is problematic. Kaye, 1967, reads it as 'or', a coordinating conjunction which connects an adverb and an adverbial phrase, thus rendering the phrase a description of four separate instances of murder: a slaying by assault, by ambush, by 'malice prepensed', or

an unseen, or hidden or nocturnal killing — *vide* Bracton, Britton and Fleta. Since the punctuation is missing, it is also possible to read the 'ou' as 'where' — 'où'.

12. 'To lawyers in the 14th century a statute was not something external to the law: it was an internal alteration, and it lived in its context so that its application was neither mechanical nor unalterable' (Milsom, 1981, 417–9). The King's pardon was, similarly, an indirect method of adjusting the law by making its application a little less insensitive.

13. 'The function of the institution is to organise the social bond as a relation of Waiting, which I write here with a capital, because the contents of this waiting vary according to the succession of political forms' (Legendre, 1988, 388–9). To wait for a fish or a god, it is the same thing: delay is an essential, not accidental, part of the process by which the law becomes our fate.

14. The problematic of intention in criminal law is the problematic of a 'cause' that does not belong to the order of bodies. Causality is derived from the necessity of the relation between corporeal and incorporeal series of events, whereas legality is born when something of an entirely different nature inserts itself into the causal series that pertains between bodies and calls itself an intention. Intention releases a soul from the laws of *physical* causality which pertain to bodies, and made it possible to affirm causality without introducing necessity. Intention is not a cause, but an incidence of bodies. Every intention has as its trajectory a series of possible effects with which it is compossible, but these effects are incidental; they belong to the ideal world of sense or meaning, and have the positive or negative validity of propositions, not the reality of bodies. *Everything hangs* on this problematic disjunction between bodies and the incorporeal effects which surround them.

15. The eavesdropper is what Braudel would call a 'deep structure' of legal history. He remains a discrete and visible figure of a social margin, and surfaces alongside his allotypes every time a policeman lacks the rigour of a cause. Thus Blackstone's reference to the statutory power of 'justice' to: 'bind over all nightwalkers; eavesdroppers; such as keep suspicious company, or are *reported* to be pilferers or robbers; such as sleep in the day, and wake in the night, common drunkards; w[h]oremasters; the putative fathers of bastards; cheats; idle vagabonds; and other persons whose misbehaviour may reasonably bring them within the general words of the statute, as persons not of good fame. [Also] such "causes of scandal" *contra bonos mores*, as well as *contra pacem*, as, for example, "haunting bawdy houses with women of bad fame; keeping such women in his own house; or words tending to scandalise the government, or words in abuse of the officers of justice, especially in the execution of their office"' (Blackstone, 1979, book IV, ch. 28). See also Kaye, 1967, 382fn. The creation of what later came to be known as 'common eavesdropping' was no doubt an indirect attempt to deal with the problem of inchoate crimes. See for example *Lincs. Rolls* (1381–96, i, at 32 (124)): A woman indicted in 1396 for 'listening by night outside the house of R.S. seeing and hearing his secrets against the King's peace'; and *Lincs. Rolls* (1381–96, i, 81 at (117)): John Singer fined for being a *communis ascultator sub tecta*, having apparently 'listened for a hundred consecutive nights under the roof of John Spicer and in no other places'.

16. The King's highway is determined by the definition of treason, which included the murder of royal messengers and highway robbery.

17. 'Fraying' is meant to denote the freudian '*Bahnung*' or breaching, pathbreaking (Derrida, 1981, 200).

18. '*Si deux de malice pretend gisont in againt lun de tuer lautre, ceo est murder, et nest material que done le primer plage, car coment qe cestuy qe done le primer plage soit tue, uncore est murder en lauter qe luy tue, par* Catlin C.J. *& auters erudits en ley, in le case*

de Stowell (10 Eliz)': *semble*, it would not have been regarded as Murder, had *cestuy qe done le primer plage* not been lying in ambush himself (Crompton, 1587 edn, fo. 21a, footnoted in Kaye, 1967, 574). Denying that combat is a good way to settle a dispute, Bonet writes: 'For gage of bataill cummys ay of forethocht felount. Bot naturaly all maner of creature naturale has a passioun of nature that is call it the first movement; that is, quhen a man or beste is sudaynly sterte, thair naturale inclinacioun gevis thame of thair complexioun to a brethe, an a sudagyn hete of ire of vengeance quihlk eftewart stanchis efter tht hete. Bot bataill taking cumis of lang forset nd forethocht purpos of malice that is nocht naturale to man' (Bonet's *Arbre des Batailles* (c.1340–1410) cited in Sellar, 1989, 45ff).

19.   The problematic of a *common* law makes itself felt as a problematic of 'dissimultaneity' in a moody aggregate ruled partly by religious law, partly under a French feudal pyramid according to hierarchies of political and administrative control. 'England' was far from being a 'simultaneous' country. It was precisely the lags in communication of the *doxa* between the centre (Westminster) and the extremities, notably on substantive issues, that instituted overhearing as the fundamental mode of transmission of common law and secured 'misreading' as its basic interpretative strategy. For a twentieth-century analogue, see Berques on French North Africa (1962, 259): 'By 1935, [Algeria] had become a simultaneous country'.

20.   See Deleuze, 1990, on the dialectic of rivalry in Plato. See also Milsom, 1981, 160: 'Just as inheritance became an abstract devolution of title, and seisin an abstract possession, so did the allocation of seisin as between rival possessors come to depend exclusively upon abstract rules rather than any actual authority of a flesh-and-blood lord. The reality must have died in the thirteenth century; and perhaps that was a condition precedent to what looks like a deliberate expansion of rights of entry in the fourteenth. But it is another question when the terms of thought were forgotten'.

21.   The Anglo-Saxon *forsteal*, like much else of the older legal language, survived only in local courts, and like its surroundings gradually sank to a petty significance. 'Forsteal' thus became 'forestall', an offence which consisted in intercepting sellers on the way to a market and attempting to raise prices artificially (Plucknett, 1956, 394). Thus a forethought that comes on the scene as a messenger, a go-between, a liaison, a rounder up, a *batonnier*, a trader, a translator and a traitor to boot.
When time belonged to God alone, the merchant's movement in time covered up his movement in space and the usance on bills of exchange was purported to measure the distance *between two financial markets — a distance which merely implied the duration of a return journey*. The King's highway was, so to speak, a usury-effect. '[I]n view of the slowness of communications, *even a sight draft gave rise to a credit transaction*, since it had to travel from the place where it was issued to the place where it was payable. However, unless otherwise specified, exchange quotations applied to usance bills. *Usance was determined by merchant customs* and, between *London and Antwerp for example, was one month from date*. It follows that a banker in London who bought a bill payable at usance in Antwerp, necessarily extended credit to the seller until it matured after one month. In the case of exchange and rechange, the delay was two months: one usance for the draft from London to Antwerp and one more for the redraft from Antwerp to London' (de Roover, 1974).

22.   The entire tension-ridden terminology of thought is derived from a Stoic episteme: note *attendre, entendre, intender*; the root of waiting, attending, intending, hearing, is the tension at the root of being.

23.   The conjoining of place and of the expressible, which comprises the notion of the incorporeal,

is the most remarkable trait of the Stoic theory of place. For the Stoics, place does not pertain to the principles which characterise bodies. Even though bodies are themselves extended, what is essential to them, force, is superior to this extension, since it is the principle in them. The incorporeality of space is analogous to a Kantian ideality. Space does not affect the nature of beings, it is not a sensible representation but a rational representation which accompanies the representation of a body, without being part of a body — something like a trust, something like an easement (Brehier, 1928, 40–1).

24. On the concept of '*demonstrare*', see Hachamovitch, 1994. Brunelleschi writes that the sky cannot be figured, only demonstrated (*dimostrare*). In his *Life of Brunelleschi*, Manetti writes that to represent the exterior of San Giovanni in Florence, Brunelleschi 'placed burnished silver where the sky had to be shown, that is to say, where the buildings of the painting were free in the air, so that the real air and atmosphere were reflected in it, and thus the clouds seen in the silver are carried along by the wind as it blows' (Manetti, 1970, 43-6). The description of this painted panel and its lentil-sized peephole is of Brunelleschi's first 'experiment' — from which many legal historians might benefit.

25. The rebellion described by Ladner is an effect of the Roman *foedus* which legitimated through a legal fiction the forced or at least expedient implantation of conquering barbarian states inside the borders of the Roman Empire. Unlike the older *foedera* had done, it no longer served to transform conquered outsiders into allied subjects, while leaving them varying degrees of autonomy.

26. 'Felony is a feudal conception applying to the breach of fidelity and loyalty which should accompany homage. Its characteristic punishment is therefore loss of tenement — escheat. On the continent, felony was often confined to this class of crime, but in England, by means unknown, there came 'a deep change in thought and feeling. All the hatred and contempt which are behind the word felon are enlisted against the criminal, murderer, robber, thief, without reference to any breach of the bond of homage and fealty. The transition may have been helped by the fact that already in Anglo-Saxon law there were crimes which put their author at the absolute mercy of the King, their property, limb and life. The King's "great forfeiture" may thus have caused these crimes to be equated with true felony which resembled it' (Plucknett, 1956, 392).

27. Consider the devolution of *entendre* in law French: 'quar si home entende de bater ascun person & en cell baterie il tua une autre, ceo este felony nient obstante son entent ne fut de lui occider' (Kaye,1967, 573). The *boke of Iustyces of Pleas*, first printed in 1506, and in 1510 by Wynkyn de Worde, still makes use of *entendre*: 'Murdre is proprely where a man by malyce purpensed lyeth in awayte to slee a man and accordynge to that malycous entent and purpose he sleeth hym'.

28. Where there was forfeiture there must have been flight. The remedy of forfeiture is the greatest clue to the *ratio* of the murder. The *reason* for the murder is 'in' the remedy; the forfeiture of land and goods to the Crown. 'A loss to theory, as well as to the sufferers from crime, was the pre-emptive practice of the Crown in the matter of forfeitures. The new feudal criminal law was succinctly explained in the *Dialogus de Scaccario* II, 16 thus: "One who has offended against the King may (a) lose all his chattels for a minor offence; or (b) lose all his lands and rents, and be disinherited, for greater matters; or (c) for great 'enormities' he will lose life or members"' (Plucknett, 1949, 80–1). Given this state of affairs, was it not almost inevitable that what is called thought should have become insolvent?

29. What then is at stake in a theory of causality? The effects or *kategorima*, which assign to a body a manner of being, are parts of the *doxa*. The question 'what is the cause' (and its response: the agent) only ever comes afterwards. Each incorporeal event remains in itself

a 'contingency' with a perpetual line of flight, or plane of possible rhetorical effects which resonates necessity. Thus legal logic operates as a logic of series which is constantly displacing 'accidents' or contingencies from one series to another, making possible the comparison, coupling and logical continuity of disparate events.

30. During the Anarchy after the death of Henry I there were briefly recreated in England conditions such as those which had so long before brought about the process of feudalisation in Europe. On each side the lands were 'escheated' and granted to supporters, for whom in turn surrender became as unthinkable as defeat. Inheritance was already the regular thing; but the trouble was that for two decades the times were not ordinary. One of the provisions of the settlement by which order was restored required that those dispossessed by the fortunes of war should also be restored. Just 40 years later, when the surviving series of plea rolls begins, claims in the right appear to be based on that provision. In a substantial proportion the King in whose reign the demandant's ancestor is said to have been seised is Henry I, and with him, though not with later kings, the assertion is more specific: the ancestor was seised in the reign of King Henry I, namely on the day that he died. That was the last moment of peace and legitimate title; and although Henry I himself recedes into the past, another reminder lasts as long as actions in the right. The ancestor's seisin is always alleged to have been 'in time of peace' (Milsom, 1981, 129). What is at stake in the King's Peace is always land.

31. *S'asseoir, assîs*: To sit, sitting; a defective verb: to sit. A difference of spelling in the future and conditional (*Je m'assoirai, je surseoirai*). Technical juridical sense is to impose a tax, lay (a foundation), base (an opinion). Reflexively it means to seat oneself, to sit down. *Assîs*, past participle means seated, equivalent to English present participle, sitting. In legal language, the verb *seoir* in its original sense of 'to sit' becomes in the participle *seant* (e.g. *un tribunal seant a* = a tribunal sitting at) and *sis* 'situated' (e.g. *une maison sise à* = a house situated at) (*Byrne and Churchill's Comprehensive French Grammar*, 1993, G376–8).

32. The grammar of the 'there' is a vise which holds the felon in place.

33. The jury was the source of all the evidence put before the court. 'Jurors were told to tell the truth to the best of their knowledge. If, however, they did not know or possessed imperfect knowledge they could not then support the prosecution, for they must not reach their verdict on the basis of mere "thoughts"' (Green, 1985, 26).

34. All the manners of the denial are mapped out in advance by means of the accusation, each count must be negated by its opposite, each image lifted, negated, conserved, unfolded, refolded, relevée, pliée.

35. *Kehre* [turning] derives from the sanskrit *vri*, and thus forms the root for the God 'Varuna', the 'Binder' and all that that implies. It is a form of the Latin *ver* which roots the entire tropological series of words relating to verb, verse, words, writing, furrows, ploughing etc. It is more specifically a turning in the sense of swinging a *pivot, a turning point*, the place where the two ends of something meet; figuratively used to indicate 'that about which everything else revolves or on which it depends'. This hinge may also describe a *swinging of speech toward the other* in the relation of analysis, specifically the 'transference-resistance' of analysand. This 'swinging' of speech tells us that the truth is nearing: 'The moment when the subject interrupts himself is usually the most significant moment in his approach toward the truth. At this point we gain a sense of resistance in its pure state, which culminates in the feeling, often tinged with anxiety, of the analyst's presence' (Borch-Jacobsen, 1990, 119). Here the justice sits in place of the analyst, and occupies both the place of an imaginary 'me' and of the symbolic Other — hence the 'paradox of [his] position'. The 'he' or the

Third is the hinge around which the subject revolves. This binding or backing of a subject who, in *speaking* (or dictating) swings himself between one 'me' and the Other. The approach of the truth — the verdict — is this swinging-that-binds the 'me' to the Other, to the Third, the King, the Common Law, more and more tightly.

36. *Le Mort*: The dead man, the 'third person', the 'dummy' or false grammatical subject, has many functions; indeed it is the 'functionary' or role par excellence. The dead man appears as the grammatical *'pseudo*-subject' (called 'dummy subject') in the usage that the impersonal *il* serves for a verb that has only a weak semantic value and which leads into the 'real subject' which in such circumstances follows the verb. In French, this occurs particularly with verbs such as *arriver* (to arrive, to happen), *se passer* (to happen, to be going on), *rester* (to remain), but is also found with many other verbs — *se souffler*, for example. Likewise in *il y a* ('there is' or 'it is (nine o'clock)') when an adverb of place or of time stands in the place of the subject of the sentence. In subjunctive clauses such as 'it was necessary that ...' (*il fallait que...*), the 'it' functions as a dummy-subject. In the situation of analysis, the analyst plays the role of the dummy — the 'other ego' and 'trustee' of the solemn speech of the unconscious. Where there is the paradox of a benefice granted, a dead man appears in the name of the donor. When there is joint tenancy the surviving tenant, the *'conjoint'*, may be the dummy for the other joint tenants who no longer exist; hence the 'I' who speaks for the 'we' or signs for the we, etc. The incipience of *le mort* is thus at the very basis of the development of juridical agency, of trusteeship, of the fiction-ridden history of the forms of action.

37. The reasonable man, Milsom tells us, did not begin as 'a sort of Mr Average: in legal English the word 'reason' was slow to lose its French connotations, and the reasonable man began as the rightful man. What lawyers first articulated, and then appropriated, had begun as something more than the decent instincts of society: it had been the same right and wrong that had once been brought to bear within ordeals, then found by jurors searching their conscience' (Milsom, 1985c, 216).

38. 'It is best not to call them a jury,' writes Maitland, 'for though we see [in the grand assize] one stage, a very important stage, in the growth of trial by jury, still in many respects trial by the grand assize to the last day of its existence — and such a trial was possible in 1834 — remained a distinct thing from trial by jury. We observe for instance that the recognitors were sworn to tell the truth not about mere facts — the separation of questions of fact from questions of law belongs to a later day — but to tell the truth about rights, to say whether A or B has the greater right (*jus majus*)' (Maitland, 1989, 21).

39. The King's court only applies a common law of inheritance. 'Its rules are not criteria for making a present choice, but reach down and back to reverse decisions made yesterday or a century ago. They are rules about the devolution of a sort of abstract ownership. To claim that ownership, one has only to make oneself out as heir to an ancestor who was seised' (Milsom, 1981, 122).

40. Overhearing is an essential part of the formula for the fantasm of a murder. The dead man or dummy is the subject of unconscious repression. The 'bar' of repression is still in place even though the previously unconscious idea has now become conscious; it still exists in two forms in two separate registers: 'a conscious memory of the auditory impression of the idea, and the unconscious memory of the actual experience existing in its earlier form'. '*[But] there is no lifting of the repression* until the conscious idea, after overcoming resistances, has united with the unconscious memory-trace' (Freud, 1963, 125).

41. *Malice prepensed* is an obscure but well-founded phenomenon: it signifies the tension inside a body, which penetrates other bodies and resonates through them. This is because

the limit of the body is ideal and incorporeal: it consists of all that can be said or cried out about a body; it is doxic, dogmatic, or decorous. The being that is cried for, that one can cry out for is *ti*, not *on*.

42.   Aulus Gellius, *Attic Nights*, II, 4, quoted and commented on in Lacan, 1968, 75.

43.   The obfuscation of the second person is in some sense a cause of the incipient staying quality of a centralised system of justice. As Milsom reminds us, (1981, 120) a pathological forgetfulness is at work in this displacement. 'To be seised of' — in the manner of a tenant — is to be seised *by* the lord *of* a tenement. A lord — a second person — seised a tenant of the tenement, and in the passive mood, 'the tenant was seised' meant *seised by the lord*. '*Seisin connoted two people*, and not a relation between a person and a thing. The verb is older than the noun.' What remains of the 'you' in the relation of seisin, 'when the lord is dissolved out and ideas which depended upon lordship survive in a world without true lords' is a neutralised, neurotic, narcissistic derivative of the 'I', *the first person*. The second person, the 'you', like the lord, becomes an *aside*. Thereafter, seisin itself — and the relation of possession it implies — 'becomes abstract and empty, a relation between one person and land, with only vestigial mysteries to indicate that once a second person had been inherent in the very word' (Milsom, 1981, 122).

The 'I''s narcissistic identification with the second person is what gives rise to 'primal reflexive fantasy'. The relation of 'being seised [by]' comes to designate a reflexive moment of the 'I' — but a moment without any real relation to an *other*. It is merely a reflection of the juridical fact of possession — or dispossession — a means by which the 'I' apprehends such a fact, makes it deliver (its sense), and thence appropriates what it can only assimilate as fantasy. The passive moment of 'being seised' is experienced as aggression, but an aggression which the 'I' turns on itself, an aggressing of itself.

44.   'You' designates the limit that the 'me' can only briefly cross; we find it in Lacan's Antigone, in 'the text of the Chorus ... significant and insistent — ektos atas eektoz ataz' (Lacan, 1966, 265–83). The 'you', the 'ata', is first an accusation, then a plea, and only then does it make itself felt as a cry, a moaning for the dead body of 'ektos' — the Other.

45.   The juridical preconscious is the translational space par excellence: it is where the (Alhazenian) *intentiones* of the object are translated into subjective structures, on the model of the heard. The pretrial jury thus serves as the screen, the filter, the mirror, the warranty or guarantor of what Freud called thing-representations and what the judges call 'facts'.

46.   For Freud, an unconscious thought is screened before it is allowed to pass into consciousness. But before being thought, such a thought 'is not yet conscious ... it is certainly *capable of entering consciousness*, according to J. Breuer's expression, that is, it can now, without any special resistance and given certain conditions, become the object of consciousness. In consideration of this capacity to become conscious we also call the consciousness system the "*preconscious*"...' (Freud, 1963, 122–3). The *prepense* or preconscious does not 'belong' to the subject, it belongs and only ever has belonged to the object. Whereas the unconscious is populated by *petite perceptions*, bitten out of thought by the real encounter, memory traces or affects read visually, the preconscious is the domain of the heard and fills with word-representations or (auditory) fantasms which move between the conscious and the unconscious systems.

47.   For Peirce, the evolution of a code requires that there be a conservation and development of forms, a logic of continuity which converts a mark into a symbol: 'the mark is a mere accident and as such may be erased. It will not interfere with another mark drawn in quite another way. There need be no consistency between the two but no further progress beyond this can be made, until a mark will *stay* for a little while; that is, until some beginning

of a *habit* has been established by virtue of which the accident acquires some incipient staying quality, some tendency toward consistency' (Peirce, 1931–5, 204).

48.   What distinguishes murder and 'simple' homicide, as Green writes, was imposed upon the courts by the country: *(par le pays)* that is, by the jury, by the jurors who had evidence of their own, who claimed the evidence of the court was inconclusive, by jurors who were near neighbours of the parties and the witnesses and knew the credit and estimation of every one of the same deponents and witnesses, and also some of the said defendants, knowing more of themselves in that matter than was openly given in evidence. Consider it: a juror deposed that six of the others said of their own knowledge that they knew the defendant was not at the felony and further said that their own knowledge was as good to them and better than any evidence given in court. Jurors said that the chief witness for the Crown was known to most of them to be of light behaviour and small credit although he was not so known to the judges (Green, 1985, 142fn).

49.   For a brilliant analogue of this off-the-record pre-trial, see McConville et al., 1991.

50.   It would be wrong to suppose that thought developed independently of the practices and reflections of a feudal society; one should rather espy that the practice of doing homage to several lords, the 'true scourge of vassalage', would in its turn have exercised its baleful influence upon thought. The fealty of a settled or sedentary thought must be studied on what Le Goff calls its two slopes, entry and exit: there is always the possibility of exit, of disavowal, of betrayal, of withdrawal or contraction of faith, repressed within thought as its negative slope of fealty, its ontological boundlessness or 'unmeasure' (Le Goff, 1980, 247; Bloch, 1993, 216–7). One must, in sum, study the felony as one form of negative fealty within the montage of feudal obligations, a montage of faith in which faith itself had become almost *unrecognisable*.

51.   See *In Re Ellenborough Park* ([1956] Ch. 131 at 184, per Evershed MR) for a curious reference back to *ius spatiandi*. By contrast, see *McKay v Gratz* for the American 'mitigation' of the strict rule of English common law by 'common understanding with regard to the large expanses of unenclosed and uncultivated land in many parts, at least, of this country'. Over these, it is customary to [hal]lucinate at will, as it were, 'to wander, shoot and fish ... until the owner sees fit to prohibit it. A licence may be implied from the habits of the country' (*McKay v Gratz* 260 US 127 (1922) at 136, per Holmes J).

52.   'And Louis XVI answered the deputies thus: "I have to use my power to restore and maintain order in the capital.... These are my reasons for assembling troops around Paris." And on the morning of Sunday 12 July the city was full of posters "by order of the king" announcing that the concentration of troops around Paris was intended to protect the city against bandits. Through these notices the city was designated as both the place and the population organised as a totality, sealed by the military action which produced it as a confined crowd. The *rumours, the posters, the news* ... communicated their common designation to everyone: each was a particle of sealed materiality. At this level, the totality of encirclement can be described as being lived in seriality.' (Sartre, 1976, 355) Reading itself against the royal armies, the city feels itself as a totality waiting for a common fate, on the basis of seriality as inert flight. But when the people of Paris began to arm themselves against the king, it was on the basis of seriality as practice.

53.   'Mes' are deeply passive in their relation to ancient messages: the stories of the grandmothers, the old voices, the old news, the ancient precedents. The fantasy of rehearing, of overhearing, of hearkening to a (grand)motherly or mothering speech at a distance of centuries is a kind of repatriation of the subjective material of heredity, a fantasy of pinning down an essentially frayed part of the 'Englishness' of English law.

54.   The problematic of the prepensed, of the easement of thought, may thus be summarily defined: the empirical element of an experience cannot be the object of thought. Thought fails at the very moment that it encounters the real. It can only recognise or judge or remember or estimate or imagine an object through and across a matrix of prepenses or 'intentions' — what Legendre has called 'the juridical montage', the assemblage of images and names through which the law makes itself loved.

55.   Is it not obvious that the original provocation is thought itself? The entire common law doctrine of provocation — the sole ground of voluntary manslaughter — is rooted in thought as this agent provocateur. Is it not obvious that the only mode of resentment that bears a 'reasonable relationship' to the provocation is thought?

56.   'Hotter never stops where it is but is always going a point further, and the same applies to colder,' says Alice (Sellar, 1989, 45ff). Cold and hot-blood — malice prepensed and chaudemellée — were 'natural signs' of unlawful temperaments. What is at stake in the blood as an index of juridical substance is the very chance of tempering, of temporising thought, and the precise danger of transmitting alongside and through nature or the natural the possibility of what is called thought. To think? It is to temper or temporalise, to mix (where the best mixture of all is the common sense of the common law). But how does one temper a pathological volume, a thought that always explodes or bursts into flames *just before it is thought*? How can one measure a blood that is always hotter or colder than thought?

57.   'Among the causes which in course of time have rendered justice more rapid we must reckon not merely good roads, organised postal service, railways, electric telegraphs, but also the principle that men can hand over their litigation and their other business to be done for them by agents, whose acts will be their acts. Rapid justice may nowadays be fair justice, because if a litigant cannot be present in court in his own person, he may well be there by his attorney and his counsel. But this principle that every suitor may appear in court by attorney is one that has grown up by slow degrees and, like so many other principles which appear to us principles of "natural justice", it first appears as a royal prerogative; the king can empower a man to appoint an attorney. But so long as litigants have to appear in person justice must often be slow if it is to be just; the sick man cannot come, so justice must wait until he is well; one must give the crusader a chance of returning. But one cannot wait for ever...' Much of the law on excuses for non-appearance, Maitland writes, has been instrumental in 'raising high the barriers between the various forms of action. In the action begun by Writ of Right, which will finally deprive one of the parties of all claim to the land, the essoins that a man may proffer are manifold; a litigant can generally delay the action for a year and a day by betaking himself to his bed; in other actions so many essoins are not admissable' (Maitland, 1903, 19).

58.   For John of Salisbury, for Agricola, for Ramus, for the medieval jurist, logic was only ever the logic of place: '*know the places...*' In Thomas Wilson's sylvan setting, invention has become hunting and Agricola's forest primeval becomes a game reserve: 'Those that bee god harefinders will soon finde the hare by her fourme. For when thei see the ground beaten flatte round about, and faire to the sight: the have a narrowe gesse by al likelihode that the hare was there a little before. Likewise the Huntesman in Huntyng the foxe wil soon espie when he seeth a hole, whether it be a foe borough, or not. So he that will take profeite in this parte of Logique, must bee like a hunter, and learne by labour to know the boroughes. For these places bee nothing elles, but covertes or boroughes, wherein if anyone searche diligently, he maie find game at pleasure. And although perhappes one place faile him, yet shal he finde a dousen other places, to accoumplishe his purpose. Therefore if anyone will

doo good in this kinde, he must go from place to place, and by searching every borough he shal have his purpose undoubtedly inmoste part of them if not in all.' The directive laid down by Wilson (*know the boroughs* in which the foxes are hiding) repeats Agricola's dictum: *know the places* (be familiar with the headings as I give them) and draw (*deducere*) out of them the arguments you are after. Wilson tricks out the arguments as foxes (Ong, 1958).

59. Lacan's division of the psyche into Symbolic, Imaginary and Real, must itself undergo a division into the *symbolic, imaginary* and *real*. The real would then designate a concrete material fragment or piece of everyday life encountered by the 'me' — what Woiekoff calls a *moveable body* and Roman law recognises as moveable goods, *things in rem* capable of being restored as real property, *terra and tenementa*. English law would assimilate such moveable goods to things personal — *bona et catalla* or chattel — capable of being restored only by personal action, founded on either contract or tort. Thus Bracton says that there is no action *in rem*: 'At first sight it may appear that the action should be both real as well as personal, *tam in rem in personam*, since a particular thing is claimed, and the possesor is bound to give it up, but in truth it will merely be *in personam*, for he from whom the thing is claimed is not absolutely bound to restore the thing, but is bound in the *disjunctive* to restore the thing *or* its price, and *by merely paying he is discharged*, whether the thing be forthcoming or not'. Quoted in Maitland, 1903, 60 (emphasis added). At the very basis of the murder is the dogma of the *murdro* — the fine as a legal and phantasmatically equivalent substitute for the thing itself, to wit, a moveable body. Here too, then, the juridical thing takes the place of the truth.

60. The Inns of Court are figures of the law's reception, and the problematic history of this reception is emblematised by these hospices or 'hostells' which are said to date back at least to the reign of Edward I. An early reference from Thomas Hoccleve makes allusion to a dining club, 'a court of Good Company', Sir George Buc traces the term Inne to Hostelry 'which in the Roman is *Diversoria*, guest Innes and Commonhouses for entertainment of all travellers for their money'. Dr John Cowell provides the same etymology for *Hospitii Curiae* derived from common inns 'instituted for passengers, for the proper Latin word is *Diversorium*, because he that lodgeth there is *quasi divertens se a via*'.

61. The common law comes *in the image* of law, as a semblance of law, *in the fashion* of law, but it is further outside a common law for commonfolk than any law could ever be. It is the law of the King not the law of the country (*com*pagne). It is never *here* but always and already *there*, like the felon. It too is on the road and on its way to become, that is to be what it is not yet — the Common *Law* and the *Common* Law, the customary Law and the common custome, the ius non scriptum or unwritten law. From the point of view of the country, *the shortest thought, the smallest thought* was that of these itinerant, ambulant justices, 'hard-worked men rushing through their business at high speed in order to get on to the next place' (Kaye, 1966, xxvi).

62. The problematic *whose?* of this legacy, these writings, is also the problematic *whose?* of the trust, of what they entrust (the unconscious), and the problematic *where?* of the beneficial interest in the trust (where does the beneficial interest lie?). Thus conjoining the problematic of the archive to that of property and possession, and therefore to psychoanalysis as an institution, to the unconscious as this institution, while introducing the problematic of the couple. A joint tenancy is, to cite Bracton, '*Quilibet totum tenet, et nihil tenet, scilicet, totum in communi, et nihil separatim per se*' (Bracton, fo. 430, vol. 4, 336). A whole in which each holds everything and yet holds nothing. This indivisible estate is vested simultaneously in each and every joint tenant. A joint tenancy confers on the one who

outlives the 'marriage' *ius accrescendi* or the right of survivorship. Blackstone's *Commentaries* (1979, vol. 2, 182) describes the joint tenancy as one wherein 'two or more persons are seised of a joint estate [their] interest is not only equal or similar, but also is one and the same. One has not originally a distinct *moiety* from the other ... but ... each has a concurrent interest in the whole; and therefore on the death of his companion, the sole interest in the whole remains to the survivor.' It is said that this 'singular infelicity' of Blackstone ('expounding' on Littleton's law-French) has misled generations of lawyers: 'seised *per my et per tout*' *would not have meant* 'by the half or moiety, and by all'. Gray tells us: 'The word '*my*' is now generally agreed to have been the *mie* which in old French served as a negative expletive particle rather than *mi* or half as Blackstone seems to have believed. (So much *should have been obvious* in any event from the reflection that there may be more than two joint tenants)' (Gray, 1987, 296fn). A permanent possibility of denegation would seem to descend through and across the smallest conjunctions and with it the permanent possibility for the reinvention of the atom, the particle, the letter, the my as well as the *my* [*mie=nihil*, not], the **smallest** unit of thought as well as the smallest unit of sense. In effect, Littleton's phrase '*per my et per tout*' is merely a reiteration of Bracton's '*totum tenet et nihil tenet*'. A joint interest in an estate means that each of the partners owns *everything or nothing*, and that *one cannot even speak* of owning a 'half-share' or a 'moiety' of a joint tenancy, without converting it, mistakenly, into a tenancy-in-common, or without misrepresenting an inchoate right as an actual right, or without presuming proleptically (that is to say, in the future perfect) a severance of the joint tenancy (which *will have converted* each joint tenant into a co-owner in equal shares). The grammar of misrecognition worked itself into the material of heredity while the unconscious remains unassignable.

63.   The not-mine as the space of equity is one of the fantasmatic but legal paradoxes of the unconscious. Paradox 1: *The unconscious does not know death*. This means that it does not know death as an other; the event of death does not sever the joint tenancy. A joint tenancy confers upon the one who outlives the 'marriage' *ius accrescendi* or the right of survivorship. Thus the unconscious as the final original tenant, the final original fantasm, does not know that the others are dead, does not know of death at all. This 'not-knowing' is instanced in the paradoxical fact that, although a tenant may die since none have a patch of their own that can devolve upon their death, none of the remaining ones may be said to have a 'larger share' since the tenancy appertains always and by definition to the *whole* indivisible joint tenancy. It is impossible to say what happened to the particle or fraction of the joint tenancy of an original that died — since the original would have originally constituted the tenancy as such, as its fantasm, as its *appareil*. Paradox 2: The unconscious *does not know time*. A joint tenant is still and will always be an originary joint tenant, not only because it is there at the birth of the tenancy, but because it will be there at the end. If there is an unconscious it is there, as the final original fantasm, the last of a series of joint tenants. Paradox 3: The history of this grammar of equity is difficult to account for, even more difficult to audit. This is because *equity abhors a vacuum, does not know the 'nothing'*, *denies* the 'not' or 'no' or, in old law-French, the *my*, the negative expletive.

64.   Here then, we are back at the problem of the archive, of what remains and what does not remain: what is it that registers the being-out of the being-at-home or being-with. Or the being-empty of the King's Bench. Finally, the being-away or the being-gone of the King. The grammar of denegation registers as *unheimlich*, as the not-being-at-home of what is written, the possibilities of this not-written [*if... then*] of a space. At least for the duration of a clause, being has flown, as it were, but what remains is the coop of a grammar, this unconscious archive of excuses. What remains is a leasehold of denial, a licence to a

mood, a leeway to play. The function of the grammar, of this archive of excuses, is not to decieve but to keep the record straight.

65. As mentioned above, the offer of battle was a ritual formality, a solemnisation of ancient law, and appellees did not expect to be taken seriously. Things, as Fleta tells us, were no longer as they had been (Kaye, 1966, xvi).

66. The formula 'Here lies' when used of a dead man is '*ci git*' — rather than *ici* (here) — which indicates a position not a place.

67. The 'policy' resonates an old Roman dogma found in a case of Justinian: 'If a dead body has been dispersed ... into pieces, and it has many sepulchres, many resting places, which is the principal tomb? To which would apply the statute of a "religious place" (*locus religiosus*)?' One responds: '... there where the head is, there is found the principal — *accessorium sequitur principal* — because it is from the head that one makes the image (*imago*) and it is from the image that one knows'. It is the head that makes the body *signify*; the face that makes the body represent, and representable, the *imago* or funereal mask that makes the dead face memorable. See Justinian's *Digest*, II, 7, 44, cited in Legendre, 1988, 7.

68. This placebo effect is the emotional condition for the possibility of law. The emotions which support the legality of law, are born in the absence of law, with the hallucinatory activation of the idea of law, which is accompanied by a *feeling* of utter reality.

69. If 'a donor should be parted with his [let us say, 'x'] *without any intention* of retaining any interest therein, ex hypothesi', then according to the law relating to trustees and trusteeships 'neither the beneficiaries named to whom such interest is given, nor the donor, are in a position to put forward any claim to the equitable interest not expressly disposed of, it necessarily falls to the Crown as *bona vacantia*', as the keeper of all goods lost at sea, of goods that have no owner (Pettit, 1989, 4). The story of the family *vacance*, of the vacance of writing, may thus be summarily recovered as the ownerless thing, to wit, the unconscious. But and of course also, writing. Recovered, discovered, this *bona vacantia* — the always and already lost [law] — would seem to be our own, all ours, *les siens*. But no. It would seem that 'les siens' is not the his, the hers, the its of we beneficiaries, we hearers, we interpreters, we translators — but of the One's, the Crown's, His Majesty's, the Baby's. There is no sanction of the unconscious, only the grammar of Equity, of what would have been written and what will have been written, essoins or excuses which put into play the conditions for the possibility of the equitable *refinding* [*retrouvee*] of the real: of what will not have been lost if writing had, if only writing could have had, the power to construct, to create, an equitable reality.

70. It is Aristotle who tells us that only the adverbs of place and time have the remarkable feature of being predicated of primary substance in the manner of nouns: 'Socrates is there'. The remainder modify something other than the subject, usually the verb. For example, 'Socrates speaks well'. What was at one time a mood of something else, its accident, in rejoinder comes to predicate the subject.

71. We see here a profound mannerism which, unlike classicism, has no need to stipulate a constant substance, upon which to confer essential attributes, but rather replaces the essentiality of the attribute with the spontaneity of manners. Thought appears — if it appears — as the last of a series of *petite perceptions* that are scarcely noticed, because they remain at first buried in the immemorial depths of the soul. This entrenched order of the immemorial remains the guiding framework and the register of the mythological 'already-known' *despite the fact that from the point of view of history such an original register is by no means justified.* The 'immemorial' was *compiled* by new proprietors after the

Conquest, to wit, Frenchmen, participants in the gains of the adventure, who had either displaced one or more English owners or had been intruded over their heads to become their lords. The tenures of those who held in-chief of the King, and some tenures at a lower level, were thus created instantly. More came into being as the King laid on his tenants-in-chief the obligation to furnish fighting men. The courts of these communities of tenants *created* the '*customs*' of 'English' feudalism and so imposed on English property law a logic as indestructible as soon as it became irrelevant (Milsom, 1981, 20–1 (modified)). In other words, the immemorial origin of the law itself was never 'legal'. The reason of the law was from the start an archive of excuses, a logic designed to encrypt, to divert.

72. On the capture of the subject by means of his representation, see Legendre, 1988, 344.

73. We find this in Sanskrit adjectives, which do not have a termination exclusively reserved for adverbial usage. Instead, the accusative singular neuter (acting as an 'internal accusative') may do duty. Hence, *sighram calati* [he moves a swift (moving)] (Coulson, 1976, 64).

74. Thus, in such constructions as *felonnessemente*, -*ment* is added to the feminine form of felon, i.e. felon*esse,* because '-*ment* derives from the Latin -*mente,* a form of the word *mens* 'mind' which was feminine, so one had constructions like *felonnessement* 'with a felonious mind' hence 'feloniously' or felonfully.' Thus also such easements of manner as *placida mente* (with peaceful mind) hence 'placidly' or 'peacefully' (Price, 1993, 474).

75. If there is a legal relation, it is not between subjects but between representations which are inherent in subjects, and are predicated of subjects.

76. This cover-up of the word (prepensed) *en souffrance* or in delivery announces the existence of a crypt — a split in the Ego — as well as its fetishisation within the uniconscious (Abraham and Torok, 1986, 81).

77. This autoplasticity has an analogue in Theseus's ship 'which the Athenians were always repairing'.

78. An Englishman is not an idiot, writes Giles Jacob (1725), if he can count to 20 pence, name the days of the week, measure two yards of cloth, or beget a child. Still, it would be wrong to suppose that an Englishman thinks. The 'I think' of the sovereign subject may be an exception which takes being along with it, an absolute accident (*pathe*) which marks the fact that a medieval idiot (*idiota*/layman) has learned to count, and now believes himself to be a thinking thing.

79. 'The word "if" or some equivalent must needs play a large part in the ascertainment and development of the law, and the subjunctive appears as the mood of hypothesis. We cannot say that "*si"* invariably governs the subjunctive; but it generally does so unless what is in form an hypothesis is in substance a statement of some fact which exists or is represented as existing. Thus it was good style to use a subjunctive after "if" (*si*) and "although" (*coment qu, mes qu, tut*), "until" (*tantqe, avant que, einz qe*) and "unless" (*sanz ceo qu*)' (Maitland, 1903, lxvii).

80. Hale tells us that the Trial by single combat was introduced by King William 1 at the same time as the 'Law de Murdro, or the Common Fine for a Norman or Frenchman slain and the offender not discovered', as part of what Gervasius Tilburiensis calls *Leges Neustriae quae efficacissimae videbantur ad tuendam Regni pacem,* and was principally designed for the securing of the Peace of the Kingdom, especially between the English and Normans, and *the establishment of King William in the Throne* (Hale, 1880, 89).

81. On the sense of this as-if, see Vaihinger, 1924; and relatedly Murphy, 1994, ch. 3.

82. The trial was always two trials: an accusation and a proof. The proof by ordeal was an Anglo-Saxon tradition, the trial by battle, Norman. Every guilty verdict had to be tried by a form of physical proof: the truth of the accused was inscribed on his body. The truth

belonged to God, it was a matter of what Lacan calls the Real. In 1215, with the assise of Clarendon, the use of the ordeal in England came to an end and the trial jury was charged with determining the date of the accused. While the 'sentimental' attachment to trial by battle was too strong to do away with it altogether, it gradually fell into disfavour during the thirteenth century. Green (1985) suggests that it is not so much that the jury was adopted as an alternative mode of proof, as that the ordeal was dispensed with. Yet one might argue that judgment has never escaped the dimension of the ordeal or the battle: that the reality at the basis of the proof was merely displaced, to an *other* scene of truth. As Milsom tells us: 'the jury was first used as a new ordeal, giving an equally blank result. Of course it reached that result by considering detailed facts. But the facts did not get onto the record so that the historian can misinterpret as a crude dispute about the commission of an obvious wrong what was really a delicate dispute about the details of an indisputed event.... A blank result settles the dispute but can make no law. What if the beating was accidental? The questions cannot be asked as legal questions until the supernatural is replaced by a rational deciding mechanism' (Milson, 1981, 4–5). See also Haldar's essay in the present book.

83. For Freud, *Ein kind wird geschaglen* (a child is being beaten) is a neutralised, neurotic, conscious derivative of the primal reflexive fantasy. This reflexive moment of the 'I' is designated by the sentence 'I am being beaten by my father'. 'It does not necessarily give a reflexive content to the "sentence" of the fantasy; it is also and above all to reflect the action, internalise it, make it enter into oneself as fantasy.' The scenario is defined by the series beater-beaten-beating but the me may vary its role in the fantasy by entering the scene as different 'verbal bodies'. The passive moment of 'a child is being beaten' is an effect of the 'turning around of the subject' upon himself: 'to fantasise aggression is to turn it around upon oneself, to aggress oneself'. Hence a derivative of the reflexive 'I' (Laplanche, 1976, 97–103).

84. This expression is manifestly important because it shows the essential place occupied by the body in the cultural and mental symbolism of the Middle Ages. The body is the symbolic site where man's fate — in all its forms — is fulfilled. It would be a mistake however to think of good intention, and its essentially dogmatic structure, in the 'framework of a simple opposition between two determined actions — an intended action and an accomplished action. Indeed, on the one hand, the willed action is an image of action, a projected action; and we do not speak of a psychological project of the will, but of that which renders it possible, that is, of a mechanism of projection tied to bodies, to physical surfaces. It is the strange knowledge of the body itself — what Freud calls the unconscious — which, far from being an agency of the depths, is a phenomenon of the entire surface, or the pheneomenon which adequately corresponds to the *coordination* of physical surfaces' (Deleuze, 1990, 207).

85. We come back then to the trauma, to the encounter with the real, to the real as encounter — *tuche* — 'the encounter in so far as it may be missed, in so far as it is essentially the missed encounter'. What first presented itself in the unhappy encounter — the 'murder' of the French — is already a repetition, already a symptom of the (original) no less unhappy encounter with the Latin (Lacan, 1986, 55).

86. 'A father seduces a daughter' is the concise formula of the fantasm of recognition. Nothing says that the subject will find his position straight away in the term 'daughter'; indeed we see it misrecognise the term 'father', and the term 'beaten' (Laplanche and Pontalis, 1986).

87. The situation of the prisoner is mirrored in the situation of analysis: there the analyst plays the role of the dummy — the 'other ego' and 'trustee' of the solemn speech of the unconscious.

88.   The role of the inquisition — the seduction — is to inscribe the fantasy into the social discourse of Fate, in order to 'reintegrate the subject into speech'.

89.   Commenting on the 'shabby trick' played by a justice on a slow-witted man, Kaye reminds us that 'the day had not yet arrived when justices would consider it their duty to act as impartial arbiters between crown and prisoners and to ensure that every point in a prisoner's favour was taken. Rather they *were* the crown, and the emphasis was on speedy and efficient clearing of the lists, not on abstract justice. When evidence in the modern sense, and the examination of witnesses were unknown, when juries decided cases on much the same basis of a prisoner's general reputation as on that of the specific charge against him, and above all when justices regarded a prisoner's defences or objections to aspects of the procedure as irritating obstacles to be overcome by any possible means, it is easy to conclude that "medieval man acted at his peril" though not for the reasons suggested by Holmes' (Kaye, 1966, xxxvi). The precedents show again and again attempts to trick prisoners into an unwary answer. 'Having been informed by the sheriff that Thomas de N was accused of having killed a man in self-defence, the justice nonetheless began his interrogation by asking Thomas to name the man *ke vous occistes en assaut purpense, felonessement com felon.* There seems little doubt that had Thomas replied to the invitation by simply naming the deceased he would have been deemed to have confessed a felonious killing, and his defence would not have been presented. Fortunately, he realised what was afoot and in his reply carefully denied felony. The justice, thwarted, remarked with professional cynicism, as he allowed the case to go to the jury, *vous avez mut enveli vostre parole et vostre defens enflori*' (Kaye, 1966, 19–20). Stoic logic was thus turned into trickery. For how could the justice be the quasi-cause of the incorporeal event, and thereby seduce the accused, if the event were not already in the process of being produced by corporeal causes, or if guilt were not prepared at the innermost depth of bodies? The function of the justice is to limit the actualisation of the event in a present without mixture, to make an afterwards, *postea*, more intense, taut and instantaneous than the lying in wait which preceded the murder, since it expresses an unlimited future and an unlimited past. This is the use of the inquisition: the mime, and no longer the fortune teller. Thought thereby stops going from the greatest present toward a future and past which are said only of a smaller present, and marches from the future and past unlimited, all the way to the smallest present of a pure instant which is endlessly subdivided (like the Road, like the King's Peace, like the body of the dead man) (Deleuze, 1990, 147).

90.   'As [Hirn] points out, *reus* was originally a genitive ending in *-os*, and replaces *rei-jos*, the man who is possessed by the thing. It is true that Hirn, and Walde who follows him, translate *res* by "legal action", and *rei-jos* as "implicated in legal action"' (Mauss, 1967, 50–1). But this is arbitrary and presupposes that *res* means legal action. On the contrary, if our derivation is accepted, every *res* and every *tradition* of *res* being the object of a legal action in public, it becomes clear that 'implicated in a legal action' is merely a derived meaning. Thus the meaning of 'guilty' for *reus* is even farther derived. Thus we would prefer to say that the word meant first the person possessed by the thing, then the person implicated in the legal action arising out of the *traditio* of the thing, and finally 'the guilty and responsible person'.

91.   It was wrong to reject the argument put forth in *Thabo Meli & Ors v R* ([1954] 1 All ER 373). One can continue to intend to kill a man irrespective of his death, one can intend to desire an object regardless of the fact that it no longer exists. It is what Freud calls *Verwefung*: a symbolic abolition, a form of negation which consists of not symbolising what ought to have been symbolised. Intentions can ride on such non-symbolisation; they have an ideal

validity which no material fact can annul. A fact can only confer upon symbolisation an ideal negative validity; the meaning or sense of a symbol is not invalidated by its missing reality.

An intention is an incorporeal event, with an ideal validity which is independent of any empirical fact. It is this ideality of validity that holds open the register of the symbolic and makes symbolisation possible. To say that a judgment has an ideal negative validity is to say that falseness, too, has an ideality; that the false judgment as a content which can become ideal and omnitemporal, can be repeated again and again, can take the place of a truth. It is therefore possible to distinguish between an ideal positive validity and an ideal negative valididity without denying the ideal validity of the intention as such. The ideality of negative validity makes it possible for a judgment to lose its validity, without losing its sense. Moreover, the ideality of negative validity keeps up a certain essential relation with the absent or exceeded truth so that a judgment which has become outdated retains its sense. It is also what holds open the eventuality of truth, what supports the problematic ideality and omnitemporality of intention. For example, the statement 'The woman was dead when I threw her off the cliff' may be false at the time it is uttered. Yet the ideal validity of sense is not altered by the fact that the woman is alive. *The sense of this false judgment is also ideal.* What is called murder is the resonance of two disjoint events which have nonetheless formed extrinsic relations of compatibility or conjunction. Both *actus reus* and *mens rea* are in themselves contingencies or accidents and do not of themselves signal liability, but rather derive their causal force from their internal resonance within a temporal series. To produce a murder — *again* and *for the first time* — it is necessary to restore the series.

92. What is beyond the active and the passive is not the pronominal, but the *event*. *Thought is the event.* What it demonstrates is the fantasy: the 'Seduction' by which the 'me' opens itself to the surface and delivers the impersonal and pre-subjectal singularities which it had imprisoned. 'It literally releases them like spores and bursts as it gets unburdened' — that is, *as it thinks* (Deleuze, 1990, 213).

93. The King's Court loooking from *outside the unit* could not think in terms of management, only of rules and some abstract right. And what is more, since its first interference had been on the basis that the management might have done wrong (thus reminding us that in a murder, like all cases going to the grand assize, the issue was often whether or not the parties were lord and man (Milsom, 1981, 131), the rules had to reach back into the past. It was not only that the eldest son must now never be passed over, however, incapable. It is that a choice made generations ago may be tested against the inflexible rule, and undone as wrong; and it follows that the person then passed over must have had a sort of ownership which had been transmitted in some abstract world to the present heir of that line. Similarly, the arrangement made for the future can no longer be just a matter of intention which in due course will be carried out: there will be no management to carry it out, and it must somehow work now by conferring a property right to take future effect (Milsom, 1981, 3).

94. We thus glimpse at what must have been said, what must have been done, to put into play a symbolic order, that is to institute the *Untouchable*. As Legendre explains, 'The Reference is a parallel for the power of the father as dead, that is to say, it marks that which it is impossible to kill. "Can one kill the Reference?" is tantamount to: "Can one abolish the order of Causality, the order of Reason, the framework of humanity?" Killing the Reference would be like duplicating the founding murder, that is to say, killing its effects' (Legendre, 1988, 357).

95. 'The wrong done to the plaintiff or demandant is a breach of law and a wrong which should

be redressed somewhere; but it is the contempt of the king's writ which makes it a wrong which should be redressed in the king's court; in the language of the old English law there has been an "overseeness" or "overhearness" of the king which must emended; the deforciant of land or of a debt has not merely to give up the debt, he is at the mercy of our lord the king and is amerced accordingly' (Maitland, 1989, 20–1).

96.   'And if he confesses that he is a thief or a murderer, robber or burglar before the sheriff in full court, but in the absence of the coroner's district, in consequence of which his confession is not entered in the coroner's roll, he may still deny it word for word in the presence of the coroners and declare himself to be good and law abiding, and in case anyone should say otherwise ready to defend himself by his body against the suspicion. This is because the coroner's roll bears record and the county court itself does not' (Kaye, 1966, 23).

97.   What becomes a prisoner begins as a form of wardship, a relationship between a dead man and his lord. The dead man's son was recognised as heir; but until such time as he should be in a position to perform his duties as a vassal a temporary administrator held the fief in his behalf, did homage and carried out the services. This *baillistre* who assumed the responsibilities of the dead man's fief, also pocketed its revenues, without any other obligation towards the minor than to provide for his maintenance. The idea that a lord should take the place of the *baillistre* would originally have been regarded as absurd; what he needed was a man, not an estate. But this was by the eleventh century contradicted by actual practice. One of the earliest examples of the supplanting, at least the attempted supplanting, of a kinsman by the lord as *baillistre* brought face to face the King of France, Louis IV, and the young heir to one of the great honours of the realm — Normandy. *The introduction in various countries of the system of seignorial wardship marks the moment when the value of the fief as a property to be exploited seemed generally to exceed that of the services which could be expected of it.* Indeed it is not inconcievable that the accusation of murder — of parricide — had the advantage of clearing the fief, once and for always, of both the interests of its tenant and his heirs. If he was convicted by the country, the lord, the King, would hold the son in custody, not as ward but as felon. The beneficial interest will have passed to the Crown, in the manner of all lost property, *bona vacantia*.

98.   There is nobody to whom the land can physically be given, so the land is kept for her as *custos*. What land might have been allocated by a tenant to his unmarried daughter was kept for her as *custos* — it could then be argued *that the allocation was never made* (Milsom, 1976, 145–6).

3 The Law of the Land: Criminal Jurisdiction 1747–1908

LINDSAY FARMER

> You will permit me however very briefly to describe, rather what I conceive an academical expounder of the laws should do, than what I have ever known to be done.... He should consider his course as a general map of the law, marking out the shape of the country, its connexions and boundaries, its greater divisions and principal cities: it is not his business to describe minutely the subordinate limits, or to fix the longitude and latitude of every inconsiderable hamlet. His attention should be engaged ... in tracing out the originals and as it were the elements of the law.
> (Blackstone, 1966, vol. 1, 35)[1]

Introduction[2]

It is far from inappropriate that an essay on the development of Scottish criminal law should begin with a quote from William Blackstone. Scots lawyers have consistently underestimated the influence of the English, preferring to believe the comfortable myth that portrays our criminal law as purely native product. However, our immediate interest lies in his suggestive use of the metaphor of mapping, rather than with any questions of substantive law. It raises two broad points which, between them, capture the object of this essay. The first is that it connects the law to a particular physical space. At one level this is a point that is both trite and obvious. Its significance, nevertheless, has been left unexplored. The power of law is always a territorial question. The law draws physical boundaries in geographical space. The law orders the interior of this space into political and administrative units. Legal sovereignty means nothing without these physical aspects of space and organisation. The law is always also the law of the land. The second point is that Blackstone sees the law as a map. This is to acknowledge, as he was clearly aware, that the law is always a representation — it can never lose its metaphorical character. Understood in this sense, the law is always a distortion of reality, though as Sousa Santos points out, this does not necessarily mean that it is a distortion of truth (Sousa Santos, 1987, 282). It is always the result of a process of selection or an attempt to impose an order by marking out the 'greater divisions and principal cities'. The mechanisms by which the law distorts reality are not chaotic but determinate. And hence the process of representation is a fitting object of study.

And in this way we come to the question of jurisdiction. This is the question of the spatial ordering and application of the criminal law, and here we find an immediate parallel with the first sense of the metaphor. The criminal law is, in a very particular way, the 'law of the land'. Our conduct is ordered by its precepts, our transgressions physically reprimanded. There is no place for the guilty to hide, we are told, from the 'long arm of the law'. To raise the question of criminal jurisdiction is to attempt to map or describe this physical apparatus of the criminal law as it is inscribed on a particular physical space. Conceptions of jurisdiction refer to the nature and limits of authority. It can be conceived as Royal or individual property or alternatively as a legal or political administrative unit. Jurisdiction can also denote questions of legal ordering. Through this concept is regulated the legal competence to judge or punish in various instances. To look at jurisdiction is to look at the way that power is actually exercised and the way that this changes over time. We are concerned with the changing physical organisation of the law in the territorial space that is Scotland.

Yet this alone would never be sufficient. Alongside these 'physical' questions, we are concerned with what might be termed the 'metaphysical', that is to say, the practices by which the law is represented.[3] Criminal jurisdiction also concerns the various criteria according to which the conceptual structure of the law is organised — the central points of the map, around which all the other elements are distributed (Sousa Santos, 1987, 285). This is the question of the rationality by which a certain field of law is ordered over time. This is the legal system's reflexive account of itself, the way that it defines the boundaries of jurisdiction and renders intelligible the practices in that system (Ewald, 1985; 1986, 137–42; 1988). This does not happen in abstract, but always in relation to a particular system and the problems of order that continually pose themselves there. And it raises the question of the power to speak the law (*jurisdiction*), to establish the true or official representation of the legal system. This is the question of legal authority, both in the narrow sense of the building of a system of precedent and in the broader one of the establishing of an authoritative account of the origins and operation of the legal system. The criminal law is made up of a complex of institutions and ideas — both the physical and the metaphysical — and it is this complex and the relation between its various parts that must be studied.

This essay raises these questions in relation to the development of criminal jurisdiction in Scotland, specifically in the period between 1747 and 1908 in which the modern criminal justice system took shape. The discussion will be divided into two sections. In the first we will look at developments in criminal jurisdiction between the dates 1747 and 1908. The former because it is the date of the passing of the *Abolition of Heritable Jurisdictions Act* (20 Geo. II c. 43), which is conventionally regarded as founding the modern criminal justice system. The latter is the date of the *Summary Jurisdiction (S.) Act* (8 Edw. VII c. 65) which, together with the *Criminal Procedures (S.) Act* ((1887) 50 & 51 Vict. c. 35), effectively codify Scottish criminal procedure. In the second section we shall go on to look at the ways that the Scottish legal tradition has attempted to make sense of, or rationalise, these changes. In particular we will look at the reception of the statutorily created area of summary criminal jurisdiction, which presents an apparent threat to the vision of order represented by the tradition.

The Power of the Sword: Jurisdiction 1747–1908

Criminal Jurisdiction, termed the Power of the Sword, is a Power of judging and punishing crimes. (Forbes, 1730, 215)

Between the beginning and the end of the period the criminal justice system undergoes a radical transformation. The major change is from a system which is composed of a number of overlapping feudal jurisdictions where central control and formal ordering is weak, to a system of hierarchical courts with increasingly detailed rules of internal ordering and a relatively high degree of central control. In legal doctrine the problem posed by the issue of jurisdiction moves from being that of who had the authority to order and control geographical areas of the country and its inhabitants towards being a more strictly technical legal question. It comes to be defined in terms of procedure and powers of disposal and only linked in a secondary way to questions of geography or the nature of the offence. We can also see that a new apparatus is constructed in the form of the statutorily created area of summary criminal jurisdiction.[4]

The following three trends can be identified: (a) there is the establishment of a system of central organisation and supervision; (b) in this process a number of the inferior courts of feudal origin are superseded by a new system of summary police courts; and (c) the idea of summary jurisdiction emerges, created by statute, and the legal rules governing jurisdiction and procedure become increasingly technical in character.

The Establishment of Central Organisation

The *Abolition of Heritable Jurisdictions Act* 1747 (20 Geo. II c. 43) is normally regarded by historians as the point at which the transformation from the pre-modern to the modern criminal justice system is made. With this Act, it is argued, was abolished the old feudal system of courts, and the foundations of the 'centralised and formally structured order were laid' (Davies, 1980, 120).[5] It is thus an appropriate starting point. The Act was passed as a result of English pressures to place the Highlands of Scotland under strict government control following the Jacobite revolt of 1745–6.[6] The aim was to subject the administration of justice to central control by breaking the traditional structures of authority that bound the courts and their officials to the local nobility. This is stated in the first section of the Act where, collected together under the rubric of making more effective provision for the administration of justice, three separate justifications are offered. These are:

> for restoring to the Crown the Powers of Jurisdiction originally and properly belonging thereto, according to the Constitution, and for extending the Influence, Benefit and Protection of the King's Laws and Courts of Justice to his Majesty's Subjects in Scotland, and for rendering the Union more complete.
>
> *(Abolition of Heritable Jurisdictions Act*, s. 1)

It is clear from the text that it is primarily an assertion of the right of the Crown to control and administer the country, although couched in terms that imply that this process is in fact the restoration of a pre-existing order. The principal effect of the Act was to (re)place the control of jurisdiction in the hands of the Crown, as it had been under the feudal system, in those cases where it had otherwise been sold or granted in perpetuity to certain families. Some courts and offices were abolished altogether, in particular the jurisdictions of justiciary and regality whose power had vied with that of the Royal courts.[7] The office of Sheriff was abolished, although the Sheriff Court was not, and his powers and duties were taken over by the newly created Sheriff depute (s. 29). In this form the Sheriff court was destined to become the centrepiece of the system of legal administration. The remaining feudal courts either had their jurisdiction reduced or more clearly defined.[8] The remainder of the Act laid down guidelines as to how central control was to operate in the system.

This was to be done primarily by the increased regulation of the inferior courts. This took place at two levels. First, by a series of regulations that establish the central importance of the Sheriff Court. At a national level the network of Sheriff Courts was to be the means by which the other local courts were to be supervised (ss. 18, 19, 24; Whetstone, 1981, 9). Courts were to be held more regularly and on a more public basis. Sheriff deputes were to be appointed on a more professional basis, according to their legal qualifications, rather than their local connections, and were to be remunerated accordingly. The intention was to prevent the appointment of poorly qualified local substitutes who would merely perpetuate the inadequacies of the previous system (Whetstone, 1981, 5–11; Young, forthcoming, ch. 3; Lenman, 1981, 24–5). The post was to be held *ad vitam aut culpam* and the judge was made subject to legal penalties for neglect of duty or abuse of position (s. 29).[9] By 1800 this seems to have had the effect of providing stronger links with the centre. The importance of the Sheriff, and the professionalisation of the personnel of the Sheriff Court, was something that was to continue to grow throughout the following century.[10]

The second level was that of providing for the proper operation of the Circuits of the High Court (ss. 31–40). The Crown had been trying for many years to extend the influence of the Justiciary Court by providing for annual journeys to certain larger provincial towns in order to try the more serious cases (which would otherwise be settled by local courts), and to review the decisions of the lower courts. This procedure was formally instituted with the establishment of the High Court of Justiciary in 1672 and purported to be a continuation of the old, and largely ineffective, system of travelling Royal Justices (Justice Ayres). In spite of further legislation the system had never fully taken root.[11] The new provisions, however, were to be finally successful in establishing this function of the Court.

It seems clear that the framework of relations with the centre that was established by the Act was vital to the developments of the nineteenth century. However, there is also an important sense in which the Act is also part of a much older movement of centralisation. And, if we place the Act in this context, it allows us to illuminate our understanding of what is specific to the later process of centralisation. We can see this if we look at the terms in which the Act deals with jurisdiction. It is quite clear that there was no desire to sweep away completely the idea of feudal jurisdiction. Most obviously in sections 20–22 there are a series of provisions stating that the jurisdiction of the proprietors of fairs, markets and mines (coal works and salt works) is to be preserved except in cases inferring the penalties of loss of life or demembration.[12] What seems peculiar to us in this instance is that such proprietorship should be regarded as 'jurisdiction', which we conceive of in predominantly legal terms. What is more, it seems stranger still that this 'jurisdiction' should be preserved if the Act were indeed the foundation of the modern order. There are other clear continuities with the older system. Many of the old courts and jurisdictions remain, albeit with their powers somewhat diminished. Some, indeed, survive well into the nineteenth century before being abolished or restructured.[13]   And it would also appear that institutions such as the army and the church continued to exercise some separate jurisdiction (Hume, 1986, 34).[14] From this point of view, then, the scope of the Act must be regarded more narrowly. It limited feudal jurisdiction only when it appeared to threaten the claim to universal jurisdiction of the central sovereign power. It only introduced reforms into two courts, and with the aim of establishing a national network of control over the others. And the provisions relating to the regularisation of circuit courts were only the fulfilment of a long existing project. There is thus a definite sense in which the Act should be read alongside the earlier history of attempts by the sovereign power to impose its authority on, or to 'civilise', the unruly peripheries of the nation (*Scots Magazine*, 1747, 58).[15] This was done by the means of creating a single law, and hence a single source of authority — though with the result that the sovereign was also to be bound by the law that they had created. From this perspective, provisions professionalising judges, protecting them against arbitrary removal and the influence of local barons, while at the same time attempting to ensure their freedom from monetary corruption and ensuring their loyalty by making them take an oath of allegiance, make perfect sense. It would thus appear that the 1747 Act was aimed at streamlining the operation of the system that had been established in the late seventeenth century rather than introducing something new.[16]

The issue up to the end of this period was clearly viewed as one of the control and regulation of the various forms of legal jurisdiction. This was a struggle over the 'Power of the Sword'. The principal concern was the removal of other sources of power rather than the intensive control of the exercise of that power (Murphy, 1991, 196–7). That this was also conceived as a political question of the control of territory, and consequently its inhabitants, merely serves to underline the fundamental connection between juridical sovereignty and territorial space (Foucault, 1991, 93). By the late eighteenth century this sovereignty was all but unchallenged. The Justiciary Court could claim an 'almost universal' jurisdiction over the territory and inhabitants of Scotland (Hume, 1986, 31). To be sure, insofar as the object was to regulate the inefficiencies of the existing economy of power, we can see the origins of the modes of administration that were to characterise the modern criminal justice system (*Scots Magazine*, 1747, 58).[17] But these were secondary concerns.

There was little interference with the substantive jurisdictions of the courts, in the sense of dealing with the internal questions of the regulation of overlapping jurisdictions. These courts did not yet comprise a system of criminal justice in the modern sense. Reform of the burghs, and other inferior criminal jurisdictions, was a matter that only came to be addressed in the early years of the nineteenth century.

The Reform of the Inferior Courts

The jurisdiction of the High Court was universal but the jurisdiction of the other courts at this stage, if it could be defined at all precisely, could only be done negatively — in terms of the cases they could not handle or the powers that they did not possess. There were still four main types of inferior jurisdiction: the Sheriff Court; the Justice of the Peace (JP) Courts; Burgh Courts, which could be either Royal or Baronial in their grant of jurisdiction; and Barony Courts. By 1800 these began to be joined by a fifth which was to become increasingly important. These were the Police Burgh courts created under local statutes from 1797 onwards (Carson and Idzikowska, 1989). The jurisdiction of all these courts appears to have been roughly cumulative and much confusion existed over the principles by which it was exercised. Writing contemporaneously Baron Hume, one of the most authoritative writers on Scottish criminal law, stated that 'the application and extent of their powers are very liable to controversy, and has not been settled by any uniform or consistent practice' (Hume, 1986, 70). They could, and did, exist within the same geographical area. The powers of a given court depended more on the particular statute or charter that had brought it into being than any rules of general application. Even then, jurisdiction could simply depend on what was deemed expedient in a given situation. In the absence of detailed historical research we continue to know little about the operation of the inferior courts at the beginning of the nineteenth century.[18]

In the early years of the nineteenth century the jurisdiction of the inferior courts seems to have been increasingly limited to minor crimes, and especially those related to the public peace but there were few definite rules of jurisdiction. Sheriff Courts were supposed to deal with the more serious crimes according to more formal procedures, but this rule seems frequently to have been disregarded in the Burgh Courts in the interests of expediency. Hume wrote that a privilege of sharp and summary coercion:

had been thought material to the quiet of those places, and the safety of their inhabitants, otherwise so much exposed to the evil practices of the many dissolute and profligate persons, who have their haunt and resort in towns.

(Hume, 1986, 149)

Prior to 1827 the only formal procedures that were strictly enforced were those for the High Court and thus covered only trial by jury (1672, c. 16).[19] In the inferior courts, these rules could have been taken as guidelines, especially in the more serious libels or those concluding for physical punishment, but they were not binding. Hume makes it clear that 'a deviation from any of those precepts, is not to be pleaded peremptorily as a nullity of the process' (Hume, 1986, 67). His sole recommendation was that cases be conducted as far as possible in a fair and equitable manner (Hume, 1986, 67).[20]

This was to change with the gradual introduction and regulation of a system of 'police courts'. This was carried out in a very piecemeal fashion, and is particularly difficult to trace because in many instances these new courts were simply superimposed on the existing Burgh Courts. Nonetheless a number of points can be made that underline the radical nature of this transformation. It is clear that the emergence of the courts was connected with the establishment of police forces and the reform of burgh administration (local government). Burgh councils had always been responsible for the provision of 'police' (in the traditional sense) inside the burghs, and from 1800 onwards many of the larger and expanding burghs began to introduce specialised police forces.[21] Indeed, the introduction of police forces seems to have been treated as a natural extension of the traditional duties of the burgh to look after the well-being of its inhabitants.[22] Initially, only Royal Burghs were given the power to establish a police force (*Burghs Police (S.) Act* (1833) 3 & 4 Wm. IV c. 46), but later, following the reform of the franchise, this provision was extended to allow new centres of population to establish forces (*Burgh Police (S.) Act* (1847) 10 & 11 Vict. c. 39).[23] A series of more general enactments followed, each of which not only provided for the creation and financing of police forces, but also created a series of 'police offences' and provided for summary procedures by which these could be tried.[24] Most of these were related to the maintenance of the burgh amenities, such as roads, lighting, drainage and licensing, but a number of minor common law crimes, such as would offend against the good order of the burgh, were also formally defined and penalised.[25] Normally the grant of jurisdiction was confined to these specific offences and the penalties that were statutorily attached to them. However, many local Acts would preserve the pre-existing burghal jurisdiction, with the result that exceedingly complex jurisdictions could build up locally.[26] As a result, it took a long time for uniformity to develop. However, the laws creating police forces brought their own internal pressure for centralisation and uniformity because in the absence of uniform provision difficulties could be created as 'problem' populations shifted from the well-policed to the less well-policed areas.[27] The unit of regulation was the country as a whole, but the level of concern had shifted to dealing with problems of internal order produced by inconsistencies and imbalances in the distribution of powers and competences. As the century progressed, these were gradually eradicated, although the process of centralisation was constrained by the absence of a government department, such as the Home Office in England, that could take overall responsibility for the collection of information and the initiation of new legislation.[28] A more general form of provision was finally made by the *Burgh Police (S.) Act* 1892.[29]

The overall effect, in combination with the development of summary procedure in the Sheriff Court, was that prosecution became much easier and more systematic. There was a massive increase in the number and types of crime that were dealt with summarily (H.H. Brown, 1895, xix).[30] Not only did the overall number of cases increase, but there was also a shift in the locus of activity and the style in which cases are dealt with. The Justiciary Court came to play an increasingly insignificant role in day-to-day business, and the percentage of cases dealt with by solemn procedure became an ever smaller part of the total. Thus, by 1898, of a total of almost 166,000 prosecutions only about 2,500 were dealt with by solemn procedure, and only about 200 of these by the Justiciary Court (*Parliamentary Papers*, 1900, 38). The characteristic feature of the new system was the legal administration of large numbers of offenders tried summarily for minor crimes. The main difference from the older system is not to be seen in the development of summary process alone, for it had obviously long played some role in Scottish criminal justice. It is that the logic of administration of the summary courts developed in a way that became increasingly estranged from the traditional models of criminal justice.

Legislation Creating Summary Jurisdiction and the Technical Character of Legal Rules

Accompanying the rise of the new police courts was a reform and regularisation of the existing summary processes which in turn led to a transformation in the way that jurisdiction was conceived. It moved away from being a question of legal competence relating to geographical space, the nature of the crime and the power of the particular court to punish. Instead, it came to be defined primarily in terms of procedure. It is not being suggested that the other questions cease to be important, for that is clearly not the case, but it is undeniable that they become secondary to the question of procedure. That this is the case is most obvious in the growth of 'summary courts' which are defined in terms of the type of procedure that they use and which cut across the 'old' type of courts. The nature of this transformation was neatly captured by a commentator on the 1908 Act:

> The forms that must be observed and the steps or proceedings that must be taken to enable a judge to exercise his jurisdiction in a case, are known and referred to as the 'proceedings' or 'procedure' in the case.... Jurisdiction is thus exercised through what is known as 'procedure'. (Trotter, 1909, 3)

Summary forms of process thus gave rise to a new conception — that of 'summary criminal jurisdiction' — which is fundamental to the organisation of the modern criminal justice system.

It emerged in two stages. Between 1825 and 1864 there were a series of statutes that attempted to regulate summary procedure in the inferior courts.[31] These produced a patchwork of different provisions, many of which only applied in a single court. The principal common feature was that summary process was not designated positively, but was seen as simply the negative of the more formal procedures. The most important single provision was that of the statute of 1828, where it was laid down that the Sheriff Court might try offences 'in the easiest and most expeditious manner', where the libel concluded for punishment not exceeding 10 pounds sterling or 60 days imprisonment. The application of this was extended to some Police Burghs,[32] and it was also used by Royal Burgh and JP courts, although the powers of Burgh Courts using these procedures were reduced by half by an Act of 1856.[33] In most burghs, however, reform of summary process was a consequence of the implementation of the various local and general Police Acts. The form of these Acts effectively provided for a certain level of local variation in procedures, for prior local arrangements could be maintained and burghs could make such rules of procedure as they saw fit, provided that this was done 'with the advice and approbation' of the senior judges (*Police (S.) Act* (1850) 13 & 14 Vict. c. 33 s. 249; *General Police and Improvement Act* (1862) 25 & 26 Vict. c. 101 s. 412). We can gain some idea of the complexity of regulation in this period by looking at an account of the local courts in Glasgow, written in 1840 by the Assessor of the Burgh and Police Courts (*Parliamentary Papers*,

1840, 115). We learn that there was both a Police Court and a Burgh Court. The former operated under a Private Act of Parliament, where there were no forms of procedure specified, although certain maximum penalties were established (£5 or 60 days imprisonment). The latter operated under its original charter, trying those offences that were considered to require greater punishment than the Police Court could give. Other cases still were remitted to the Sheriff Court, where the forms of procedure of the 1827 *Act of Adjournal* were used. No part of the general Police Act had been adopted. The writer, not surprisingly, is critical of the lack of more general regulation:

> In the Courts in which summary procedure takes place, such as the Police Courts held by the magistrates of burghs and justices of the peace throughout the country, the form is different; and even in the same court in some places the same form is not invariably observed. (*Parliamentary Papers*, 1840, 325)

Between 1864 and 1908 this patchwork of provisions was gradually consolidated under the rubric of summary jurisdiction. This was carried out by a series of statutes that were of increasingly general application, and which introduced increasingly specific rules for the conduct of summary prosecutions. The *Summary Procedure (S.) Act* 1864 (27 & 28 Vict. c. 53)[34] was the first statute to deal exclusively with summary procedure (ss. 2–3). It introduced a system of prosecution that was to be available, but not compulsory, for all offences punishable by summary conviction. The schedules provided more detailed forms to be used for complaints and the recording of procedure. By the *Summary Jurisdiction (S.) Act* 1881 (44 & 45 Vict. c. 33)[35] the option of using the old forms was removed, subject to certain exceptions (s. 3). Finally the *Summary Jurisdiction (S.) Act* 1908 (8 Edw. VII c. 65) repealed and consolidated all the previous statutes on summary procedure.[36]

With the passing of this Act we can see that what has emerged, in contrast to previous periods, is a positively defined summary jurisdiction. In addition to the fact that summary process is started by complaint, and conducted without written pleadings and with only a limited record of the proceedings, we can now see that a dense body of regulation has emerged covering procedure before, during and after the trial in the event of the occurrence of various likely and less likely situations.[37] There is a special procedure of appeal by stated case which, though it does not supersede existing forms, was specially tailored for summary trials.[38] These general rules on procedure have the effect of flattening the differences between courts. Different types of courts still exist, but these differences are now of only minor importance. The primary differentiation is in terms of procedure. It is now possible to speak of 'summary courts' and a domain of summary jurisdiction which has been developed and ordered within the sphere of criminal jurisdiction.

It is worth briefly drawing the main threads of the argument together. I have argued that, in spite of certain continuities, we cannot regard the process of development since 1747 as the continual evolution of a centralised system. On the contrary, it is clear there has been a qualitative shift in the nature of the criminal justice system. Along with the movement of the primary locus of operation to the summary courts, and the involvement of many more people in the system, there has been a concomitant shift in the way that jurisdiction is conceived. It has now taken on a distinctively legal meaning, that refers primarily to decisions about the administrative distribution of people in the criminal justice system. The concern with territory has been displaced by a concern with population (Foucault, 1991), and the concern with sovereignty by internal ordering and regulation. These are the principal characteristics of the modern system.

Legal Competences

Thus far we have concentrated almost exclusively on the development of new courts and legal structures, presenting the evidence of massive changes in the nature of legal practices. But to leave the story here would be also to leave it incomplete. If we have looked at the 'physical', we must now look at the 'metaphysical'. And here we immediately come face to face with an important question. If this account of the physical changes in the practices of the criminal law is true, and if they are as fundamental as they appear to be, why is it that so little attention has been paid to them by lawyers? Or, to put this question differently, how has their potentially radical impact been neutralised? To ask this is to require that we look at the way in which lawyers have represented the question of jurisdiction. We shall approach this in two broad stages. First, we must establish the broad categories in terms of which jurisdiction is thematised between 1747 and about 1830, the days of the 'old' system. Then, second, we shall go on to look at some of the ways in which the 'new' system is written about in the contemporary case law and doctrine.

This brings us to a central fact of the development of criminal jurisdiction. In the discussion which follows, we must bear in mind the question of the extent to which the High Court can be said to constitute its own jurisdiction. To put this slightly differently, it will be necessary to bear in mind that the

High Court, as a consequence of its position as the supreme court, was often called upon to determine questions relating to the scope of its own jurisdiction. Its legal authority was constituted by reference to the system whose activities it reviewed. But, at the same time, it constructed a reflected version of this system, in legal concepts and reasoning, which was essential to the practical solution of the problems that came before it — and, hence, was no less important to the exercise of its authority. It has continually to provide an authoritative account of its own authority to settle the questions that come before it. The mapping of the law is always conducted within this circular process.

Natural Jurisdiction 1747–1833

In our first period, the prime concern was that of establishing exclusivity of jurisdiction. The discussions of jurisdiction and the perception of related problems were couched in a language that stressed and reinforced the sovereignty of the Justiciary Court over all matters criminal within the bounds of Scotland. Just as the law was to be a universal code for the people, the supreme court had a jurisdiction that was to be universal over territory, persons and crimes.

Hume set the tone by arguing that the jurisdiction of the High Court was 'almost universal' (Hume, 1986, 31). It could and would try all crimes, whatever their degree of seriousness and regardless of whether they were committed against private individuals or the public economy and police. It was only necessary that they should be 'infringements of our ordinary ... universal code of law; that which is administered by the secular courts of justice, and is common to all the inhabitants of the land' (Hume, 1986, 34).

This point is underlined by Alison who, in phrasing his justification of public prosecution in similar terms, also makes clear the need for a proper machinery to enforce this universal jurisdiction:

> He [the Lord Advocate] is now invested with [these powers] in the fullest and most unlimited extent — so that his title to prosecute crimes is now universal; embracing not only public crimes of every description ... but also those of a private nature, which more immediately affect the welfare of individuals.
>
> (Alison, 1989, 85)

The clearest example is in the discussions of the sources of criminal jurisdiction (Hume, 1986, 49–57; Alison, 1989, 70–83). Both Hume and Alison reject the previously accepted arguments, drawn from Roman law, that it can be based on birth (*forum originis*), domicile (*forum domicilis*), or the place of arrest (*forum deprehensionis*). They declare that such principles are not relevant to the practice of 'independent sovereignties', although perhaps being of some application between inferior and limited jurisdictions. Jurisdiction was to be based on the place (*forum delicti*) where the crime was committed. The reception of the *forum delicti* and the rejection of the other grounds was founded in the same principles. Indeed, Hume's argument is constructed in such a way that by eliminating the other possibilities, first on theoretical grounds and then because there was no record of them in the practice of the law, the *forum delicti* stands alone. The reasons for this are stated in the rejection of the *forum originis*.

> [T]he peace of the land has not been broken, and the society of its inhabitants has not been shocked or disturbed by his deed, as they are by one which passes at home; nor are they likely to feel so much the propriety or necessity of executing the vengeance of the law on him in such a case. (Hume, 1986, 51)

The authority of the law is accordingly based on a combination of the right moral sentiments of the people and a compact between states and those individuals to whom the protection of the law was offered.

This power is universally recognised by the laws of all civilised countries; since every foreigner who comes to a state, and, *pro tempore*, obtains the benefit of the protection of its laws, is bound, in return, to yield obedience to them (Alison, 1989, 81).

Hume concludes in terms that stress the supervisory role of the High Court in the administration of jurisdiction. He points out that the inferior courts 'receive the aid of the Supreme Court towards explicating their jurisdiction', because they are connected by a 'common interest and mutual regard' in the enforcing of one law in every part of the country (Hume, 1986, 57).

The terminology of this argument, founding criminal jurisdiction within the bounds of the sovereign and independent nation state, is important. This jurisdiction is presented as the natural state of affairs and, as the language of the common law demands, an age-old legal practice and part of the 'ancient constitution' of Scotland. The issue of Scotland's independence does not raise itself directly here, since the boundaries of legal sovereignty were not considered to have been affected by the Act of Union — although the peculiarity of establishing the grounds of jurisdiction on the basis of national borders at a time when control of these was passing away deserves mention.[39] The nationalist twist comes with the reference to the moral sentiments of the people which were not to allow the development of universal principles but to entrench the differences from England (Farmer, 1992, 25–43). This also points to an important shift in the purpose of the law. With the privileging of the *forum delicti* the law is moving away from the face to face control of individuals towards the control of actions within a particular legal space. The legal subject is abstracted from particularities of place, time and biography. It is a further index of the concerns of these writers that there is virtually no discussion of the inferior courts. There is little interest in discussing particular powers in particular localities.

Reconceiving Jurisdiction 1833–1908

As we would expect in the later period, the concerns of Hume and Alison, particularly in relation to the establishment of political sovereignty, diminish considerably in their practical importance. Instead, discussions of jurisdiction take on an increasingly technical character, as jurisdictional issues become more involved with the internal management of competences in the criminal justice system. However the transformations wrought by summary jurisdiction were not, at a doctrinal level, to be the main, or even a significant, object of reflection. It appears that to recognise this would have been to require recognition of the changes brought about by summary jurisdiction. The theoretical reflections on the changing nature of the system tended to focus on problems of the relationship between common law and statute law. Here, the breadth of the concept of universal jurisdiction was to have important consequences, minimising the impact of the developing summary jurisdiction.

The growth of legislation regulating criminal procedure led to an increasing body of case law on the interpretation of these statutes. By looking at some of these cases we can begin to see how the High Court constructed a particular understanding of the summary courts and their role in the operation of the criminal justice system. This works to reinforce their own superior status by a continual reference to the idea of the universal and natural scope of the territory of the common law. A prime example of this sort of argument is to be found in the case of *Bute v More* ((1870) 1 Coup. 45). This case, which concerned a summary conviction in the Burgh Court for offences against the laws against trading on a Sunday, raised the question of the scope of summary jurisdiction. And, although in the particular case it was held that the prosecution was incompetent, the leading judgment by Lord Justice General Inglis laid down the authoritative version of the origins of summary jurisdiction. This, it was considered, was not a statutory creation. All inferior courts had practised, and therefore possessed, a summary jurisdiction at common law,[40] even if the statutes had subsequently spoken of conferring jurisdiction on those courts. The statutes, from the 1829 Act onwards, had merely defined and regulated that procedure. This, of course, undoubtedly contains some truth. However, it is at least arguable that the 1829 Act and subsequent changes had created new processes that superseded the earlier, irregular ones,[41] and that with the 1864 Act there was the creation of that new entity, summary jurisdiction. It cannot be argued that prior to, at least, the 1829 Act the inferior courts had possessed summary jurisdiction. The conclusion is that the origins of all jurisdiction are common law, and therefore the superior common law court has an implicit right to regulate the inferior courts, a right that could only be surpassed by statutes under limited conditions. This point was elaborated by Lord Justice-General Dunedin in the case of *McPherson v Boyd*, an early case of speeding.

> I have always understood it to be the law of Scotland that in the case of statutory offences, which are not offences at all until they are created by statute, the jurisdiction must be conferred on any courts which have not universal jurisdiction, and the only courts which have universal jurisdiction are the Sheriff Court and this Court.... When I say universal jurisdiction, I mean an inherent universal jurisdiction, which may, however, be curtailed in many ways. But there is an underlying universal jurisdiction in both the Sheriff Court and this Court, and it seems to me, therefore, to be settled by quite long practice that, where Parliament is going to give jurisdiction to courts other than the Sheriff Court or the Court of Justiciary, it must say so. (*McPherson v Boyd* (1907) 5 Adam 247 at 254)

Statutorily conferred jurisdiction can only add to this independent and universal jurisdiction. Statutorily created crimes were in general a strengthening of this common law jurisdiction, rather than its replacement.[42]

The classic statement was made by Lord Justice-Clerk Macdonald, a senior judge and author of an influential treatise on criminal law and procedure:

> Here we come face to face with this difficulty, that there is nowhere any definition of summary procedure, or summary jurisdiction. It is assumed all through the Acts of Parliament that these words are perfectly well understood, and the statutes all refer to it as perfectly well understood, and as already existing.

He then discusses various modes of proceeding under Scots law, before going on:

So far as I know, there is no other way to explain the term summary procedure, except that it means procedure where there is no induciae, no indictment, and no notice of the witnesses to be examined, and where there is no objection to the proceedings because no agent appears for the accused.

(*Lamb v Threshie* (1892) 3 White 261 at 271)

This remains the standard judicial definition of summary criminal jurisdiction. It is remarkable for the collection of negatives that call to mind the early history of summary jurisdiction, and seem to put its legitimacy into question. It seems to imply, moreover, that it is something that does not have a proper legal existence. It is hardly enough to point to the fact, as commentators usually have, that 'many of these negatives are superseded by positive statutory requirements' (H.H. Brown, 1895, 7).[43] Rather, we have to concede that the picture is indeed, from the point of view of the common law, an accurate one. From this point of view it appears that summary process arose as a means of avoiding the formalities associated with the common law. It did so only in the inferior courts and for offences that were to be considered inferior. The practice only arose by leave of the common law and the jurisdiction that it granted. As we know this picture is inaccurate. Thus, if we ask ourselves why a senior judge should produce such a negative definition, and why this definition should be so well received, it is difficult to answer this question except in terms of the preceding analysis. There is a relentless privileging of the common law made possible by the wide contours of the concept of universal jurisdiction — and this amounts to a negative definition of all the other courts. Common law courts and rules, with their long history and Royal connections, are superior even to parliamentary legislation. This, it must be stressed, necessarily implies that there is a further privileging of the visions of community and order represented by the common law and its view of independent Scottish sovereignty. Within the Scottish legal tradition the construction of summary jurisdiction does not force a reconsideration of the bases of jurisdiction.

There is one further, and rather less obvious, consequence of this. The above statements perhaps convey either the impression that the common law has been bypassed by new forms of law[44] or, from the point of view of the common law, that things simply stayed the same. Neither one of these positions is true. The important point about these procedural rules, though, is not that they bypass or render insignificant the common law but rather that they are the means of its continuing application. The law is still a vital social institution, but in order to ensure its continuing social relevance it must respond to the new administrative demands that are imposed upon it. The procedural rules, as they become more complex and specialised, mediate between the administrative demands of the interventionist state and the more traditional juridical forms (which are still important to political sovereignty). The procedural rules are the essential techniques for the balancing of the differing demands of law and administration. The truth is that the criminal law is defined through these procedural practices rather than by moral categories.

Conclusions

The Scottish legal tradition was thus able to construct a vision of itself and its history, that was sufficient to explain the existence of summary jurisdiction. And this vision is incorporated into the decisions and the doctrine as a vital part of the conceptual machinery that makes those decisions possible. The reflexivity of the Scottish system thus has two components — the physical and the metaphysical. By the first we mean that the High Court has been always in the position to determine questions relating to its own jurisdiction and that of the other courts. Though this is undoubtedly true for all areas and systems of law, its significance becomes particularly clear in relation to jurisdiction and competency. The second, the metaphysical, is the complex of ideas both legal and 'extra-legal' that are referred to by the Court to account for its own practices. This is not something that is rigid and monolithic, but something that is in a continual process of reconstruction in response to changing circumstances. The tradition forms itself around other developments. It cannot deny the existence of certain features that make up the landscape of the law, but it can represent in such a way as to place them on the periphery. The central point of this map of jurisdiction — the metaphysical point of reflexivity — has been the idea of universal and natural jurisdiction.

And so with the aid of the map we come to the end of our journey. And what we have found is that this map, like all others, is only really an accurate guide to itself. So, in the course of this journey, because we chose to look, we have seen some unexpected things. Some surprising, others less so. And we have not strayed too far from the well-marked path. The common law map is not an accurate one, but it is not perhaps untruthful. The question that we now face is one that was familiar to Blackstone. How is the 'academical expounder' of the law to approach the subject? Are we to use the same map? And if not, then which?[45] It will not do to simply invent a new one. We must remain truthful to the physical features that make up the landscape of the law. We may, and indeed we must, distort reality, but we should beware distorting the truth. There is no new territory that is waiting to be discovered by an academic Columbus who dares to journey beyond the boundaries of the existing maps. The boundaries of the law have been mapped. This critical positivism must exploit the fact that there is a disjuncture between the representation and the reality, and in this way seek to construct better representations, new projections, different scales. The map of the law can be redrawn.

Notes

1.   For a more detailed exploration of the metaphor of mapping in relation to the law, see Sousa Santos, 1987.
2.   An earlier version of this chapter was presented to a seminar at Lancaster University Law Department, and I would like to thank the participants for their comments. I would also like to thank Sean Smith, Peter Young, Beverly Brown, Gunther Teubner and Arpad Szakolczai for their comments on an earlier version.
3.   This would be analogous to the projection of a map (Sousa Santos, 1987, 291–4).
4.   Very little has been written about the rise of summary criminal jurisdiction in spite of its obvious impact on the functioning of the modern criminal justice system. For the little that there is, see Radzinowicz and Hood, 1985, 618–24; Gattrell, 1980, 274, 302–5; Manchester, 1980, 160–2; and McBarnet, 1981, 138–43.
5.   See also Irvine Smith, 1958, and Young, forthcoming, ch. 3.
6.   See *Scots Magazine*, 1747, *passim*, for an account of the debates on and amendments of the Bill. See also Phillipson, 1990, ch. 1; and Lenman, 1981, 1–2, 24–5.
7.   See McNeill, 1984, 90–3, for a detailed account of the powers of a regality.
8.   For example, the capital jurisdiction of the Baron Courts, which in theory had meant that they had powers of punishment equal to those of the Supreme Court, was abolished — although it had fallen into desuetude. It was left competent to deal with 'Assaults, Batteries and Smaller Crimes' (ss. 17–19).
9.   Cf *Claim of Right* 1689; Hume, 1986; vol. 2, 66.
10.   See generally Whetstone, 1981, ch. 1; Carson, 1984/5, 215–6. Also see for example *Sheriffs Courts (S.) Act* (1825) 6 Geo. IV c. 23; *Bank Notes Act* (1828) 9 Geo. IV c. 23 s. 22; and *Sheriffs Courts (S.) Act* (1838) 1 & 2 Vict. c. 119 s. 28. By 1877 all substitutes were appointed *ad vitam aut culpam* by the Crown.
11.   For an account of these failures, see Hume, 1986, ch. 1, pt. 1; Cameron, 1988, 366–79; cf Davies, 1980, 150.
12.   This is a reference to the servitude of colliers which was not abolished until 1799 (*Colliers (S.) Act* (1799) 39 Geo. III c. 56).
13.   The Admiralty Court with maritime jurisdiction (*Great Yarmouth Haven and Pier Repairs* (1681) 1 Ja. II c. 16) was not abolished until 1830 (*Court of Session Act* (1830) 11 Geo. IV & 1 Wm. IV c. 69). As late as 1827 this Court tried a case of culpable homicide. See Hume, 1986, 192.
14.   Cf England, where military jurisdiction also survives until the 1820s (Cockburn, 1991, 87–90).
15.   See K. Brown, 1986, 269–72, for the earlier history of this project.
16.   Cf Beattie, 1986, ch. 11, where a similar periodisation is argued for in the English system.
17.   Here the reform is justified in terms of the speed, economy and utility that it would offer; cf Foucault, 1977, 78–9.

18.   By far the most lucid nineteenth-century account is to be found in Moncrieff, 1877, chs 1–2; see also Spens, 1875, ch. 2.

19.   The new forms of process made after the 1747 Act also made some provision for trial before the Sheriff without a jury. See Moncrieff, 1877, ch. 1.

20.   See the case of Banks and Sutherland 1735 cited there.

21.   See generally Carson and Idzikowska, 1989.

22.   This may explain why the introduction of police forces met with less resistance than in England, where historians have drawn a sharp distinction between the 'old' and the 'new' police, and summarised in Gattrell, 1990.

23.   See Lenman, 1981, 162–4, on electoral reform.

24.   For example, *Court of Chancery of Lancaster Act* (1850) 13 & 14 Vict c. 43; *Exchequer Court (S.) Act* (1856) 19 & 20 Vict. c. 48; *General Police and Improvement (S.) Act* (1862) 25 & 26 Vict. c. 101.

25.   See for example *Burgh Police (S.) Act* (1892) 55 & 56 Vict. c. 55, ss. 380–453. Police jurisdiction could also normally cover the minor common law crimes, provided that they were not committed with certain aggravations, such as serious assaults or property crimes over a certain value.

26.   For example, see Moncrieff, 1877, 48, where he points out that Edinburgh's regulations were derived from at least five different sources.

27.   The punishment of banishing individuals from the burgh or county in which they had committed their offence was abolished in 1830 (*Criminal Law (S.) Act* (1830) 11 Geo. IV & 1 Wm IV c. 37); see Wilson on the problems of vagrancy in *Parliamentary Papers*, 1895, 1; see also Carson and Idzikowska, 1989, 288–97, on the policing of Lanarkshire.

28.   A situation that did not change immediately with the introduction of the Scottish Office in 1885 since the Lord Advocate retained overall responsibility for the criminal justice system. See Hanham, 1965, 205–44.

29.   Imposing a limitation of 60 days imprisonment or a fine of 10 pounds, following the *Summary Procedure (S.) Act* (1864) 27 & 28 Vict. c. 53. As this Act did not extend to the rural areas of Scotland and the larger cities (Aberdeen, Edinburgh, Glasgow, Dundee, Greenock), that provision was still not completely uniform.

30.   Cf J.F. Stephen, 1877b, 735–59; Gattrell, 1980, 274, 302–5, on the easing of prosecution in England.

31.   The principal statutes were the *Act of Adjournal of the High Court* 1827, under the authority of the *Sheriffs Court (S.) Act* (1825) 6 Geo. IV c. 23 s. 5; *Circuit Courts* (1828) 9 Geo. IV c. 29 ss. 19–20 and Schedule C; see also *Criminal Law (S.) Act* (1830) 11 Geo. IV & 1 Wm. IV c. 37 ss. 4–5; plus various local and general police Acts.

32.   Those taking advantage of the *Police Burghs (S.) Act* (1833) 3 & 4 Wm. IV c. 46.

33.   *Exchequer Court Act* (1856) 19 & 20 Vict. c. 48. That is, 5 pounds sterling or 30 days imprisonment. Parliamentary burghs that had already adopted the 1828 procedures could continue to use the old powers, since they were not mentioned by the Act – 'probably by oversight' (Moncrieff, 1877, ch. 1).

34.   For a discussion of this, see Moncrieff, 1877, ch. 2; Anon., 1865, 51–9.

35.   This also applied some provisions of the English *Summary Jurisdiction Act* (1879) 42 & 43 Vict. c. 49.

36.   For discussion see Renton, 1908, 219–22; Trotter, 1909.

37.   The 1908 Act runs to 77 sections and 18 pages of schedules.

38.   See *Summary Prosecutions Appeals (S.) Act* (1875) 38 & 39 Vict. c. 62 and 1908 Act, ss. 60–73. Under the 1864 forms of process (27 & 28 Vict. c.53) no note of evidence was kept, making review impossible.

39.   Legal authority was considered to derive from the sovereign, rather than Parliament. The Act of Union had dissolved the Scottish Parliament but left the 'Kingdom' intact. See for example Hume, 1986, 1–16, where he works hard to dismiss the suggestion that the office

of Justiciary had derived its authority from the Scottish Parliament.
40. It speaks of the jurisdiction as being conferred by the recited Acts. That is not the case, because it certainly belonged to these inferior Courts before the recited Acts were passed (*Bute v More* (1870) 1 Coup. 495 at 515).
41. See for example the argument of Sheriff Logan: 'Previously to the passing of the Acts referred to the Sheriff had no summary jurisdiction. They conferred it on him, but only under the restrictions imposed by them' (*Byrnes v Dick* (1853) 1 Irv. 151). This was rejected by the High Court. See also the discussion in Spens, 1875, ch. 2.
42. *Clark & Bendall v Stuart* (1886) 1 White 191 at 207; *Paton v Neilson* (1903) (J.) 5 F 107 per Lord J-G Kinross. Cf Alison, 1989, 8: 'Common law jurisdiction remains unless removed by statute either by direct words or unavoidable inference'.
43. Cf Trotter, 1909, 4.
44. See Murphy, 1991, for example.
45. This is also the question of 'critical positivism'; see for example Ewald, 1986.

4 From Experts in Responsibility to Advisers on Punishment: The Role of Psychiatrists in Penal Matters

GERRY JOHNSTONE

I am a psychiatrist. But do not think of me as one of those 'alienists' called to the witness stand to prove some culprit 'insane' and 'irresponsible' and hence 'not guilty'. I abhor such performances worse than you, dear reader, possibly can.

(Menninger, 1977, 5)

What, then, is the role of the psychiatrist in penal matters? He is not an expert in responsibility, but an adviser on punishment. (Foucault, 1977, 22)

Introduction

Legal and penal reformers frequently complain about the criminal law's refusal to amend its practices in response to developments in the scientific understanding of criminal behaviour. The law assumes criminals to be 'rational creatures who intended the consequences of their acts and, moreover, thought consciously and deliberately about them in advance' (Morris, 1989, 43).[1] Knowledges which put the legal view of persons in question are, reformers claim, ignored by the courts. A much cited example is the law's adherence to the M'Naghten Rules — as its criterion of responsibility — despite the fact that these rules are based upon outdated psychological views.[2] As a consequence, reformers argue, many mentally disordered offenders have been hung (Morris, 1989, 45) and, while this problem no longer exists, many are still sent to prison for punishment when they ought to be sent to psychiatric institutions for treatment.

The reformers clearly have an important point. In making it, however,

84

they tend to ignore the other ways in which the human sciences in general, and psychiatry in particular, have shaped the practices of criminal law. While it may be true that psychiatric thinking has made little impact upon the substantive law of crime, it has had a considerable influence upon the 'operational principles' of criminal justice. In order to understand this, it is necessary to distinguish between two distinct ways in which psychiatrists have challenged the law's near monopoly over decisions in the criminal justice process.

First, psychiatrists have questioned the law's right to be the sole decider of matters of responsibility. In this, psychiatrists have failed. As the critics of the M'Naghten Rules point out, the law refuses to allow psychiatry any significant say in such matters. Secondly, however, psychiatrists have questioned whether the law should be the sole decider of what happens to offenders once they are convicted. In this psychiatrists have had greater success, gaining considerable influence over the way offenders are processed once they have been convicted.

This paper explores the birth of this second psychiatric challenge to the law. It focuses upon a shift in psychiatry's ambitions in the field of criminality which occurred, in Britain, during the 1860s and 1870s.[3] Until this time, medical-psychologists (as they were then called) saw themselves as experts in responsibility and engaged in fierce battles with the law over this issue (R. Smith, 1981). During the 1860s psychiatrists began to see themselves, less as experts in responsibility, more as advisers on the disposal of offenders. In this role they continued to criticise the law, but the nature and temper of their criticisms changed. The paper also looks at the background to this shift in psychiatric concern, which is crucial to an understanding of how psychiatrists succeeded in establishing themselves as advisers on punishment, where they had failed to displace lawyers as experts on responsibility.

From Responsibility to Control

In 1862 the medical-psychologist Thomas Laycock summarised the deep disagreements that existed between law and medicine over the definition of insanity and the proper response to the insane offender:

Medicine maintains that a theoretical and practical study of mental diseases and defects is necessary to a proper understanding and detection of defect; law denies this, and says it is a fact to be determined by any dozen of ordinary men in consultation on the case. Medicine says a man may be insane and irresponsible, and yet know right and wrong; law says a knowledge of right and wrong is the test of both soundness of mind and responsibility to the law. Medicine says restrain and cure the insane and imbecile offender against the law; law says hang, imprison, whip, hunger him, and treats medical art with contempt. (Laycock, 1862, 593)

Laycock was saying little that was new. The 'antagonism' between law and medicine which he described had been brewing for some decades and had come to the boil during the 1840s and 1850s. Whilst the law was quite happy to excuse those 'offenders' who were insane at the time of their crime — provided of course that they were not released from custody but were confined in a secure place — it insisted on restricting the defence to those who were suffering from gross delusions or severe disturbances of the intellect.[4] In order to be excused on the ground of insanity defendants had to be so devoid of reason as to be unable to understand the nature of their actions or the difference between right and wrong.[5] Moreover, the law insisted that the question of whether defendants were insane at the time of their transgression was to be decided by a jury, consisting of ordinary persons with no specialist knowledge of mental disorders (R. Smith, 1981, 77–9).

For medical-psychologists this was unacceptable. The legal definition of insanity failed to take account of their recent discovery of 'partial insanities' such as 'moral insanity' and 'homicidal mania without disorder of intellect' (Prichard, 1833; 1847; Robertson, 1860). These were conditions in which the person's powers of comprehension were sound, but other mental abilities — such as the ability to feel for others or to control one's behaviour through an act of will — were disordered. In cases of moral insanity, for instance:

The intellectual faculties appear to have sustained but little injury, while the feelings and affections, the moral and active principles of the mind, are strangely perverted and depraved; the power of self-government is lost or greatly impaired; and the individual is found to be incapable, not of talking and reasoning upon any subject proposed to him ... but of conducting himself with decency and propriety in the business of life. (Prichard, 1833)[6]

The law dealt with such persons as if they were sane, fully responsible for their conduct, and deserved to be punished. For medical-psychology, such persons were mentally disordered and ought to be pronounced insane and excused punishment.

Medical-psychologists also objected to the law's procedures for deciding such matters, arguing that if the law were to extend its definition of insanity to include emotional and volitional — as well as intellectual — disorders, it would also have to change its method of 'detecting' the insane offender. The ordinary juror could easily recognise, as insane, the raving lunatic and those suffering from gross forms of intellectual disorder. But to the lay person, the morally insane offender might appear to be mentally normal and simply dissolute or eccentric.[7] In order to detect these more subtle forms of insanity one required considerable expertise and clinical experience. James Cowles Prichard, who coined the term 'moral insanity', had himself only become convinced that such persons were in fact insane after many years of observing patients at the Bristol Infirmary where he held the post of Physician (D. Leigh, 1961, ch. 3). Hence, for medical-psychology, the decision about insanity had to be entrusted to medical experts, whose wide experience of dealing with the insane made them competent in the detection of insanity (R. Smith, 1981, 79; Johnstone, 1990, 194–9). Only the medical expert was able to distinguish the genuinely insane from those who feigned insanity in order to escape punishment (Davey, 1859).

I have suggested that this 'antagonism' between law and medicine had reached its climax by the 1860s, when Thomas Laycock wrote his lecture summarising the issues. Laycock did, however, mention an aspect of the discord between law and medicine which, if not entirely new, was only beginning to emerge as a major issue in the 1860s: 'Medicine says *restrain and cure* the insane and imbecile offender against the law; law says hang, imprison, whip, hunger him' (Laycock, 1862, 595). Laycock was hinting here that medical intervention could achieve something else, besides wresting the insane offender from the hands of the executioner. It could also cure such offenders of their mental disorder, the cause of their propensity to crime. Previously medical-psychologists had merely asked the law to excuse certain offenders from legal responsibility and hence from the normal punishment for their offence. Now it was criticising law's methods of dealing with insane and imbecile offenders, arguing that instead of punishing such offenders, the law should employ medical art to restrain and cure them.

A few years later Laycock's concern with the insanity defence had faded into the background. In an article on 'medico-mental science' and the prevention of crime he confidently asserted: '[t]hat medico-mental science is often at variance with the doctrines and decisions of the courts of law is a fact too well known and too generally admitted to need formal proof' (Laycock, 1869, 334). His attention had, by then, shifted to a rather different and — in terms of numbers involved — much larger problem:

> There is a large number of criminals termed in France the 'classes dangereuses' and in English phrase 'known to the police' and another still more numerous body, not exactly of this class, but incorrigible vagabonds, drunkards, mendicants. All these, numbering tens of thousands, are really so constituted corporeally that they possess no self-control beyond that of an ordinary brute animal ... They are, for the most part, immoral imbeciles, so that however frequently they may have been subjected to prison or other discipline, the moment they are set free, they resume their vicious and criminal course. (Laycock, 1869, 342)

Laycock was not alone in losing interest in the insanity defence and becoming interested in the problem of controlling the criminal class. Rather, he was part of a more general trend. In the 1850s the *Journal of Mental Science* — the major outlet for medical-psychological writing on criminality in this period — published numerous articles concerned specifically with the scope of the insanity defence. From the mid-1860s on, fewer articles on this subject appeared, while a new concern emerged and began to dominate: a concern with the psychology of the 'criminal class' and the problem of their control. For a brief period these concerns were intertwined, and articles would give equal attention to both matters (Symonds, 1864/5; Haynes, 1864/5). But, within a few years, articles on the new subject — the psychology and control of habitual criminals — began to make at most only passing reference to the issue of the insanity defence (Thomson, 1870; Thomson, 1871). Within the space of a few years the insanity defence had become almost a peripheral issue for 'medico-legal science'.

Of course, the conflict over the insanity defence did not die out. To the contrary, the dispute was given fresh impetus by the acceleration of the campaign for the abolition of the death penalty during the 1860s (Radzinowicz and Hood, 1990, ch. 20; N. Walker, 1968, ch. 6). Because of its bearing upon the debate about capital punishment, the *Royal Commission on 'Capital Punishment', 1864–6* (*British Sessional Papers*, 1866, vol. 21), explored the issue of the insanity defence with much thoroughness and so became the forum for yet another heated debate between law and medicine. More generally, for many psychiatrists, the insanity defence would remain the main — or even the sole — area of conflict between them and the law (Stafford-Clark, 1963, 270–6). The legal-psychiatric conflict over the insanity defence continued to erupt, at various intervals, over the next century.[8]

But for many psychiatrists — especially those who worked in the prison medical service and quasi-penal institutions (Gunn et al., 1978; Sim, 1990) — the insanity defence became of less interest. Although they continued to oppose the law on this issue, they didn't labour the point. Eventually, as I will show, they even came to accept the legal definition as appropriate in criminal trials, albeit with some remaining reluctance. But this slow withdrawal by medical-psychologists from their battle with the law over the insanity defence did not mean an end to hostilities. To the contrary a new, and in many respects much larger, dispute emerged — a dispute over how best to handle and process habitual criminals. Medical-psychologists continued to criticise the practices of criminal law, but the nature of their criticism changed profoundly.

First, there was a shift in the scope of the conflict. Previously, as we have seen, the dispute was over how many offenders should be entitled to use the insanity defence. While there was a great deal at stake in this conflict,[9] the number of offenders affected was relatively small. Because a successful plea of insanity led, not to straightforward acquittal, but to confinement as a lunatic, the defence was only attractive to those charged with capital offences. Hence, in practical terms, the disagreement was over how many of those who committed capital offences would be confined as lunatics, rather than receive the death penalty. Relatively few offenders were affected by the outcome of this debate and the numbers would get fewer as the death penalty became used less and less.[10] In the 1860s medical-psychologists became interested in a much larger group of persons — 'the dangerous classes' — whose inability to abide by the law and live respectable lives was caused by mental abnormality. In the above quotation from Laycock, he estimates the number of these 'immoral imbeciles' as 'tens of thousands'. The concern is no longer with those relatively few 'mad criminals' who commit capital offences without rational motive, but with the vast number of habitual offenders; non-respectable persons, lacking moral sense, who frequently end up in the courts and prisons, usually for the commission of petty crime (Johnstone, 1990, 59–63; Radzinowicz and Hood, 1990, ch. 8).

Secondly, this expansion of medical-psychology's interest formed part of a shift in the *nature* of its concerns. Previously, its central concern was to obtain *compassion* for those offenders whom it considered to be insane. It argued for a relaxation of the strict rule of law, not just for those without reason, but also for those without moral sense or the capacity for self-control. Now its concern was to ensure that mentally abnormal offenders — and practically all recidivists were considered mentally abnormal — were subjected to *effective forms of control*. Medical-psychologists criticised the law's policy of regarding these offenders as fully responsible, rational beings — not because this was unsympathetic or unjust — but because this policy prevented the law from exercising adequate control over habitual offenders. If habitual offenders were recognised for what they were — mentally disordered — then the procedures designed for mentally normal offenders could be deemed inapplicable to them. This meant that such offenders should not be punished, but it also meant that they could and should be confined and treated on the same basis as dangerous lunatics.

> It is better ... to deposit a brain-sick man in a hospital for the insane, where he may be *cured* as well as kept out of the way of harm to himself or others, than to allow him to remain at large till he has committed some crime which will cause him ... to be maintained at the public expense as a convict ... or executed.
>
> (Symonds, 1864/5, 273–5)[11]

From the 1860s on, medical-psychologists proposed not just a minor (albeit symbolically significant) shift of the line between the culpable and non-culpable but a much more fundamental change in official attitudes and policies towards habitual offenders. Habitual offenders were to be dealt with, not as rational persons with a capacity of free will, but on the same basis as dangerous lunatics.

The Problem of the 'Criminal Class'

The problem of habitual offenders had its genesis in the industrial revolution and the accompanying acceleration of the trend towards urbanisation. These developments created new problems of social control (Thompson, 1981). Partly this was because traditional mechanisms of social control were weakened, due to the impact of industrialisation and urbanisation upon established bonds of obedience and deference and settled structures of authority. But, in addition, industrialisation and urbanisation required new standards of behaviour from people. Modes of conduct and lifestyles which were acceptable in pre-industrial, pre-urban times, became unacceptable in industrial, urban society (Thompson, 1981).[12] Hence, there was a change in the *objectives* of social control. New mechanisms of social control were required, not just to maintain public order, but to promote new standards of conduct.

Throughout the first half of the nineteenth century there were massive developments in social policy as a multitude of 'projects' were launched to deal with the huge problem of 'moralising' or disciplining the people. These projects varied enormously in terms of their specific concerns, mechanisms and goals. However, a general, pervading concern was that of cultivating self-control and self-respect. The people had to be 'educated' in such a way that they *internalised* values such as industriousness, temperance, domesticity, sobriety, thrift, self-help, decency, rational recreation, and lawfulness (Wiener, 1990).

The criminal law played a central role in this project of fostering disciplined behaviour and a broad ethos of respectability among the people. With the decline of more traditional, less formal mechanisms of social control, and with the need for higher standards of discipline, the more formal methods of criminal justice began to play a much greater role in policing the 'lower orders' than they had previously. Criminal justice did not simply replace more traditional forms of social control. Rather, it began to enforce new norms. Behaviour which had previously been ignored by the authorities, such as vagrancy, public drunkenness, prostitution, and disorderly behaviour by juveniles, was 'criminalised' (Wiener, 1990, 50, 261–3).

By the 1860s policy-makers began to form the opinion that the vast majority of the population had been moralised and had become respectable (Wiener, 1990, ch. 5). However, they also thought that a significant number of people had not. These people continued to lead unacceptable lifestyles and behave in undesirable ways. Hence, they frequently ended up in the courts, charged with criminal offences. No matter how many times they were punished, they did not adjust their behaviour. Penal policy makers argued that a large portion of crime was attributable to such people. Hence, distinctions began to appear, in the discourses of social policy, between the respectable labouring classes, who had adapted their lifestyle and conduct to the demands of industrial-urban society, and the *residuum*, who had not been moralised.[13] The residuum — or, as one commentator called them, 'the lowest class — occasional labourers, loafers and semi-criminals' — remained unattached to the social order.[14] They had failed to become respectable. They had not internalised the values of industriousness, sobriety, domesticity, thrift, lawfulness etc. They were therefore seen as a nuisance and a danger to respectable society. During the 1860s the emphasis of social policy began to shift from projects designed to moralise the people in general, to programmes designed to control and discipline the residuum or 'criminal class'.

The Psychiatrisation of Habitual Offenders

The vast complex of social control institutions, established in the first half of the nineteenth century, had succeeded (or so it was thought) in making respectable the vast majority of the population — but it had failed to discipline a significant minority. Why was this so? Medical-psychology's answer to this question involved explaining this institutional failure as a result of individual mental deficiency.[15] Just as those whom schools could not educate were labelled 'imbeciles', implying that they lacked the intellectual capacity to grasp the school's lessons (Garland, 1985, 224; N. Rose, 1985, ch. 4), those whom the criminal justice system failed to moralise were labelled 'moral imbeciles', implying that they were incapable of learning morality: 'Habitual criminals are, as a class, moral imbeciles' (Thomson, 1871). This psychological defect explained why these persons had failed to learn the lessons of morality and why they persistently committed crime despite the threat of legal punishment. Habitual criminals behaved as they did because they lacked the faculties of moral sense and self-control. While the reasoning faculties of habitual criminals were often well-developed, their faculties of feeling and will were underdeveloped. While habitual criminals had the intellectual capacity to understand moral obligations, they had no intuitive feeling for these obligations and no ability to control their behaviour in accordance with them. Habitual criminals behaved badly because they lacked conscious control over their actions and were at the mercy of some inherent drive towards anti-social and criminal behaviour.

The psychological explanation of habitual criminality neatly explained (away) the failure to integrate into respectable society a whole class of persons. This complex social problem was reduced to a matter of mental inferiority: the lowest classes lacked the mental capacity to appreciate the value of respectability or to resist the temptation to indulge in bad habits. If this were simply a matter of crude labelling it might have failed to convince despite its appeal to class prejudices. But, in fact, the concept of moral imbecility was well in line with central developments in medical-psychological thought (Johnstone, 1990, ch. 5; Donnelly, 1983).

The concept of moral imbecility was closely linked with the concept of 'moral insanity' which was formed in the first half of the nineteenth century (Carlson and Dain, 1962, 130). As we saw briefly, earlier in this chapter, proponents of the concept of moral insanity had questioned the conventional assumption that the essential and defining feature of insanity was loss of reason: 'It is generally supposed that the intellect or the reasoning faculty is principally disordered in persons labouring under mental derangement ... this is by far too limited an account of madness' (Prichard, 1833).[16] Prichard, the leading proponent of this concept, argued that were other types of insanity, such as *moral insanity*, in which the person's capacity to reason was unaffected, the intellectual powers remained intact, but the *emotions* and *will* were impaired. While Prichard argued that 'moral insanity' was a form of mental disorder, he made it quite clear that he did not regard the morally insane as mad in the conventional sense of the term. Rather, for Prichard, the mind was divided into different compartments or faculties. In particular, the faculty of reason was distinct from the moral faculty. It was possible that the former could be healthy while the latter — the moral sense — could be impaired. This left the person incapable of *appreciating* the difference between right and wrong or, alternatively, of controlling his behaviour.

Behavioural problems — an apparent inability to conduct oneself with decency and propriety — were both a symptom and a sign of this condition. Hence, through the concept of moral insanity, psychiatrists could interpret deviant behaviour as a sign of mental disorder, even where this behaviour was not accompanied by delusion of reason or aggravated disturbance of the intellect. Morally insane people behaved in a deviant manner, not because they had chosen to do wrong, but because one of their mental faculties — their moral sense — was damaged.

It is important to note, however, that as used by Prichard and many other medical-psychologists, a diagnosis of moral insanity was only considered appropriate in cases where there had been a sudden change in a person's disposition — where a person began behaving in a way which was foreign to their previous character. Persons who suddenly, and for no explicable reason, underwent a substantial change of character and conduct were to be diagnosed as morally insane. So, although moral insanity was diagnosed upon the basis of departures from behavioural norms, the norms departed from were not simply 'objective', they were also 'subjective'. The norms were established, to a large extent, by the person himself in his own past conduct. For example, an honest person who suddenly, and for no apparent reason, started to steal things, might be diagnosed as morally insane, whereas a person who had a long history of dishonesty would not — in the strict sense of the concept — be diagnosed as such. This point was made clear by Henry Maudsley, a later proponent of the concept of moral insanity, who described the phenomenon as follows: 'What we shall often observe is this — that after some great moral shock, or some severe physical disturbance, in a person who has a distinct hereditary predisposition to insanity, there has been a marked change of character; he becomes "much different from the man he was" in feelings, temper, habits, and conduct' (Maudsley, 1973, 173–4).

This limited the scope of the concept considerably. But, as Michael Donnelly has pointed out, the concept of moral insanity was often employed more loosely. The term was frequently used to refer to the 'irrational' behaviour — such as criminality and habitual drunkenness — of the labouring classes and the poor (Donnelly, 1983, 137–8). Such behaviour now became seen as a result, and a sign, of moral insanity — a lack of *moral sense* among the lower classes — caused by their living in an uncivilised environment which was not conducive to the cultivation of moral sense (Johnstone, 1990, 188–94). In this looser usage the concept was used to interpret almost any deviation from norms of respectable and prudent behaviour as a sign of mental disorder.

This tendency to interpret crime — and other forms of behaviour which were considered to be irrational or anti-social — as symptomatic of mental abnormality was taken much further in the second half of the nineteenth century through the concept of *moral imbecility*. The crucial distinction between moral insanity and moral imbecility was that reference in the former was to persons whose moral sense had been damaged, whereas the latter referred to *persons who had never developed moral sense* in the first place. Moral imbecility was considered to be an hereditary, or inborn, and permanent condition (Maudsley, 1973, 179–81; Skultans, 1975, 186ff). Hence, whereas diagnoses of moral insanity were based upon an individual's deviation from norms of conduct established by himself in his own past conduct (even though the term was often used more loosely), diagnoses of moral imbecility could be based upon a person's habitual transgression of 'objective' norms.

With 'moral imbecility', habitual criminal behaviour came to be regarded, in itself, as a product and sign of mental disorder. It was not considered necessary to provide independent evidence of mental malfunctioning, such as intellectual disorder or 'slowness'. Rather, the existence of mental disorder was inferred from anti-social conduct alone. Recidivism was deemed to be, in itself, sufficient proof of moral imbecility. Hence Havelock Ellis, who did much to promote the concept, argued that all those who constituted the criminal class (i.e. persistent delinquents) could be seen as moral imbeciles (Ellis, 1910, 33, 285–6). For Ellis the 'born criminal' and the 'moral imbecile' were one and the same thing; there were 'no clear lines of demarcation between the insane and the criminal' (Ellis, 1910, 292, 288). This did not mean that criminals were thought to be mad. Rather, they were deemed to be suffering from a form of mental abnormality which was significantly different from ordinary madness.

Psychiatrisation and Criminal Policy

What implications did psychiatrists draw from their 'discovery' that habitual offenders were moral imbeciles? One implication they might have drawn was that, since moral imbeciles lacked responsibility for their conduct, they should be excused punishment when they broke the law. This inference was, however, seldom drawn and certainly not stressed. What concerned psychiatrists more was the implication of their discovery for attempts to control habitual offenders/moral imbeciles.

The law attempted to control the behaviour of these offenders through judicial punishment. When they came before the courts, habitual offenders were tried, sentenced, and punished in the same way as ordinary offenders. In particular, they received a sentence roughly proportionate to the offence which they had committed. Such punishment, it was assumed, acted as a deterrent; it dissuaded the recipient and others with similar motives and opportunities from committing further crimes.[17]

During the 1860s and 1870s penal reformers began to argue that punishment was not deterring habitual offenders. The very fact that 'the same individual is convicted over and over again, to even more than a hundred times' (*Parliamentary Papers*, 1872, para. 3),[118] proved that the existing system of penal sanctions was failing to influence the behaviour of this section of the population. This argument led to a search for ways of making punishment more stringent, in order to increase its deterrent effect, and to the exploration of other means of controlling and 'neutralising the residuum' (Radzinowicz and Hood, 1990, part 4).

The significance of the concept of moral imbecility was that it helped explain why habitual criminals were not deterred through ordinary penal measures. The notion of deterrence assumes that actions are determined by volition and that they are the product of a careful — but not necessarily conscious — calculation of profit and loss, or pleasure and pain (Johnstone, 1988, 321–2). Punishment could only deter those with the capacity to control their behaviour on the basis of rational calculation.[19] Since moral imbeciles lacked this capacity the threat of punishment could make no impact upon their conduct. No matter how much they might fear punishment, they would continue to commit crime because they lacked the capacity to stop themselves from doing so. They were governed not by rational calculations of pain and pleasure, which could be influenced by the lessons of punishment, but by an instinctive and uncontrollable drive towards delinquency. Moral imbeciles were, in this respect, similar to lunatics who also lacked volitional control over their behaviour.

The likening of habitual offenders to lunatics pointed the way to the best means of controlling them. Society's reaction to habitual offenders should be modelled, it was argued, not upon its reaction to mentally normal wrongdoers, but upon its reaction to lunatics (Ellis, 1910). The procedures and operational principles developed by medical-psychology, for the control of the mad, should be applied to habitual offenders/moral imbeciles. In particular, society's response to moral imbeciles should be guided, not by the principles of justice and punishment (which were inappropriate in the context of persons with no responsibility for their conduct), but by the principles of restraint and treatment. When faced with the lunatic the authorities' guiding principles were restraint and cure (Symonds, 1864/5). Lunatics were confined as a means of protecting the public — and lunatics themselves — from the harm they would cause if left at large. In addition, medical art was used in an effort to restore lunatics to a state of reason, so that they could resume their place in society.

Penal authorities, it was suggested, should adopt a similar approach when faced with the habitual offender/moral imbecile. This meant that habitual offenders should be restrained (i.e. confined) for as long as they remained a danger to society. They should be confined in an institution — which would be a place of treatment rather than of punishment — until they developed moral sense and a capacity for self-control. They should be released only when expert medical opinion had determined that they were cured of their moral imbecility.

In particular, this meant a change in the principles governing the *sentencing* of habitual criminals. The main principle governing the sentencing of offenders was that of *proportionality*. The amount of punishment which offenders received was determined by the gravity of their offence. Minor offences attracted small punishments; serious offences met with severe punishments. For example, those who were found drunk and disorderly in a public place could expect a small fine or a short prison sentence, while those who committed murder could expect to be sentenced to death. Medical-psychologists argued that, while the principle of proportionality was appropriate for the sentencing of ordinary (i.e. mentally normal) offenders, it was entirely inappropriate for the sentencing of moral imbeciles. The sentencing of habitual criminals/moral imbeciles should be based, they argued, not upon the gravity of the crime committed, but upon a medical assessment of the offender. Offenders should be assessed to determine the extent of their dangerousness and their capacity for reform. The sentence should be determined by the offender's 'treatment' needs, rather than by the gravity of the offence. In many cases the offences of habitual criminals were minor. Under the principle of proportionality they attracted only small fines or short periods of imprisonment. The 'sentencing' of habitual offenders according to their capacity for dangerousness and their treatment needs, would lead to them being placed under much more stringent control (Johnstone, 1990).

In addition, new types of penal institution were required. Prisons were designed to discipline and punish ordinary offenders. Ordinary prison discipline was, however, unsuitable for habitual offenders (Gunn et al., 1978, ch. 1). These offenders had to be sent to institutions where they could be subjected to more intensive disciplinary training, in order to teach them moral sense and self-control (Johnstone, 1990, ch 3). The inebriate reformatory, an institution designed specially for the reformatory treatment of habitual drunken offenders, was the type of institution required (MacLeod, 1967; Radzinowicz and Hood, 1990, ch. 9; Harding and Wilkin, 1988; Johnstone, 1990, ch. 3).

Havelock Ellis's Proposals

Many of these arguments appeared in the work of Havelock Ellis who, as we saw earlier, was an advocate of the view that habitual criminals were, as a class, moral imbeciles. I will sum up the points I have just made with a brief account of Ellis's proposals for the reform of criminal justice procedures.

Ellis was highly critical of both 'the antiquated traditions concerning "responsibility" which rule in our courts of law' and attempts to deal with habitual criminals through 'the antiquated blunderbuss of punishment' (Ellis, 1910, 24–5). Relying upon the concept of moral imbecility, Ellis supported three sets of penal policy proposals: eugenic proposals for the sterilisation of habitual criminals; the introduction of indeterminate sentences for habitual criminals; and proposals for prison reform.

Sterilisation of habitual criminals In keeping with his view that moral imbecility was an hereditary condition, Ellis supported eugenic proposals for the sterilisation of habitual criminals and other methods — e.g. permanent segregation — of preventing moral imbeciles breeding offspring whose moral sense would be even more defective than their own, and thereby 'lowering the level of civilisation in the community' (Ellis, 1910, 13).[20]

The indeterminate sentence Whereas others had used the concept of moral insanity to attack the right to punish, Ellis employed it in order to point to the inadequacies of punishment 'as a practical tool for dealing with criminals in a civilised state' (Ellis, 1910, 33).[21] The policy of punishing habitual criminals,

Ellis pointed out, was based on the presumption that they were, like other persons, responsible beings. According to Ellis, however, it had now been established that the habitual criminal was not in fact a responsible person, that he was a moral imbecile. This being the case it was useless to punish the habitual criminal as if he were a normal offender (Ellis, 1910). The habitual criminal could not be controlled in the same way as the ordinary person, for whom the threat of punishment was generally sufficient to prevent delinquency. Rather the control of the habitual criminal should be put on the same basis as the control of other dangerous lunatics. In particular, it was necessary to reject the principle of proportionality between crime and punishment when dealing with these moral imbeciles. Habitual criminals could not be dealt with by 'simply meting out to them "punishments" in the form of a term of imprisonment roughly equivalent to what social opinion and the judge considered to be the size of the offence, a method which is merely a transformation of the old *lex talionis*' (Ellis, 1910). Instead of punishment being determined by the crime the 'treatment of offenders must be so far as possible individualised and directed not so much towards the crime as towards the criminal' (Ellis, 1910). The habitual criminal, in other words, must be confined for as long as he remained a threat to society: 'The indeterminate sentence ... is really as cardinal a principle in the treatment of prison inmates as of hospital inmates, while from the point of view of social protection it is even more necessary' (Ellis, 1910).

Prison reform Ellis proposed the establishment of a 'moral hospital', an institution which would be the equivalent in the domain of moral disorder, to the lunatic asylum in the world of intellectual disorder: 'We used to chain our lunatics. Our lunatic asylums during the past century have become mental hospitals. Our prisons must now really become what it was long ago said they ought to be, moral hospitals' (Ellis, 1910). Ellis advocated the Borstal institution as a good example of a prison run on modern and intelligent lines (Ellis, 1910).[22] The ideal institution would incorporate certain features of the hospital, most importantly the principle that patients were not discharged until they were 'better'. It would also incorporate elements from other institutions, such as the technical school: 'It is now becoming recognised that the prison must have in it elements borrowed from the hospital, the lunatic asylum, and the technical school, while yet remaining distinct and apart from all these' (Ellis, 1910).

The Transition Complete

The argument that habitual criminals should be regarded as moral imbeciles — and managed through psychiatric, rather than juridical, procedures and methods — eventually led to the problem being taken up by the *Royal Commission on the Care and Control of the Feeble Minded* (The Radnor Commission) which reported in 1908 (*Parliamentary Papers*, 1908). The Radnor Commission expressed concern with those:

> Persons who are not idiots or lunatics, or at least are not regarded as either — persons of weak mind who are socially dangerous. In the affluent classes there are numbers of weak-minded lads ... who are not thought to be certifiable, but allowed to go about uncertified though obviously weak-minded. Among the poorer classes, there are, no doubt, great numbers of moral incapables who are not certified, who are moving about and are socially dangerous.
>
> (*Parliamentary Papers*, 1908, ch. 23)

The Radnor Commission wanted such persons certified as moral imbeciles, so that they could be confined and treated in special institutions. But, to avoid the possibility of its motives being misunderstood, the Commission made it quite clear that — in arguing for the legal recognition of the category of moral imbeciles — they were not trying to deprive the criminal law of its right to convict and punish these people if they committed offences.

> In the case of persons who are charged with offences and are alleged to be mentally defective, the principle should be adopted of keeping the question of committal of the alleged offence separate from the questions of alleged mental defect, the relative responsibility of the offender and his appropriate treatment.
>
> (*Parliamentary Papers*, 1908, para. 26)

> It is not ... necessary or desirable that the precedents under the Trial of Lunatics Act, 1883 ... should be pushed further ... The question of fact may go to the jury, and when that is settled, the question of mental defect may be settled by the court in modification of the sentence. (*Parliamentary Papers*, 1908, para. 460)

> It is of course true ... that a person must be either responsible or irresponsible; that in the matter of criminal procedure these two terms cover the whole ground, and that where the question is 'guilty or not guilty' it would be impossible for the law to admit the existence of any doubtful territory between the two.
>
> (*Parliamentary Papers*, 1908, para. 458)

The question of moral defectiveness was to become pertinent only at the sentencing or *disposal* stage. So, accused persons would be tried in the normal way. If found guilty, the question of mental defect would then be raised, *as pertinent to the question of disposal*. Those who were found to be suffering from a mental disorder such as moral imbecility — which did not amount to insanity — could be subjected to special forms of control instead of, or in addition to, receiving the ordinary (proportionate) sentence for their crime.[23]

The shift in psychiatric concern, which started in the 1860s, was practically complete at this stage. Psychiatrists, in order to establish their new role within the penal system as advisers on the disposal of offenders, insisted that they had no intention of interfering with the law's power to judge and punish. To take one further example, this time from Hamblin Smith, a prison medical officer who did much to promote the psychological approach to crime:

> It is not meant that this medical examiner is to supersede, in any way, the proper purpose of the court. The investigation of the outward facts of the alleged offence is a matter with which the court alone is concerned. The court can, and should ... remand a case for special medical examination and report. But it is probably better that this report should not be considered until the facts relating to the alleged offence have been legally determined. Again, the ultimate decision as to what is to be done with the case ... lies with the court. And it is not for a moment suggested that the medical examiner should encroach upon the court's prerogative, or its responsibility in this connection. (Hamblin Smith, 1922, 27)

Hamblin Smith was willing to concede to the law's demand that it determine the question of the legal responsibility of offenders. This compromise was necessary in order to increase psychiatry's influence over decisions of disposal (Hamblin Smith, 1922, 32). By not insisting that they be recognised as experts in responsibility, psychiatrists enhanced their chances of being recognised as advisers on the disposal of offenders.

While critics of the 'psychiatric approach to crime' often overstate the extent to which offenders have become 'medicalised', there is no doubt that psychiatrists have gained a firm foothold within the criminal justice system (Gunn et al., 1978; Walker and McCabe, 1973; Carlen, 1986; Johnstone, 1988; Sim, 1990). It is true that the substantive law of criminal responsibility has changed little, in response to psychiatric arguments. In the criminal trial, psychiatric witnesses occupy much the same position today as they did in the middle of the nineteenth century. However, once the offender has been convicted, psychiatrists have a considerable say in how they are processed.

Psychiatric reports can influence sentencing decisions (Prins, 1986, ch. 3; H. Allen, 1987, ch. 4) and, once an offender has been sentenced by the court, psychiatric advice plays a considerable part in determining how the offender is actually dealt with. The whole penal process, to a very significant extent, has become 'psychiatricised' (Johnstone, 1988; 1990).

Conclusion: A Tentative Hypothesis

Where psychiatrists failed in their battle with the law over the issue of the insanity defence, and eventually conceded to the law on this point, they have gained a firm foothold within the criminal justice system as advisers on the processing of convicted offenders. In order to explain psychiatry's failure in its first battle with the law (i.e. over the issue of responsibility) and its relative success in its second campaign, we need to consider the social functions which criminal justice performs. One important function of criminal justice is the public denunciation of crimes. In the past, this ritual condemnation of crime usually took place during the execution of the sentence, which often occurred in public (Garland, 1990, 71). In the modern criminal justice system, the actual execution of the sentence has become hidden from the public (Foucault, 1977). Hence, the task of expressing public indignation has shifted from the execution of the sentence to the trial, which still takes place in a public setting (Garland, 1990, 72). Because the task of publicly censuring crime and criminals now tends to fall mainly on the courts, they have been reluctant to recognise knowledges, such as those of psychiatry, which interfere with condemnation. Psychiatry, to put it bluntly, is too equivocal on the issue of moral responsibility — it is too hesitant about blaming people for their criminal actions. Although some psychiatrists have insisted that to *explain* criminal behaviour in psychiatric terms does not necessarily mean *excusing* that behaviour (Moore, 1984), it does not always appear that way, especially to the public. There is a widespread perception, which some psychiatrists have re-enforced, that psychiatry seeks to undermine notions of moral responsibility, that it seeks a relaxation of law and ethics. The courts, no doubt recognising that the notion of moral responsibility is indispensable to the functioning of modern society, have therefore been reluctant to recognise psychiatric doctrines *in the courtroom*. Once the criminal and the crime have been censured, however, the objection to psychiatry becomes less noticeable.

At this stage another concern of criminal justice — a concern with the efficient management and control of offenders — begins to take over. Here, psychiatry becomes *useful* to criminal justice. Many writers have pointed out that psychiatry is useful to the criminal justice system because its medical justifications of confinement help to 'legitimise' the subjection of offenders to forms of restraint and control which cannot be justified in purely legal-punitive terms.[24] However, while this ideological function is important, it is just one part of the explanation of psychiatry's utility to criminal justice. In addition, psychiatry — through its experience in handling the insane — has developed strategies and mechanisms for the management of very difficult people which are quite useful in the penal system (Carlen, 1986; Sim, 1990).

Notes

1. Cf: 'The law is based on an assumption that, in the absence of evidence to the contrary, people are able to choose whether to do criminal acts or not and that a person who chooses to commit a crime is responsible for the resulting evil and deserves punishment' (Smith and Hogan, 1992, 4).
2. 'The Rules, being based upon outdated psychological views, are too narrow, it is said, and exclude many persons who ought not to be held responsible. They are concerned only with defects of reason and take no account of emotional and volitional factors whereas modern medical science is unwilling to divide the mind into separate compartments and to consider the intellect apart from the will' (Smith and Hogan, 1992, 207).
3. For a similar transition in France, see Castel, 1975; Foucault, 1988; and Nye, 1984.
4. On the history of the insanity defence, see N. Walker, 1968. For a comprehensive summary of the current legal position and modes of 'disposal', see Smith and Hogan, 1992, 192–215. Norrie is a useful guide to the debates about the insanity defence and their political context (Norrie, 1993, ch. 9). For a riveting study of the insanity defence in Victorian trials in its cultural, intellectual and political context, R. Smith, 1981 and 1989, are also very interesting.
5. In response to a series of decisions which threatened to expand the scope of the insanity defence the judges had, in 1843, formulated the famous M'Naghten Rules which *re-affirmed* the 'loss of understanding' definition of insanity: 'To establish a defence on the ground of insanity, it must be clearly proved that, at the time of committing the act, the party accused was labouring under such a defect of reason, from disease of the mind, as not to know the nature and quality of the act he was doing; or, if he did know it, that he did not know he was doing what was wrong' (per Tindal CJ, cited in Smith and Hogan, 1990, 191).
6. Quoted in Skultans, 1975, 180. On Prichard and the concept of moral insanity, see Johnstone, 1988, 339–47; D. Leigh, 1961, ch. 3; and Carlson and Dain, 1962.
7. 'It is often very difficult to pronounce, with certainty as to the presence or absence of moral insanity, or to determine whether the appearances which are supposed to indicate its existence do not proceed from natural peculiarity or eccentricity of character' (Prichard, 1847).
8. See, for example, Morris, 1989, 43–5, 80–1, for a discussion of the dispute during the 1940s and 1950s.
9. The most important thing at stake was, of course, the lives of offenders, but that was not all. The conflict over the insanity defence intersects with a number of larger cultural battles: between traditionalism and modernity; between 'common sense' and science; between advocates and opponents of the idea that individuals should bear the full responsibility for who they are and what they do; between those who like to deal harshly with miscreants and those who favour a more sympathetic response; and between advocates and opponents of

the death penalty. It is because it has such symbolic significance, as well as practical importance, that the issue of the insanity defence has received so much attention from, among others, philosophers and film-makers.

10. For statistics on the insanity defence and related matters in this period, see Walker, 1968.
11. Emphasis in original.
12. See also Storch, 1976; Harrison, 1971; and Johnstone, 1990, ch. 2.
13. For an example of such distinctions see Charles Booth's *Life and Labour of the People in London*, as discussed in Williams, 1981, ch. 7.
14. Charles Booth, quoted in Williams, 1981, 316. On the emergence of the concept of a criminal class in England, see Radzinowicz and Hood, 1990, 73–84.
15. An explanation frequently found in the discourses of penal and social policy: 'It is perhaps typical of a much broader strategy that the failure of a normative institution should be displaced onto the character of the "failed" individuals, who are then deemed "beyond control"' (Garland, 1985, 224).
16. Quoted in Skultans, 1975, 180.
17. On the philosophy of deterrent punishment see Honderich, 1971, ch. 3. For the view of mid-nineteenth century prison administrators on the subject of deterrence see McConville, 1981, 241–3.
18. On the overlaps between the problem of habitual drunkards and that of habitual offenders see Johnstone, 1990, 60.
19. Hence Bentham, the leading theorist of deterrent punishment, held that punishment was pointless, and ought not to be inflicted, in cases where the recipients lacked control over their behaviour (Bentham, 1830, 23–4).
20. For Ellis's views on eugenics, see his 1922 essay 'The Individual and the Race', in Ellis, 1939. On the rise of eugenics and its 'infiltration' of criminal law, see Radzinowicz and Hood, 1990, ch. 10; and Garland, 1985, 142–52.
21. Ellis often used the term 'criminals' to refer to habitual offenders, whom he regarded as 'true criminals', rather than to anybody who committed an offence. Ellis's typology of offenders is set out in Ellis, 1910, ch. 1.
22. Preface to 4th edn.
23. The recommendations of the Radnor Commission led to the *Mental Deficiency Act* 1913 (2 & 3 Geo. V c. 28) which made legal provision for the control of moral imbeciles (s. 1 (d)). For a discussion of this provision, see Burt, 1944, ch. 2.
24. For example, Box, 1980, 121; and Ramon, 1986, 214–40.

5 Words with the Shaman: On the Sacrifice in Criminal Evidence

PIYEL HALDAR[1]

'I is an other.' That is the secret told by the mystic. (de Certeau, 1986, 96)

Are we capable of atheism? (Lacoue-Labarthe, 1993, 13)

Preparations for a Journey[2]

Dislocated in between two worlds of mysterious violence, the laws of Criminal Evidence hold a unique place in all penal systems.[3] Judicial pronouncements of the sentence generate from a violation of substantive law, a breach necessitating evidence of the event. Thus it is that evidence connects the violation of the law, of a criminal code, to the violence of punishment. However the usual history of the evolution of the modern trial procedure assumes that the rules of evidence are discrete, disjunctive and disengaged from Criminal Law.[4] The place of evidence is merely supplementary to the substantial rules and exist in order to prove facts to which those substantive laws may be applied.

This notion of proof is one which supposedly engages a procedure that is objective in its fact-finding process; a process which, under the Rule of Law, is impartial and non-arbitrary. Whatever theory of truth might underlie this supplementary concern — correspondence, pragmatic, ideological — its method is grounded in the Enlightenment assumption that the truth of an event can be proved by 'man'. Modern Law denies any intimacy with the more 'primitive', 'illiterate', and 'violent' premodern rituals of proof which, by and large, centred around practices of divination. In the premodern scheme of things, as for example in the Thomist branch of scholasticism — the point at which Christian metaphysics took to an otherwise pagan philosophy — the Divine exists as the sustaining cause of the community. Such a presidency,

104

not only ruled and ordered every contingency, but was considered to exist prior to any knowledge. The principle of reason represented the discursive conceptualising faculty of human beings, the function of which was to draw conclusions based on commonsense observation, yet this form of rationalism belonged only to a lower order of truth-production than that of spiritual knowledge. Pre-modern trial procedures were thus dominated by the assumption that truth was to be revealed by an omniscient, authoritative God; the 'founding reference' as Legendre puts it (Legendre, 1990). There was, in general, no need to find evidence that the accused was guilty because God would reveal by providing *certain*, and not merely probable, proof. If, in the medieval mind, God existed as this 'founding reference', that to which all things referred, then the rituals of proof, the sacrificial tortures and the *judiciae dei*, might be seen as the 'theatre of the founding reference' — for each performance of these rites establishes the mythical order and mystical authority of the divine sovereignty. The rationalism of modernity in general, and modern law in particular, would lay claim to the fact that acts of divination could not hold individuals to account, for this would imply the existence of an external norm which interferes in order to guide the individual (Goldman, 1964, 31). Modernity, then, is characterised by the loss of an encounter between a deic authority and His mortal subjects. It is characterised by the elimination of the mysterious, the fancy, the curious or the miraculous, and by the remoteness of its problems from the cult of Gods, religious rites and liturgical functions that had constituted the 'dark ages'. In the rational scheme of things, Man's behaviour within a community can only be governed and explained by reference to his isolated, autonomous, and unfettered will. The claims of the *philosophes* in particular were accompanied by this disappearance of a God (Goldman, 1964, 32). Even in the strict theism of, for example, Pascal and other theological responses to the Deists, God was considered to be in hiding (*deus absconditus*). But it should be remembered that a hidden God is also a God who had once been unconcealed; a *deus absconditus* refers also to a God who had once been a *deus ex machina*, a device which had enabled the unfolding of a particular and certain narrative.[5] That is to say that God still exists as a sovereign figure in the rational philosophy of the Enlightenment but only as a first cause, an *ens entium*, located within the originary moment that founds a scientific universe. However, once the Earth had been set in motion upon its axis, the authority of God was to make way for the sovereignty of those individuals created in his image. Such were the dictates of the age of Reason at least until Kant provided his synthesis of Empiricism and Rationalism in the *First Critique*. Within this new order, Modern Law is perceived to be altogether more civilised and rational, less violent in its methods of proof and in its concern for the sovereign and autonomous will of the individual.[6] Toleration, reason, or 'just measure', have to be exercised with respect to all individuals in the social contract, even in the moment of punishment (Goldman, 1973, 22). Thus, the principles of juridical proof were separated from those which derived from theological and religious discourse, and formulated in concordance with the techniques of the objective and neutral sciences. Seemingly, therefore, the current trend to allow into the courtroom advanced technological and 'man'-made inventions as records of an event (new computer, camera, or recording techniques), or as proof of an identity (DNA), operates within this rational and technical modern order. What seems to be at stake in the modern laws of evidence is the ability to prove the truth of an event, and assign responsibility for an action upon an isolated individual, without hint of violence, in order that that same individual be punished.

In this chapter, it will be argued however that, through the laws of evidence, modern criminal justice is an energetic and virulent system of *decriminalisation* with a violence that knows no bounds. For the purpose of the argument, the term 'decriminalisation' is used to suggest a two-fold aspect of criminal justice. First, the term is suggestive of a judicial devotion (*devotio*) to public duty, to rid or cure a peaceable public of its criminal element. Secondly, it reminds us of those arguments in favour of converting a criminal back into a citizen. That is to say that the wayward individual who, as if playing truant, has strayed from an order and has breached an obligation under the social contract, must be brought back to law, requalified as a legal subject. In this respect it is not a matter of mere facetiousness to make connections between Law and other institutions based on the performance of pedagogy.[7] Indeed, bearing in mind the uncertainties of legal proof and the Enlightenment opinion that only probable, rather than certain, knowledge was possible (Shapiro, 1983),[8] punishment may have a more symbolic rather than an utilitarian or humanitarian function. For what is symbolised in this notion of decriminalisation if not a normative behaviour and a sense of social order. This being so, the criminal process shares elements of an institution it tries to reject, an institution within which the individual is the expendable cost of prescription and cure; an institution based on sacrifice and a religious sovereign order. This chapter sets out first of all to reinstate the notions of the sacrificial (*Katharma*) and the curative back into an understanding of modern criminal procedure and evidentiary practices, to seek out what has been hidden (*absconditus*), and then to speculate upon their rejection or repression. The concern here is not to call for a return to religious or Christian dogmatics but to recuperate those other repressed traditions and their obsession with the unseen as that which can never directly be represented, in order to deconstruct the epistemological assumptions that ground the principles of rational evidence. Or to put it conversely, an understanding of the history of criminal evidence necessarily entails an appreciation of the violent procedures or rituals of divination, sacrifice and cure; rituals the performance of which still order the criminal law trial and exist as those traumas and ordeals in the symptoms of their repression. As we shall see, the commemoration and 'incantation' of these religious and medical origins of evidence, the performance of this 'theatre of the founding reference', problematises the figuration of the individual; that autonomous site or image upon which punishment is inscribed. For what is sacrificed in the juridical act of decriminalisation is all that which is other to the principle of the individual, all the unwanted profanities of a social order. In recuperating these repressed notions of the sacrificial to the understanding of modern problems of criminal procedure the figure of the Shaman, borrowed from Gregory Ulmer's reading of the art of Joseph Beuys and the literature of deconstruction, will later be used to refer both to the decentred subject in law, as well as to the return of these supposedly dead, buried, and forgotten traditions. For, as Ulmer points out, 'the shaman's power derives specifically from his special relationship with death — his ability to "detach" his soul from his body temporarily (without having to die) and thus journey to the land of the dead and return' (Ulmer, 1985, 219).

Sacrifice and Healing

Defrock the erminous splendour of the judge and beneath the horsehair wig, squirrel skins and the red plush gown lurks a primitive space within which rattle the bones of a legal anthropology. That is to say, the metaphor of judge as medicine man, of justice as a curative procedure, and of the trial as sacrifice extend back into a presentable history. Within such excavations are the resurrected remains of violent and mystical procedures of Evidence central to the understanding of Criminal Law.

The status of the sacrifice as a historic ritual which inaugurates, causes to begin, and binds together religious communities (Freud, 1940), is primarily a religious state of affairs which orders a divine rather than secular law, thus enacting its religious set of prohibitions through the totemic law of the father. In addition, much of the foundational treatises on the fixture of the sacrifice deal largely with anthropological, cross-cultural accounts of Pagan, Aztec, or

Mithraic cults. However, here we are not so much concerned with a *type* of sacrifice which will determine the structure of the (English legal) community. The sacrifice, it has to be stressed, is a symbolic ritual and its import into Western thinking makes it doubly symbolic (Bataille, 1988; 1989; Freud, 1940).[9] The 'sacrifice' has literally been appropriated by Western academics and *thrown within* (symbolic, *symballein*: to throw with) Western culture. It has been made to 'coincide with something else' (Eco, 1986, 153) and accorded symbolic and totemic status on its own merits. What is addressed here then is the status of sacrifice as the origins of a symbolic and evidentiary order of truth, which in turn (in)*augurates* a legal community.

However, it is not simply a question of the community. Rather, if the sacrifice is a symbolic ritual, then it is also a question of the individual — for the symbolic is the determining order of the subject. What the concept of the sacrifice does is to problematise the notion of the individual. In its regulation, the sacrifice seeks not to punish an individual but to cure (*pharmakon*) and restore sanctity to the profane existence of a community.[10] The victim (*katharma*), sacrificed and repressed for the good of the community, is a substitute or a surrogate replacement for the absent source of malevolence which infests a community. In the modern trial the punishment has to be enacted both on and in the presence of the guilty defendant. Yet even in the sacrificial order of things the victim is already an individual, already consecrated as a recognisable and chosen figure, already radiating 'intimacy, anguish, the profundity of living beings' (Bataille, 1988, 57). The victim is thus an individual under the occupation of the community, for it is within the space of the victim's body that a community invests its hopes of an intimacy with the divine order.[11]

Two points need to be made here in connection with evidence and evidentiary practices. First, the sacrifice is made of objects taken from the order of lost intimacy. This is more than what Bataille calls 'the real order', it is the order of proven existence, of an empirical world of material and evidenced objects, of the dumb things we intimately know or of which we have knowledge. Indeed if the sacrifice reflects the temporary and temporal transformation of spiritual malevolence (*pharmakon*) into beneficent cure (*pharmakon*), if it reflects a shift from an 'obsessional sickness' of the taboo to a state of purification (Freud, 1940, 79), it must first of all be that these objects are tainted with the 'symptoms' of the profane, symptoms of otherness. (In this light it has to be remembered that the Aristotelian notion of 'proof' is that of 'symptom': *tekmerion*.)[12] Thus the individual who is set up as sacrificial object is one who is made known to the community, one who is grounded in a proven, yet forgotten, existence, but also one who bears the evidential symptoms of impurity. The victim is thus the 'other' of the community and represents the heretical threat to the vision (*evidere*) of social order.

The second point to be made is that the sacrifice itself is *proof* of an invisible divinity (*deus absconditus*), of a variety of sacred things which cannot be circumscribed by vision or apprehended by ordinary mortal senses. The divinity is that authority which remains absent and anonymous. Through the institution of the sacrifice, which lies in place of the inadequacies of mortal perception, there is some sort of attempt to provide proof of the infinite, of that higher being which extends beyond the sphere of everyday objects and beings. The nature of sacrifice, along with superstitions and dreams, is thus of that religious form of proof — divination. In these terms, the sacrifice is a theory of representation, a practice of representing that which is absent (Bataille, 1989, 46).[13] It limits and trains its imaginary dimensions, it controls the image of its divine referent, by reducing itself to an authorised and consecrated meaning. Furthermore sovereign authority, made known through sacrificial evidence, is not of the same status as authority made known through an oracle. Where the oracle attempts to pierce, to speak about, and to determine the truth of the future, the sacrifice (as with all forms of evidence) proves a past state of affairs — that which has already existed and has existed from a beginning. Authority is that which derives from the past, from precedent, from the *priori*. It is that which exists from the beginning and gives witness to a succession of events. The principle of authority is thus authorial in that it derives from an originary moment and takes the form of the textual or the scriptural (testament). That is to say, authority demands its own iconic repetition, for the condition of writing itself lies in its putative capability of that originary time being repeated or disseminated.

As an evidentiary concept, the sacrifice is bound up in a ritual of proof which maintains a hierarchy, celebrating the dominance of the Gods over the subservience of humanity. For there is here the sacrifice of a lower order of evidentiary objects, the profane and idolatrous victim (the order of negative *pharmakon*), in order to attain a higher and iconic order of the evidence of Gods (the order of positive *pharmakon*). But what authorises the violence of the sovereign sacrifice is that such proof is also the proof of an order, a dictum which heals and binds (*nexus*) the community back to the institution of the sacrifice. It is thus an institution which demands the principle and the 'act' of belief, that other evidentiary notion which invests in the truth. In the context of the modern trial it must be said that this notion of belief exists not simply as dogma, but as the investiture of the subject in a proposition. Thus, for example the practice of oath-taking (whether in the space of a modern trial or in the ancient custom of compurgation) is important for its act and not necessarily for its content; it is a modality of affirmation, a belief in the institution which in turn provides the witness with a quest for credibility and identity within that same institutional space.[14] But it is through the dynamics of belief, through the believable and therefore the evidential, that the reason of law becomes humanised, incarnated, or violently inscribed upon the body of an individual. This sacrifice, this textualisation of the individual in the name of humanisation, is what is at stake when evidence, in practice as in theory, becomes believable. However, to say this is not yet to say that the institution of courtroom practice is the repetition of sacrificial rites. What must now be charted is an analysis of other forms of criminal trials and procedures, of what the medieval lawyers called the *lex ordinandi* in order to *ordain* and distinguish the law of procedure from the substantial, a typology that runs through trials by battle, ordeal and finally jury, in order to establish this ritual of sacrifice as the determining factor in legal representations of the body.

Trials by Battle

The battle (*battel*) or judicial combat, as a form of trial[15] in which the question at issue was to be decided according to the result of personal combat between the contesting parties or between their champions, is not considered to be essentially an appeal to physical force. Rather it is accompanied by a belief that providence will give victory to the right. The personal combat refers to an organised attempt to call upon a divine authority to decide the justice of a claim or an action or the truth of an accusation. However, as with all other trials by ordeal, such legal proceedings were also formal tests employed under fixed conditions to determine, and thus prove, the will of God. Christianity transfers this appeal from heathen deities to the God of battles, where a legal position could be affirmed by an appeal to divine judgment. Thus a dispute over the title to the ownership of real estate, for example, or any other legal difference, could be settled by duel under the shadow of the church. The combat, whether between two or many, was in its uncertain issue connected with unseen powers, and in the years of its unfolding history became regarded as the greatest test of truth, the *judicium dei* par excellence (Brace, 1886, 163).[16] The use of the various forms of trial by battle tested the truth by empowering the victor even at the risk of sacrificing his own blood, although it should be remembered that the battle made no allowance for difference in strength. It was considered that God could and, where appropriate, would empower the weaker of the two parties; such was the parabolic message of the fight between David and Goliath (Aquinas, 1990, 2, ii, Q. 95, art. 8). As the author of *Beowulf* points out, 'God alone knows who will control the place of battle, who will win' (*Beowulf*, 1980, 94–5). It is interesting to note at this point that a particular etymology of the word 'evidence' is connected to the word 'evince': to conquer, to overcome, to cast down, to eject judicially or to make a victor or a victim (*vincere*) (*Oxford Dictionary of English Etymology*, 1966; T. Thomas, 1587).

The formal and legal organisation of these combats took the form of the medieval equivalent of advocacy. Lawyers were given the task of counting or telling the tale, putting the plaintiff's case in formal terms according to custom. Such performances, which might be considered to precurse both pleading and advocacy, were understood to be the central activity in combative litigation. Thus the earliest professional lawyers were known as *narratores* in token of the description of the plaintiff's case, or counts (*contes/narratios*). The plaintiff's case would be formulated and then met by a word-for-word denial by the defendant. Only then would the dispute be settled by incorporating both claim and denial in an oath to be submitted to the *judicium dei* and the battle, the judgment of God supporting the truth of one or other of the statements.[17] Consider, by way of example, a case involving one Millicent de Cantelou who is joined by John de Hastings in denying the right of Roger de Seytom to assert his claim that a piece of property had descended to him (Selden Society, 1963, B16a–d). The trial proceeds with both parties proposing their elected champions, certain free men, to enter into duel. Once the justice has formally asked each of the champions to undertake battle,[18] the tenant's champion is asked to swear that the land is not the right of the demandant, whereas the demandant's champion swears that the tenant has perjured herself because the count is true.[19] What follows, we are told in the *narrationes*, is an exchange of gloves. The two champions then proceed bare-footed, bare-headed, and in only their single coats with 'arms undone', to a church to offer five pennies in honour of the five wounds of Christ (Selden Society, 1963, B16b) — the ultimate sacrificial victim in the Christian order of things. In the context of proving the iconic, it is interesting to note that this part of the proceedings is known as '*la forme de la veou des champyons*' or 'the form of the *view* of the champions'. Battle would then commence with pomp and ceremony, to the sound of fifes and trumpets, and in full battle array. That the champions would often be dressed in tunics of white sheepleather (*tunicas armaturas*), seems significant and serves to remind us of those biblical images of the sacrificial lamb.

Amongst the different modes of early trial procedures (including compurgation and ordeals), the structure and performance of the blood feud most resembles the modern adversarial procedure. It is indeed a procedure based upon a concept of *defensio* (Holdsworth, 1956, 134) that is to say a procedure based upon a battle between appellant and defendant. Unlike the sacrifice, the cause of the trial and the trial itself occurs within that personal, private and metaphysical space between the two parties involved, the *appellée* and *appellant*. However this space can only be described as a *'privête'*, or privity within which there is the exchange of battle scars inflicted by one upon the other. These visible wounds or traces that are symbolically inscribed upon the individual autonomy of the loser mark, not only the dominant imposition of the victor upon the victim, but also the inscription of rank and standing within a feudal community. For, according to the outcome of such trials, the victor maintains and relegitimates his feudal standing whilst the loser loses all in death and dishonour. There is in the event a proscription of (re)cognition, of belonging or not belonging to an order. Here it is interesting to note that victory may be obtained if one of either party proves recreant and surrenders to the fight, when one 'pronounces the horrible word of *craven*' (Blackstone, 1979, vol. 3, 338–44) which comes from the mouth of the conquered party as the consequence of 'his' defeat. The word conjures such feelings of condemnation that the loser is assigned and recognised by the order of infamy not to be accounted a free and legal person; *'liber et legalis homo'*. The word *craven*, it should be remembered, means spiritless and its pronouncement is proof of the lower order, the profane existence of the infamous, and idolatrous, which must be ridden of legal rights. The victor, on the other hand, by virtue of championship achieves an intimacy with that higher, noble order of the *legalis homo*, and is given his share of life. The sacrifice, in this case, is seen as a notion of expenditure and gain, 'a positive property of loss from which spring nobility, honour, and rank in a hierarchy'.[20] The battle symbolically names (*appellatio*) the champion and the loser and, in doing so, it seeks to redress an imbalance by reasserting a hierarchy. The loser becomes an accursed share taken on account of the surplus debt owed to the victor. This (pre-capitalist) notion of being bound by a debt refers also to what Georges Dumezeil has called the principle of *nexum*, in order to describe 'the insolvent debtor who was, very literally, bound and subjugated by the creditor' (Dumezil, 1988, 99). In the curative agenda of the duel, distinguished from the violence it seeks to avenge only by a legal or formalised procedure, we see the birth of a system which tries to escape the contamination of the sacrificial. It is through the procedure of law, rather than through its substance that Law attempts to create this space of purity, a space which denies the presence of the sacrificial. Yet in and through the aporia, the wounds, created within the space of a 'privity', in between the blows of battleaxes, the cut and thrusts of swords exchanged within the adversarial scheme of things, there emerges only that same ritual of the sacrifice; a ritual of proving the iconic order of the unseen, of representing the mystical and absolute authority of the sovereign divinity, and of symbolically reasserting a social order.

Trials by Ordeal

Like the trial by battle, the trial by ordeal (*ordele*, great judgment) rests upon belief in divine intervention, that God would actively interpose to establish an earthly right.[21] However, judgment is given not on the strength of any individual victor favoured by God. The 'judgment of God' is obtained by sign or miracle in order to determine a point of issue. Such divine signs were made known through tests which involved the use of fire, water, poison,[22] sacred libation, or the balance. The use of the latter in divine tests may be thought of as an interesting derivation of the scales of justice. The accused would be placed upon the scales, by a judge, twice in succession. If the individual, by the second weighing, had increased in weight s/he would be guilty. If, on the other hand, that person were equal in weight, or lighter, then s/he would be found to be innocent. For only the balance knows 'what mortals do not comprehend'.[23] In general, however, the person who is able to carry a red hot poker iron, who can plunge an arm into boiling water, who will sink when thrown into water is deemed to have right on their side.[24] Or, as Thayer cites in his *Preliminary Treatise on Evidence at the Common Law*, 'He whom the blazing fire burns not, whom the water soon forces not up, or who meets with no speedy misfortune must be held veracious in his testimony on oath' (Thayer, 1898, 35).

What is interesting about the ordeal, in its relation to the sacrifice, is the condition of divine proof required in order to appease a sense of disorder within the community. Ordeals, it should be noted, were largely public affairs. Many of the 'offences' which called for use of the ordeal arose out of public condemnation and hunting; mass hysteria. However trials by ordeal were usually reserved for victims who were regarded as profane others: the servile or the 'unfree', the foreigner, the friendless, witches and other heretics and idolaters. However their crimes were false doctrines and thus invisible. Thus, even the unwitnessed event, the hearsay or invisible statement, were tried by ordeal. Yet another citation from Thayer's treatise notes that ordeals were to be administered 'if an offence has been committed in a solitary forest, at night, or in the interior of a house...' (Thayer, 1898, 35).[25] It was thus the role of the ordeal — as *'lex parabilis*, or *apparens* or *aperta* — the manifest proof' (Bartlett, 1986, 33) — to deal with these invisible crimes and to make manifest the judicial decision of God. Thus, the guilty are those who manifest through the ordeal, evidence of that profane order of superstition as those other theological heresies and those other forms of divination. The ordeal becomes the excessive means by which the demands of a desire are to be met, to be given up, and sacrificed for satiety. Like the sacrifice, the ordeal in its viciousness takes the victim away from a surplus, in order to recall that other intimate order; an order which represses otherness.

The abolition of the ordeal as proof of guilt or innocence by the Fourth Lateran Council of 1215 may be seen to mark a turning point in the history of evidence and in the genealogy of sacrificial forms of proof. However, what is prefigured in this decision is not the dwindling power of a clergy who had a vested interest in mediating ordeals. The abolition of the ordeal instituted by Lateran IV, amongst other decrees against heretics, arose out of the Romanisation of Canon Law and the Latin Church during the Hildebrand reforms of the twelfth century. Papal authority had turned to the laws of Justinian as a means of social control and governance.[26] Although firmly legitimated by divine authority, ecclesiastical law became, through this bureaucratisation, a political and legal entity, thereby establishing the principal dogmatic doctrine of papal infallibility. That this Council was instrumental in carrying out the Hildebrand reforms is evidenced in the following decree:

> We excommunicate and anathematise every heresy that raises itself against the holy, orthodox and catholic faith ... secular authorities, whatever office they may hold shall be admonished and induced and if necessary compelled by ecclesiastical censure, that as they wish to be esteemed and numbered among the faithful, so for the defence of the faith they ought publicly to take an oath that they will strive in good faith and to the best of their ability to exterminate in the territories subject to their jurisdiction all heretics pointed out by the church.[27]

It may be added that the institution of the ordeal perhaps never reached the sacrificial status of the duel which might account for the abolition of the former and the retention of the latter. Amongst the papal decretals of the twelfth century, arguments attacking the legitimacy of the ordeal were already common. The ordeal, it was claimed, had never really been authoritatively, i.e. canonically, instituted. To be sure, whilst the ordeal was regarded as some sort of incantation of divine judgment, it had not been sacramentalised (*sacere-facere*) (Bartlett, 1986, 72–88).[28] What was instituted by the abolition of the ordeal was, thus, an even greater sense of proof as a sacred and iconic principle, even if its accepted form was in the secular trial by jury. It is of no surprise, therefore, to find that the thirteenth-century legal mind perceived the temporal law to be holy (*sacerdos temporalis, qui est judex*) (Kantorowicz, 1957, 122), and the status of the judge to be hallowed, 'as human priests'.[29]

It might be further added that, within the Anglo-Saxon scheme of things, the divine order, intimately bound up in a power accorded to the clergy, never totally gave way to the secular order of a reformative crown. For, as Kantorowicz points out in *The King's Two Bodies*, through a close reading of Bracton, the political figurehead symbolised by the Crown has a dual nature. The King is at once human and divine, temporal and spiritual. Mortal man would invest the King with a spiritual body, where God has created his temporal one. The deification of the sovereign's body, however, is not to be thought of as an apotheosis, or 'the transformation of Man into God', but rather as a consecration, or the 'transferral of profane space to sacred space' (Dupont, 1989, 399). It is to become this sovereign body which, through the conjunction of its physical and spiritual beings, determines any law. For it is the union between the political (or the body politic) and the divine which provides for the fantasy of an undivided social body, a homogeneous and dogmatic order, that recognises no exteriority or otherness to itself. The courts of law, whether spiritual or temporal themselves, become the absolute representation and proof of this singular royal sovereignty and unique constitutional supremacy which in itself is of an invisible realm,[30] an unseen and unwritten order. The status of the legal subject as a victim sacrificed in appeasement of this new spiritual order, made known through the human form of the monarch, can be seen in the context of the development of the jury trial. Far from providing an objective verdict upon the evidence heard, juries may be considered to have been an imprisoned collective of individuals, 'bound over' by the force and dogmatism of law.

Trial by Jury

If the symbol of sacrifice were to be offered merely as an analogical relation of the modern criminal trial, it would accord the judge the status of the sacrificer-priest. As in the figure of the shaman, which has been read as an emblem of the decentred subject (Ulmer, 1985, 9), the judge participates in evidentiary proof, that 'visionary' activity, through techniques of self-displacement. Before a judge can pronounce judgment upon a point of law, s/he must rely on the satisfaction of proof through the separate body of a tribunal of fact. The jury become the somewhat displaced, and even dislocated, eyes and ears of the judge. As witnesses to a sacrifice it seems more than coincidental that the number twelve becomes the usual number of the jury, redolent of the number in that other apostolic corpus of witnesses to the Christian sacrifice. Coke, however, had argued that the biblical reference was precisely the reason why we have 'twelve good and lawful men jurors'. It is 'that the law delighted itself in the number twelve. For there must not only be twelve jurors for the trials of matter of fact but [h]e that wageth his law must have eleven with him which think he says true. And that number of twelve is much respected in Holy Writ, as twelve apostles, twelve stones, twelve tribes, etc' (Coke, 1853, 155).

Whilst seemingly crude, these analogies do serve as an interesting illustration of the way in which jury service binds its members to a faith in judicial sovereignty. The jury itself is educated by the part it is required to take in the administration of justice. For de Tocqueville, this pedagogical performance of Law is to be regarded as the chief value of the system (de Tocqueville, 1969). Not so much a measure or guarantee of proof, jury service becomes but performance which teaches respect for law and order, respect for judicial attitude, respect for social obligations to the constitution. The early modern accounts of jury trial, to be found in *Spelman's Reports*, tell of the conditions under which jurors were kept in order that they consider their verdict. Having been charged 'to do in this manner as God will give you grace, according to the evidence and your conscience' (Selden Society, 1978, vol. 2, 112), the jury would be kept in the custody of a keeper or bailiff without meat, drink, fire and candle. They were not permitted to speak to anyone until they had agreed upon their verdict. Any conduct to the contrary, the mere possession of 'comfits, dredge, sugarcandie, raisins, plum jam and dates' for example (*Earl of Arundel's case* (1500) 99 SS 64),[31] was punishable and would render their verdicts unsafe. Curiously, however, if food and drink were taken after the jury had reached an agreement, but before delivering their verdict, the verdict was accepted, but the jurors still punished, as in the *Earl of Arundel's case*. The consideration of evidence was thus a responsibility to be treated with sanctity, and one which had to remain uncontaminated by the profanity of everyday life.

Indeed the sanctity of the jury, the subjection of the individual to the spiritual order of legal procedure (*ordinandi lex*), can be seen to have been constituted according to the union between the two levels of political and divine sovereignty. If it is to be believed that the popularity of the jury coincided with the demise of the trials by ordeal and the lessening importance of the combat, it is only because the jury rearticulated the form of the *judicium dei*.[32] It is poignant that where the private duel had once been a routine procedure in criminal cases, by Bracton's age felonies could only be challenged in public by the King. However, because the King does not fight in person, his elected champions became the jury. Consider Bracton's words: 'When the appellee offers to defend himself by his body he will not be heard, because the King does not fight, nor has he any champion other than the country' (Bracton, *De Legibus*, fo. 142b, 2, 402). The word 'country', in this case, is used as a synecdoche for the jury of the neighbourhood.[33] Not only were the jury considered to be participants in this new articulation of the combat, but they were also representatives and proof of the political order of sovereignty, fighting on behalf of the monarch, yet chosen from the lay and unordained community of people (*laos*).

On another related or conjoined level, the decision of the jury was still considered to be a judgment of fact given by the grace of God. A chronicler describes an early trial in 1249[34] between travelling merchants and local robbers, in which several men were convicted of highway robbery by a jury of the Winchester neighbourhood, but only after a previous jury had been thrown into a dungeon. That first set of jurors had refused to convict the accused men. It is reported that the jury had been intimidated by these local thieves, most of whom were members of the King's household: royal-keepers, cooks, retainers, and archers of the monarch. The second set of jurors, finding the men guilty, were thus said to have been in fear of the King, who wished to have his name and household purged of these unsavoury associations, and who was responsible for ordering the fate of the first jury. The lesson to be learned, or the reasons why 'these events have been so fully and diffusely described', is that finally the malefactors, who had indelibly stained their neighbourhood with their crimes, had been disposed of by the vengeance of God.

What is sacrificed in these early examples of trial by jury is the very body of a juror itself. The jury, far from providing an objective judgment upon the facts, a lay truth, were governed by the doxic nature of law. Yet it is not simply respect for law and order that is represented in these tribunals of fact. Rather, the corpus of the jury articulates the very incarnation of the sovereignty of law. In so doing the juror, as legal subject, determines her or his vision of facts (*evidere*) by virtue of this very sovereignty alone. To explain by way of a further example: During the period when procedural rules become increasingly more and more modern, there occurs a reduction in the amount of evidence for the jury to consider. The premodern trials operated by way of oral pleadings where each and every element of the appellee's counts were met, orally, by the defence. In 1540 the Statute of Jeofails introduced paper pleadings, purportedly, to combat the indeterminate trivial errors made in oral pleading. It was the power of the court to exclude irrelevant evidence. Once paper pleadings, which contained all the details of the charge, were entered into court, the details of those charges could no longer be debated. The jury, therefore, can only rely and determine their judgment upon what is allowed in court: a textualisation and reduction of determinate and immutable evidence based upon the growing exclusionary rules of the common law system. As a corpus, the jury is only articulated by what writes it, can only see the facts by virtue of what governs their vision.

Modern Problems: Legal Forensics and *Mens Rea*

One important epistemological difference between these medieval ordinances and the sacrifice is the status of the victim. The original sacrifice took as victim a surrogate, an arbitrary and symbolic figure, which was offered back up to the gods as catharsis.[35] There is, in the sacrificial order, no notion of vengeance or retribution, there is no principle of culpability for the profanity s/he represents. Where, however, the sacrifice represents the absence of culpability, the trial marks its putative presence. The medieval and modern forms of trial exact punishment upon the ever-present body of the individual miscreant, with the more rigorous and virulent force of judicial authority. Attention is paid to the culpability of the delinquent just as ecclesiastical laws look primarily at the state of mind of the individual sinner.

Ancient law had no machinery with which to accomplish inquiries into the question of intent and so punished upon evidence of acts, and proof of causation alone.[36] We might, however, place the evidential requirement of *mens rea* within an evolution of discourses of truth. The driving force in the production of truth, as has been well recorded, is the confession. The sacramental confession is in the nature of a judgment. Here, the Priest acts as a judicial figure. The penitent, on the other hand, becomes an accuser, or self-accuser. The governing principle is that the sin of the penitent-accuser affects the whole body of the church. The ecclesiastical corpus is therefore bound to deal with the penitent for the sake of its own purity. Remedial penance was thus conceptualised as being medicinal (Aquinas, 1990, 1, xvi, 6). The punishment of those who had chosen to fall from the order of a holy life, and thereby partake in the destruction of the common good, was considered lawful as a heavenly medicine which heals the wounds afflicted by sin. However, through the confession, what is abstracted from its hiding place in the soul is the ultimate truth about an individual, her/his intentions, desires, motives and fantasies (Foucault, 1979, vol. 1, 59; du Bois, 1991) — but also her/his knowledge and mental capacities. In short, what the sacrificial body becomes is proof of a state of mind.

In terms of the doctrinal rules of modern criminal law, what is on trial in the contingency of *mens rea* is purely a state of mind rather than a state of soul. The trial measures, against a notion of rationality, a defendant's ability to foresee consequences, or appreciate risks (*R v Moloney* [1985] 1 All ER 1025; *R v Hancock & Shankland* [1986] AC 455; *R v Nedrick* [1986] 1 WLR 1025).[37] But how is the court able to try and test a suspect's state of mind in relation to the elements of the *actus reus* of a particular crime? Upon what clues are they able to conduct investigation? For Foucault, the answer might simply be held in the confession. In itself the confession is a clue, a scriptural trace extracted from the defendant's mind, left by an autonomous and anatomical body, signed by hand or thumbprint. A confession speaks to the court of intention or recklessness, of purpose or lack of care. In the absence of confession however, *mens rea* is proved by resorting either to the torture of the forensic, or to behavioural signs, or even to both. So, for example, proof of intoxication through body samples and/or police statements as to the behaviour of a defendant may prove the *mens rea* of recklessness. We will return to the question of proving the defendant's capacity to think (*capacitus rationales*), in terms of intoxication, briefly. Whichever way, forensic evidence becomes an analysis of bodily functions and body movements, as proof of an (ir)rational mental capacity.

In the classical sense of the word forensic, what is argued here is that truth is appropriated as belonging to courts of law, through a process of what has been described to be the oldest branch of semiotics, that of symptomatology. The application of medical knowledge to the elucidation of doubtful questions in a court of justice, empowers law with the authority to dictate the truth about life itself. Classical symptomatology may be seen to measure life, at least its quality, in the decipherment of disease. This observationalist approach to medicine, it is often claimed, stems from the *Corpus Hippocratum*, probably in itself a synthesis of two previous medical schools: the Coan school which was concerned with disease in general, and the Cnidian school concerned with manifestations of disease. Hippocratic practices centred around a concern to decipher the causes of disease, from things which enter or quit the body, in order to find a cure. The symptom is thus *anamnestic* (signifying what has happened), *diagnostic* (what is happening) and *prognostic* (what will happen). In broader philosophical terms, the symptom becomes only a temporal instance located in signification upon a corporeal space.

Similarly the notion of 'proof', it has to be remembered, was classically associated with a medical prognosis and fate of the body (the Greek term *tekmerion* covers the three technical terms — proof, clue, and symptom). In the difficult operation of prognosis, of proving an illness, of representing the invisible, hidden, and inner sanctum of a body, the *Corpus Hippocratum* suggests nothing more than proceeding by clues. Indeed, with the fifth century BC medics, Parmenides and Hippocrates, lie not only the roots of medical semiotics or symptomatology,[38] but also the roots of evidence as anatomical prognosis, taking part in a curative scheme of things. In Freudian terms, we might add that the symptom is also that which has been substituted for the repressed.[39] Symptoms become indices of what has been sacrificed from the conscious order and prohibiting agency of the ego.

Consider, in this respect, the forensic examination of the body and the taking of body samples as proof of *mens rea* in cases involving behavioural impairment through the use of drugs or alcohol. On one level, the medical examination of a suspect represents a bureaucratic mode of observation and interrogation, an analysis of symptoms, through a coercive intrusion into what has been hatched in the private repositories of the mind. Forensics represent a sacralisation of the self through modern technology. On another related level, forensics has more than mere epistemological significance. The extraction of bodily fluids — saliva, urine, breath, blood — also represents the placing of a body at the disposition of the bureaucracy. It is a transfer in the property and dominion of what is as essential as the marrow of a bone, life itself. The abstraction of blood is thus the symbolic sacrifice of what is essential to corporeal existence. The iridescent medium of blood in particular is a testimony to both these points. In its dark fluidity it is a poignant symptom, a witness-substance par excellence. It is upon furious bloodshed that Michelet judges history, and it is upon the blood of relation and pedigree that a law recognises the identity of lineage or bastardy (*a stranger in blood*) (Barthes, 1987, 119–25).[40] In the decremental terms related to an act of sacrifice however, blood signifies the profane otherness of life itself (Valery, 1964). The sacrifice, notably in the Christian tradition, is an act of oblation, the offering up of life, the religious transfer of property through the presentation of life before God. The ablation of blood from the human form, its violent separation from the flesh, consequently transforms the body into a signifier. '[B]lood stains everything with the colour of death' (Girard, 1977, 34), it becomes a signifier of death, of a life installed elsewhere; outside of its own anatomy and otherwise than its own being. However blood, or any body fluid for that matter, is a medical humour; and therefore susceptible to the laws of corruption, of loss and expenditure. Which is also to say that, in its corruptibility, there is a condition and pledge of resurrection. The ritual of blood-letting, for Girard, takes a community away from the profane to the resurrected realm of the pure (Girard, 1977, 104–6), and sacrifices the image of otherness for the image of a controlled autonomous order, preserving the 'objective' whole by discarding the objectionable other.

In the laws of criminal evidence, what is at stake in this resurrection? Technologies of abstraction, as Barbara Stafford has pointed out, take their place within a tradition of decontamination, 'seeking eternal, immutable principles' (Stafford, 1991, 132). Its practice is dealt with in terms of bringing about a rational knowledge about the body, in order to systematically order and control every aspect of life (Stafford, 1991, 133). In this respect it is not surprising to learn that, in law, the evidence gathered and condensed from the ablation of body fluids becomes public knowledge. In *R v Chancellor of Chichester Consistory Court, ex parte News Group Newspapers*, it was held that a court or tribunal had no power to exclude the public and the press from its proceedings because of the intimate or embarrassing nature of the evidence, for according to Mann LJ 'the English system of administering justice requires that it be done in public'.[41]

In terms of proving and reiterating the immutability of law's rational principles, the taking of fluids to prove *mens rea*, or whether a defendant's rational capacity to think has been effected by drink or drugs, might be considered to operate upon the principle of loss, or upon the notion of expenditure. But it is also the taking of an excess of detail, of the minutiae of symptoms which paint, in evidential and rational terms, the portrait of the mind of an accused. In setting the defendant up as the resurrected other, as one who is either innocent or who, through guilt 'takes away the sins of the world', the law aligns itself intimately along that invisible axis of all that is sovereignly rational and reasonable, the antithesis of a drunken, hallucinogenic order. Hallucinogenics and alcohol thus represent that other, denied order of seeing the world (the etymology of the word 'alcohol' stems from the Arabic *al-Kohl* meaning: to mark the eye). Doctrinally the point is made in the context of voluntary intoxication where a defendant who cannot contemplate a risk (*incapacitus rationales*) is at least as culpable as one who can but nevertheless runs that risk (*capacitus rationales*) (*DPP v Caldwell* [1982] AC 341). One of the basic principles of pharmacology, it should be remembered, is that the effects of non-medical drugs cannot be predicted. So the sanctions related to particular forms of *mens rea* become indicative of a community losing control over its minds, its rationality, its sovereign and intentional subject, its faith. On a general level the broadest evidential question to be asked of the defendant in all criminal trials — 'is s/he guilty?' — proves the rational sovereign order by denouncing both the act and the thought, *actus reus* and *mens rea*, and sacrificing the actor from the order of the universe.

Such proof, whether through confession or behaviour, places the body symbolically at the centre of attention. The body is accorded sacrificial status, it is taken away from a lost but visibly proven order of (ir)rationality and (un)reasonable behaviour, so that the court regains and secures an intimacy with that invisible realm of juridical categories of norms that *mens rea* measures: intention, motives, foresight of consequences. The performance of trial binds us to a fictional sovereign, the sovereign-self, one whose power it is to dwell within, occupy and possess the internal private domain of an individual.

Ek-stasis

The evidentiary practices of a criminal law, concerned with those values of proven truths and falsities, with good behaviour and bad symptoms, and, in the sacrificial scheme, with the mortality of the individual bound to the vitality of an institution, is ultimately involved in a metaphysics which constructs the legal subject. It is through the complexities of evidential procedure that the identity of an accused and the identification of the criminal mind is asserted. Through confessions and/or evidence of the body, through the interrogations of the bureaucracy, through the trial process of examinations and cross-examinations, proof becomes an affirmation of subjectivity. It is, as perhaps Heidegger might have put it, a degradation of the spirit to the rational, an incorporation and sublation of the spiritual to the temporal.[42] That is as much as to say that the sacrifice posits the subject within or without a sovereign order, a sovereign order made intimate through the rationalities of Law, for the subjective attachment to the institution always requires a sacrifice in order to consecrate that social body. As Derrida puts it: 'carnivorous sacrifice is essential to the structure of subjectivity, which is to say to the founding of the intentional subject and to the founding of ... law' (Derrida, 1990, 953). Law is thus written upon the destruction or repression of the profane other in the same way as it defines itself upon the denial of the mythic realm of its sacrificial origins of proof; a reading of which allows us to reconceptualise the repetitions of the violence and force of law.

To connect modern day trial procedures to the medieval trial is in itself not a new idea. Jerome Frank had recognised that the trial by battle, for example, still characterised the 'fight theory of justice' which in turn constitutes the adversarial trial, and himself sought to save modern court procedures from being too closely associated with these 'private out of court brawls' (Frank, 1949, 80–102).

What I have tried to argue is that what forms the connection between the pre-modern and the modern is the notion of the sacrifice which is both decisive and foundational to the juridical ways of fact-finding and to the sovereignty of Law. What this argument offers, however, is the thought that every trial enacts and therefore re-enacts a sacrifice through a supposed logic of mimesis. Such a logic of repetition is made possible only by the idea that a new sacrifice will reveal something that an old one has neglected. The new repeats only by default of the old. Hence, the old modes of sacrifice, the *judicium dei*, are merely the crude prototypes of a sacrifice that was to come: an apocalyptic and revelatory sacrifice. Whatever truth is to be revealed by these new procedural orders, instigated during the seventeenth-century intellectual crisis of epistemology, it must be maintained that this truth can only be revealed through such a logic of mimesis. What 'perishes', what is extinguished, in these sacrificial orders is thus not simply the profanity of otherness but the singularity of the other which defies imitation, repetition or mimesis. This singularity of the other is thus a painful 'being-thrown-out', a degraded existence expelled from a rational and sovereign jurisdiction. Such another existence of the subject is what we could call the painful *ek-stasis* of being's *hypostasis* or stable essence. But this other being, which is outside of its essence, must also be a *pre-sacrificial ek-stasis*. For the shamanic ecstasy of the singular is exactly what is being sacrificed. To think apart from the sacrifice, to think otherwise than the violence of law, or the virulence of decriminalisation, must be to think of this ecstatic ekstasis which lurks from within sacrifice itself. For this other stasis, or existence, which is thrown out does not exist in some obscure place outside of law's jurisdiction. Neither can it be calculated or rationally proven. Rather it remains to haunt from the within of what can no longer be called a rational order. The sacrificial gesture of criminal procedure must surely have to contemplate this ecstatic and unevinceable spirit of otherness which undermines any attempt to turn towards a rational order.

Notes

1. I should like to thank Sharon Halliwell for her computer skills, Peter Goodrich, Colin Hay and Michael Salter for comments and the provision of references, and Peter Rush who patiently read, and extensively commented upon, the numerous draft copies this paper has been through.
2. The preparations for a journey are, in some forms of shamanism, the most significant part of ritual ceremonies. The journey itself is regarded as something of a rupture, both in terms of space and in terms of introducing the unforeseen to a community of habits and rituals. It is of course not just the word 'journey' which names this process, but also the word 'travel' which in Old English was originally the same word as 'travail' meaning trouble, work, or torment, which in turn comes from the Latin *tripalum* — a three-staked instrument of torture.
3. This essay deals with the adversarial system. For an account of the inquisitorial trial, and its connection with the sacred, the spiritual, and the demonology treatise, defined in terms of torture, see Ginzburg, 1986.
4. See for example, Thayer, 1898; Holdsworth, 1956; Hale, 1820; and Bellamy, 1973.
5. For an account of modernity and modern law as a narrative form, see Fitzpatrick, 1992b.
6. For an analytical breakdown of the differences between primitive and modern conceptions of civilisation, violence, and order, see Girard, 1977. See also Girard, 1976.
7. I am grateful to Peter Rush for pointing out this argument.
8. The failure of the laws of evidence to adequately prove the truth is dealt with by many commentators, and is seen either as a failure in particular methods of proof or in the rules of court procedure. See Twining, 1985; Eggleston, 1977; J.D. Jackson, 1988.
9. Horkheimer and Adorno, 1973, offer, from the standpoint of Western culture, evidence of the mutual implication of Enlightenment and primitive myth. The attention paid to mythology is also important to the nineteenth-century jurisprudes such as Henry Maine. For a brief account of this, see Haldar, 1994.
10. See Girard, 1977, on the curative agenda of modern civilisations. Durkheim equates the profane and the sacred with illness and health respectively (Durkheim, 1965, 53–4).
11. For Bataille, the victim is an individual who stands out from the rest of the community, a consecrated surplus taken from a mass of wealth, taken from the material order of things and destined for violent consumption. This destruction of that which is consecrated, the accursed share, removes the victim from the material world of dumb things and mere objects, and restores the divine order of religious intimacy, of life in its fullest splendour. Hence, the 'sacrifice is made of objects that could have been spirits ...' (Bataille, 1988, 50).
12. For a discussion of the relation between 'proof' and 'symptom', see Eco, 1984. On the phylogeny and ontogeny of the medical symptom, see also Baer, 1986.
13. In a different context, see Goodrich, 1990, ch. 3.
14. On the question of the asserting, through the dynamics of belief, the identities of the subject and of the 'other' within institutions, see de Certeau, 1985, 194. See also de Certeau, 1986, 31–4. De Certeau argues that the institution is borne of, and created by, belief as that process which transforms the heterogeneity of texts into the dogma of institutions by articulating the real. For an early anthropological account of oaths and belief in legal systems, see Crawley, 1934. In effect, the oath is a vestige of the medieval 'wager of the law' or trial by compurgation, in which the accused was allowed to purge (*purgatio*) or clear herself by

swearing on oath with the assistance of oath-helpers or compurgators. That the principle of belief is far more important to the (trial by) oath, than the principle of proof, is pointed out by Thayer: for 'although called by the ambiguous name testis, [the compurgators] were not witnesses' (Thayer, 1898, 19). It was not requisite that these fellow-swearers should have knowledge of the facts. They swore merely to their belief in the oath of the accused. For Sir Robert Chambers, the 'original' oath seems to be tied to the notion of allegiance to the sovereign, it is through this allegiance that the citizen defines his relation as a subject (Chambers, 1986).

15. Thayer seems to believe that the word 'trial', if used to describe the older modes of judicial procedure, is anachronistic. The word or its Latin equivalent *triato* was seldom used or cited by Bracton et al. Rather, the words *probatio, purgatio*, and *defenso*, were used instead. It was not until the fourteenth century that the word grew common (Thayer, 1898, 16).

16. Here it is argued that the potency of the various forms of combat derived from the experiences of perjury and falseness, introduced by the ancient custom of compurgators oath which 'offered irresistable temptations to swearing'.

17. For a description and examples of these proceedings, see Selden Society, 1963.

18. 'Will you undertake the battle and the right of your Lord as the Sergeant Counter has offered?' It is interesting to note that the affirmative response of each of the champions is 'Sire, Oil' (Selden Society, 1963, B16a). The word 'yes' is almost half that of the French word for 'eye' or *oeil*. What is at stake here is of course the visualisation of divine proof (*evidere*).

19. The oath is taken in the form of the following words: 'Hear this, O Justice, that I will say truly who has the greater right in a messuage ... R. de S. to hold it as he holds or M to have it as she demands; and not for any reason will I fail to tell the truth' (Selden Society, 1963, B16a). It ought to be remembered at this point that all trials by battle were conducted with such spectacle and ritual. For those feuds that took place without such procedure, if anyone killed in revenge or self-defence, they were obliged to lay out the body of the slain upon his shield, with his head to the west and his feet to the east. This would suffice as proof of a justified killing to whoever had jurisdiction over the locality and to the relatives of the deceased. See Chambers, 1986.

20. Bataille deals with the 'notion of expenditure' (Bataille, 1991, 122). Bataille's language here vividly evokes the connection between sacrifice, the reassertion of hierarchy, and catharsis. The gift must be considered 'as a loss and thus a partial destruction, since the desire to destroy is in part transferred onto the recipient. In unconscious forms, such as those described by psychoanalysis, it symbolises excretion, which in itself is linked to **death'**.

21. There is some debate in much of the literature on these medieval forms of proof as to whether or not trials by ordeal is a generic term used to include the combat as a particular form of the ordeal. Certainly, the judicial duel must have constituted some ordeal for the parties involved, if not for their champions. However for the purposes of this argument it seems necessary to distinguish between the two. The 1215 Lateran Council, which forbad the ordeal as a form of truth-telling, did not expressly mention the trial by battle. Indeed in the history of Anglo-Saxon trials, at least, the battle was not prohibited until 1818 (*Ashford v Thornton* (1818) 1 B. & Ald. 405). The decision of Lateran IV to abolish the ordeal was incorporated into Anglo-Saxon medieval law in 1219.

22. Sometimes sanctified bread would be used instead of poison. If the accused was guilty, her/his throat would be narrowed and the food rejected (Thayer, 1898, ch. 1).

23. From a ritual solemnisation of the scales by the judge, quoted in Thayer, 1898, 35.

24. For examples and details of the various trials by ordeal, see Lea, 1973. The trials of witchcraft were usually determined by a well-known but peculiar logic. Examiners would 'swim' a suspected witch. If the suspect floated, she was guilty; if she sank, she was innocent. See the 1603 illustration 'witches apprehended and executed' reproduced in

D. Thomas, 1972, facing 102.

25. For an interesting account of the English sense of tradition as represented by the sanctity of the home, and of the iconoclastic nature of invading the house/home, see Goodrich, 1994.

26. The importance of the Romanisation of Canon Law as a political form of social control and dogma is central to the work of Pierre Legendre.

27. Cited in Tierney, 1988, 277.

28. Indeed Bartlett goes on to hypothesise that if the ordeal had been made a sacrament, with proper ritual formalities, the ordeal might have 'survived the critical scrutiny it received in the twelfth century' (Bartlett, 1986, 88).

29. 'And among the priests, some are divine priests, such as presbyters; others are human priests because they dispense with things holy, that is laws' (Kantorowicz, 1957, 121).

30. Peter Goodrich makes a similar argument that where the constitution is described as the unwritten and therefore invisible law of laws which founds the English state (Goodrich, 1990, 59).

31. According to Spelman, drinking ale was the commonest offence. Jurors, in exceptional circumstances, may have been given food or drink for medicinal purposes. Punishment of jurors is reported to have either been imprisonment or fines. In a case of 1523, jurors were fined 6s. 8d. and the bailiff 20s. for eating bread and fish, and for drinking ale after their retirement. For further examples, see Selden Society, 1978, vol. 55, 110–15.

32. In theory, during the mid-thirteenth century, trial by jury or by the testimony of fallible men, had to be chosen by the accused. There are thus reports of various pressures applied to compel the accused to choose the jury trial. Other reasons for the decline in the number of trials by battle during this period suggest that it may have been due to the fact that the duel was limited to the feudal classes.

33. The 'jury of the neighbourhood' were initially composed of individual jurors who ascertained facts and determined controversies through their local knowledge of the region. They were deemed likely to know who was in possession of neighbouring land, and the feudal status of the parties involved in a dispute.

34. Known simply as the 'Alton Robbery', originally to be found in *Matthei Parisienis 'Chronica Majora'* (Luard, 1872–83).

35. The argument that the sacrifice is a way of appeasing a community's desire to seek vengeance is also made by Rene Girard (Girard, 1977, 10). See also Nietzsche, 1909.

36. 'If a man's sword has been used to kill, the owner is liable' (Holdsworth, 1956, vol. 2, 482).

37. On recklessness, see particularly *Elliott v C (a minor)* [1983] 1 WLR 939.

38. Thomas Sebeok claims, perhaps incorrectly, that symptomatology is the oldest branch of semiotics (Sebeok, 1986).

39. 'Symptom-formation' and 'substitute-formation' are considered by Freud to be coincident processes. As Freud states, 'repression leaves *symptoms* in its train' (Freud, 1950, 93).

40. In law, an illegitimate child is treated by the Inland Revenue authorities, for the purposes of death duties, as a 'stranger in blood'. See *The Stamp Act* 1815 (55 Geo. III c. 184).

41. Ironically, the exception to this rule occurs only if it is reasonably necessary to order exclusion of the public (*The Independent*, 10 September 1991). See also *Scott v Scott* [1913] AC 417.

42. On the affirmation of the subject within interrogative procedures, and the relationship between spirit and rationality in Heideggerian philosophy, see Derrida, 1989.

6 Femininity as Marginalia: Conjugal Homicide and the Conjugation of Sexual Difference

ALISON YOUNG

Operator:	Ambulance Emergency.
Sara:	Hello, good afternoon, I've just killed my husband. I have stuck a six-inch carving knife in his belly on the left-hand side.
Operator:	Where are you, love?
Sara:	Bring an ambulance and the police around straight away.
Operator:	Where are you?
Sara:	I'm at 73 Church Walk, Atherstone, Warwickshire. My name is Mrs Sara Thornton, my husband is called Mr Malcolm Thornton and I think he's dead.
Operator:	73 Church Walk, Atherstone.
Sara:	Warwickshire.
Operator:	Yes, darling, your name is, again, Mrs Thornton?
Sara:	Thornton, shall I pull the knife out or leave it in?
Operator:	Leave it where it is, darling.
Sara:	Leave it in.
Operator:	That's right.
Sara:	Thank you, goodnight. (Nadel, 1993, 113)

Despite all this, the appellant wished to hold the marriage together, partly because of her sense of duty as a wife and partly for the sake of the children.

(*R v Ahluwalia* [1992] 4 All ER 889 at 892)

Introduction[1]

This essay is concerned with the processes of judgment faced by a battered woman who kills her abusive partner. My objective is to provide a reading of two cases in which a battered woman killed her spouse after undergoing

127

repeated violence at his hands. Such a reading will suggest how law operates to judge the abused woman who kills, not merely in terms of the formal doctrines of criminal law, but also through recourse to the laws of gender difference. The abused woman's judgment, then, occurs not only in the court's application of legal rules, but also through its representation of propriety in identity and in femininity.

The essay is concerned with two contrasting cases: *R v Thornton* ([1992] 1 All ER 306) and *R v Ahluwalia* ([1992] 4 All ER 889).[2] My account will clearly be partial, in the two exact senses of the word. First, my reading is partial in that I am concerned to look no further than the two case(report)s I will examine. Each and every conjugal homicide case deals with love, death, violence, betrayal and terror: emotions and experiences which should require no quantitative validation for an investigation of their creation and elaboration. To that extent, this text affirms the limited and local narratives of each event. Secondly, my account is partial in that I write as a feminist, with feminist concerns: here, this requires the interrogation of the extent to which conjugal violence and its judgment in law operate as a question of sexual difference. In short, while it may be thought that there is a good deal of morality in this partiality, it is more a questioning of the ethics of judgment by fleshing out the difference that inhabits judgment as law.[3]

In reading these cases, my aim is to retrace the judicial drawing of a body in law — a body that is gendered, sexed and stretched across the conjunction of assailant and victim. The cases to be considered are no doubt well known. For a time, the media took considerable interest in Sara Thornton — through her failed appeals against conviction, her hunger strike, and the persistence of a campaign demanding her release (the Free Sara Thornton campaign organised by Justice For Women), and finally her release. Kiranjit Ahulwalia's conviction for murder was quashed in July 1992 and she pleaded guilty to manslaughter by reason of diminished responsibility in September 1992. Her case is regarded as a feminist victory, both in respect of its judicial outcome and in terms of the success achieved by campaigning groups such as Justice for Women and Southall Black Sisters who supported the case and organised the appeal.[4] While similar in their narratives which bespeak violence by a man against *his* wife who eventually kills him, the cases differ enormously in result and the case reports differ greatly in their construction of the facts of the two women's situations. Sara Thornton had married a man who turned out to be a violent alcoholic. He beat her regularly; he threatened her life and that of her daughter. She had, on several occasions, called the police for emergency assistance, asked neighbours for help and contacted Alcoholics

Anonymous. To one neighbour, one day, she said: 'I don't know what to do, I could kill him'. One night, her husband Malcolm returned home very drunk. They had argued earlier in the day. Thornton went to speak with him where he lay on the sofa. He swore at her, accused her of selling her body to other men, and threatened to kill her later. She went into the kitchen, found a knife and returned with it to the sofa. She said later that she had been advised to do something like this by Alcoholics Anonymous, in order to protect herself and to make him see that she was serious. They spoke again; she asked him to come to bed; again he swore at her. To frighten him, she would later say, she raised the knife and slowly brought it down, stabbing him in the stomach. She said later that she expected him to stop her; also that she believed he would have killed her later. She told her son to call the police; when the police and an ambulance arrived and were attempting to help her husband, Thornton said: 'I don't know why you're bothering, he deserves to die'. He died four hours later, from loss of blood. Sara Thornton was charged, prosecuted and put on trial for the murder of her husband.

Kiranjit Ahluwalia had entered into an arranged marriage with Deepak Ahluwalia. She had suffered violence at his hands since the very beginning of their relationship. After ten years of abuse, one evening Deepak Ahluwalia told her that he was having an affair and would leave her. He also threatened to kill her the next morning. While he slept, Ahluwalia took petrol and caustic soda, lit a candle and threw them on top of him. He ran outside the house, on fire. Neighbours saw Ahluwalia standing at a window, with her child in her arms. She opened the window to tell neighbours that she was 'waiting to join [her] husband' and closed it again. The house was now ablaze. She was persuaded to hand the child out through the window and eventually emerged herself. Her husband died six days later and Ahluwalia was charged, prosecuted and put on trial for the murder of her husband.

These would be a rough summary of 'the facts' of each event, a wide-eyed presentation of its details. Versions corresponding to something like these narratives appeared in newspaper and television reports; magazine features on women who kill; television programmes about battered women. However, when the narrative appears in its legal form — the report of a judgment — subtle mutations, manipulations and metamorphoses occur. This is not to suggest that the above media accounts of the event, or indeed my version of it, have any purchase on 'the truth' and from which the legal account could be claimed to deviate. Rather it is to emphasise that the event, if it is to exist for us, must be articulated — and here and there, it will have been articulated in numerous contexts and in a variety of ways. How the various participants in the event articulate their experience of the event will, I would argue, be dramatically different. (We can see this clearly in the Canadian case of Erica Eboli, charged with attempted murder: she pleaded 'battered women's syndrome' and was acquitted. Her husband claimed he was the battered one, and offered an account of their relationship and the event which differed in almost every detail from Erica's, coinciding only with the fact of his having been stabbed on that night.[5] Similar variations are found in the American case of Lorena and John Wayne Bobbitt.[6]) In the context with which I am concerned, the law report should be regarded as embodying a particular version of the event; and importantly, one that has been filtered through the representational and doctrinal structures of criminal law. Whereas most of the critique of legal interpretation has focused on the teaching of propositional rules of law, my intention is to trace how the interpretation of *facts* is constructed to have an effect upon the interpretation of legal rules.[7] Thus, although both cases contain similar narratives of the facts and deal with similar questions of legal doctrine, I will show how it is the interpretation and reconstruction of the events as facts that ultimately determines the outcome of the case, delivers the judgment.

Biograph/Thanatograph

In their representations of the details of the narratives, both case reports offer a highly abridged version of each appellant's life-story. *Thornton* begins:

> The appellant, who began to suffer from a personality disorder while at school, met her husband in May 1987 and realised from the start of their relationship that he was a heavy drinker and was jealous and possessive. In August 1988 they were married. There was a history of domestic violence and assaults by the husband on the appellant and in May 1989 he committed a serious assault which led to charges being laid. (*Thornton* at 306)

Sara Thornton is referred to in this passage and throughout the case report as 'the appellant'; Malcolm Thornton is here referred to as 'the husband' or 'her husband'. The woman is assigned to the impersonal, isolated place of the legal subject, the appellant, the one appealing against conviction. Her position as 'wife', 'woman' or 'battered wife/woman' is forgotten, left behind. She has been re-categorised. Malcolm Thornton remains defined in a relationship of matrimony. Instead of being called 'victim' or 'deceased', he is 'the husband', emphasising therefore the location of the event within their relationship, while Sara Thornton's relationship is now with the law, to which she appeals. The same device figures in the report of Ahluwalia's act of killing. The report begins its headnote: 'The appellant was an Asian woman who had entered into an arranged marriage with the husband and had suffered many years of violence and abuse from him from the outset of the marriage' (*Ahluwahlia* at 889), and in his judgment, Lord Taylor CJ opens with the statement that '[t]his is a tragic case which has aroused much public attention. On 9 May 1989 the appellant, after enduring many years of violence and humiliation from her husband, threw petrol in his bedroom and set it alight' (*Ahluwahlia* at 891).

Within the first sentences, we are told things about the women which are crucial to the subsequent structure of the legal narrative. With Sara Thornton, we are first told that she 'began to suffer from a personality disorder while at school'. At trial, Sara Thornton pleaded that she was suffering diminished responsibility at the time of the homicide. This was not accepted, due to differing psychiatric reports (the defence reports supported the claim that her responsibility was impaired at the time of the homicide; the prosecution psychiatrist disagreed). Despite this, the introduction to the case report deems Sara Thornton's personal mental abnormality sufficiently important to include it as a fact in the first sentence of the report. Locating the inception of her personality disorder in her schooldays also serves to emphasise that she was 'not normal' before she became involved with Malcolm Thornton. (Later the reader is told that she was asked to leave her school: she is unstable and subject to problematic behaviour even then.) Implicitly, such a move makes it impossible to claim, as proponents of 'battered women's syndrome'[8] might, that her violent reaction was inspired by the violence she herself had experienced at her hands of her husband. Sara Thornton was unable to plead diminished responsibility and thus avoid a conviction for murder; however, the legal institution introduces her as an actor in its narrative who has a disordered personality. Her story thus becomes one of illogic, yet it is an illogic that cannot justify, exculpate or mitigate. In doctrinal terms, the abnormality of mind that is the concern of the defence of diminished responsibility must *cause* the loss of self-control that leads to the homicide. Sara Thornton is represented as having a personality disorder long before she met Malcolm Thornton; therefore, she cannot claim — or at least, it is made difficult to claim — that the homicide was perpetrated in a state of diminished responsibility owing to a mental disorder which arose through his violence towards her. In short, and from the very start, the representation of illogic is placed outside the legal chronology of diminished responsibility.

The second part of the opening sentence is equally important. We are told that she 'met her husband in May 1987 and realised from the start of their relationship that he was a heavy drinker and was jealous and possessive'. Immediately, Sara Thornton is blamed for her own miserable situation: she knew what Malcolm Thornton was like; he did not attempt to pretend he was a different type of person; there was no misrepresentation on his part. She is held to have given a valid and informed consent to this violent liaison. Despite any mental disorder she was suffering, the judgment represents her as voluntarily and knowingly entering into a relationship with a violent alcoholic. She is portrayed as the agent of her own suffering. Thornton herself states that she believed she could help Malcolm Thornton to change (*Thornton*; L. Walker, 1979; 1987; Browne, 1987).[9] The legal narrative shows no interest in such a motivation: knowledge (of alcoholism, jealousy and possessiveness) leads inexorably to its consequences ('a history of domestic violence and assaults' which followed upon the marriage). The report also tells the reader about Sara Thornton's previous relationships:

> After several relationships with young men which did not work out she met her first husband. She was then 23. She gave birth to a daughter the following year and initially the marriage was happy. However ... she found [her husband] had begun to drink heavily. He was violent towards her, so she left him.... On several occasions she attempted suicide, but it is questionable whether she actually intended to take her own life. (Thornton at 308)

According to those who argue for the specificity of the position of the battered woman, Sara Thornton was existing within a matrix of experiences which could only spiral downwards: problems at school, at least two relationships with men who were alcoholic batterers. However, the court presents this in terms rather of her failure to create a successful family unit and even goes so far as to dismiss her suicide attempts as not meaning to take her own life.[10] So far, the narrative has created a central character who is deliberately fickle, falls in love with men who will beat her, and cannot sustain family relationships. In this, she is both passive (she 'began to suffer from a personality disorder') and active ('she realised from the start of their relationship').

The introduction to Ahluwalia's case presents a marked contrast to the inauspicious beginnings of Thornton's legal narrative. The judgment emphatically marks Ahluwalia as ethnic: she is 'Asian' and has 'entered an arranged marriage with the husband'. Whereas Thornton was the autonomous and consenting party to the marriage, Ahluwalia is represented as marrying only through coercion (or, if any voluntariness existed in her getting married, it is her wish to satisfy the desires of her family). The report goes on: 'They had not previously met' (*Ahluwalia* at 892). Ahluwalia therefore cannot have known of her husband's violence; they have no biography together and are brought to marry by cultural circumstance and familial obligation rather than the voluntary romantic choice that is used to characterise Thornton's act. The implied voluntariness of her act is used to condemn her, while the implied coercion behind Ahluwalia's describes her innocence. Further, Ahluwalia, we are told, 'suffered many years of violence and abuse from him from the outset of the marriage' (*Ahluwalia* at 889). She is personified as a victim from the outset: her precise relationship to her husband (his victim) is made clear. In Thornton's case, 'there was a history of domestic violence and assaults'. Her suffering is not represented, his agency as abuser is not attributed; it is the impersonality of the past. We are also given some biographical information about Kiranjit Ahluwalia: 'The appellant is now 36. She was born in India into a middle class family. She completed an arts degree and then began a law course, but came under pressure from her family to marry' (*Ahluwalia* at 891). Ahluwalia is thus an educational success, unlike Thornton (where all we are told relates to her failures: with no information given as to her success in business).[11] The report also confirms its hint as to coercion: Ahluwalia married under family pressure (and thus had to abandon her relationship with the law as its student). Lord Chief Justice Taylor continues: 'A marriage was arranged between her and the deceased. They had not previously met. The marriage took place in Canada. They then came to England and settled in Crawley. Both had jobs. Two boys were born to them' (*Ahluwalia* at 892). Ahluwalia married a man she did not know in a foreign country, then came to live and work in a country equally foreign to her. She is immediately constructed as 'out of place'. As I will show later, her out-of-placeness does not mean that she lacks a community; rather, it is Sara Thornton who will be constructed as outside the community.

Lord Taylor goes on to elaborate her experience of violence at the hands of her husband. This occurred 'from the outset.... He is a big man; she is slight' (*Ahluwalia* at 892). The asymmetries of size which are general in comparisons between women and men are given specific and additional detail: for a man, he is big and for a woman, she is small. Sexual difference is thus magnified. Detailed description then follows as to the type and severity of abuse she suffered: 'hit three or four times on the head by a telephone'; 'thrown to the ground'; 'pushed' while pregnant; a hand bruised, a finger broken, attempts at suicide (with no doubts as to her intentions, unlike Thornton's); her husband 'tried to run her down at a family wedding'; he 'held her throat and threatened her with a knife'; 'he threatened to kill her and threw a mug of hot tea over her'. She sought and was granted injunctions against him twice. Despite these court orders, we are told 'the deceased continued his violence, which intensified after January 1989' (*Ahluwalia* at 892). A further paragraph describes the evidence given by her doctor and her work supervisor as to her injuries over the next few months. Her emotional condition is also mentioned:

> The state of humiliation and loss of self-esteem to which the deceased's behaviour over the ten years of the marriage had reduced her is evidenced by a letter she wrote him after he left her for three days about April 1989.... In the course of begging him to come back to her and to grant her ten minutes to talk it over, she made a number of self-denying promises of the most abject kind.

The letter is then quoted:

> Deepak, if you come back I promise you — I won't touch black coffee again, I won't go town every week, I won't eat green chilli, I ready to leave Chandikah and all my friends, I won't go near Der Goodie Mohan's house again, Even I am not going to attend Bully's wedding, I eat too much or all the time so I can get fat, I won't laugh if you don't like, I won't dye my hair even, I don't go to my neighbour's house, I won't ask you for any help. (*Ahluwalia* at 892)

In addition to supplying additional signifiers of 'foreignness', the letter follows on from the catalogue of brutal behaviour to complete a picture of victimisation. Kiranjit Ahluwalia is represented as a woman who at all times in the relationship was a victim of her husband. In her abjection, her utter passivity, the law cannot find any autonomy of self. She reacts; she does not act. Thornton's situation — and the legal assessment of her place in the register of victim/criminal — is expressed rather differently, in substance and in tone.

The report states: 'there was a history of domestic violence and assaults by the husband on the appellant and in May 1989 he committed a serious assault which led to charges being laid' (*Thornton* at 306). No details are afforded at any point in the narrative for the reader to understand what kinds of violent acts fall into one category rather than the other. Many commentators have criticised the legal fondness of the term 'domestic' in relation to violence between intimates.[12] As a descriptive term, it is unnecessary and functions only to diminish the seriousness of the term 'violence'. This is exemplified in the statement that '*domestic violence and assaults*' occurred: this implies that 'domestic violence' might be less than an 'assault'. Note also that in *Ahluwalia*, the report writes of 'violence and abuse' (*Ahluwalia* at 892) rather than 'domestic violence'. In *Thornton*, no information is provided about the violence Sara Thornton suffered, only the bland blank terms of 'domestic violence', 'assaults' and 'a serious assault'. The precise nature of the injuries, the horror, pain and betrayal are excised. The corporeal reality of such violence cannot — or at least must not — be signified in the legal text. On the other hand, as I will discuss, the details of her acts are examined closely under the legal microscope. Not so much the wide-eyed presentation of the details of a 'tragedy', but the narrow focus of legal guilt.

I shall now consider the representation of the homicide committed by each defendant, in order to show how criminal legal discourse follows on from its earlier construction of each woman's background, biography and personality. In *Thornton*, the next piece of information included in the legal narrative relates to Sara Thornton's so-called 'revelation' to a colleague, Mrs Thomas, that she was going to kill Malcolm Thornton. Walker's study of battered women who killed their abusers showed that many battered women engage in homicidal fantasies which are simple wishes for the abuse to end (L. Walker, 1987, 1–6). A statement such as 'I am going to kill him' (*Thornton* at 308) should not be taken as a straightforward confession of an intention to commit murder (as it appears to be in the case report). Even without the specificity lent to such a statement by Sara Thornton's position as a battered woman, it could express exasperation, frustration, anger or despair, without necessarily meaning that she was planning the homicide. If it was simply a wish, then its expression would fulfil its function, without implying malice, intentionality or the formation of a plan. The narrative accepts the possibility: 'but for subsequent events Mrs Thomas might well have dismissed this as no more than an expression of exasperation' (*Thornton* at 309).

Are we to conclude from this that any such statement followed by a killing will automatically be understood to evidence murderous intent?[13] In a retrospective interpretation, which sees the homicide and the statement as part of a *sine qua non*, the present is judged by the past. The legal institution appears to have closed off the possibility that a battered woman could say such a thing, and later kill her husband through provocation, through diminished responsibility, through self-defence, as manslaughter: in short, as anything rather than murder. The subsequent events which appear so compelling are described as follows:

> On the following day [Malcolm Thornton had been drinking and had threatened
> Sara Thornton, had broken a window by hurling a chair through it; Sara Thornton
> had attempted to drug him with Mogadon in order, she stated, to get him into
> hospital where he might get treatment for his alcoholism] Monday, the appellant
> telephoned Mrs Thomas telling her she had found drink concealed in the house.
> She talked about the difficulties of divorce as they had only been married a short
> time [two months short of the one year bar to a petition for divorce] and she spoke
> of the difficulty of financial settlements ... [Malcolm Thornton was drunk that
> night, and drunk and violent the next day. He ordered Sara Thornton out of the
> house.] Shortly afterwards she spoke on the telephone to Mrs Thomas saying: 'I
> am going to have to do what I said I would do', which Mrs Thomas understood to
> be a reference to the threat to kill the deceased made the previous weekend.
>
> (*Thornton* at 309–11)

What was formerly considered to be an understandable expression of
exasperation has become a threat to kill. The Court accepts as correct Mrs
Thomas' interpretation of the latter statement as referring to a threat to kill
(the court does not question Mrs Thomas' automatic association of the second
statement with the first); although it seems equally possible that Sara Thornton
was saying that, despite all its difficulties, she would have to apply for a
divorce.[14] This is not even mentioned in the judgment. And this is an effect
of the narrative function of Mrs Thomas, as an actor in the drama: she recounts
opinions and relays views. She is acquaintance and *confidante*: in the
courtroom she is represented as a gossip. Rather than a malevolent gossip
who will speak ill of another, the judgment accepts her views as correct.
Gossip convicts.[15]

On the evening of the homicide, Sara Thornton's behaviour leading up
to the homicide is described in a form that complies with the report's
construction of her as wilfully unstable, threatening and potentially violent.
Note that the narrative has already dwelt in considerable detail upon an incident
two days before: Malcolm Thornton had threatened Sara and, apparently,
her daughter. Sara Thornton had responded to this by holding a knife towards
Malcolm and stating 'you touch my daughter, you bastard, and I'll kill you'
(*Thornton* at 309). This was witnessed by Malcolm Thornton's son, Martin,
who is said to have intervened, making Sara put down the knife. Later, Sara
Thornton had attempted to get her husband committed to hospital by giving
him Mogadon tablets (*Thornton* at 309).

That evening, Sara went out for a drink with Martin, Malcolm's son.

The report states that, before leaving the house, she wrote in lipstick upon her bedroom mirror: 'Bastard Thornton. I hate you' (*Thornton* at 310). At this point, Malcolm is said to be asleep on the couch (he had been drinking). The comments written on the mirror function as an index of Sara Thornton's increasing inversion of the norms of femininity: she uses her lipstick, not to rouge her mouth (in the gestures of conventional femininity), but to inscribe a message of violence to her husband. Instead of seduction, her mouth speaks violence. She writes the message upon a mirror, converting its function as reflector of an image of femininity into the medium through which she can actively communicate her hatred. When Malcolm Thornton looked into the mirror, he would see not himself (as he would if the mirror were to function as a reflective device), but rather his wife, mouthing obscenities.

I regard the recounting of this moment within the text as paradigmatic of the law's imagining of Sara Thornton's situation. In the anecdote, Sara Thornton is the embodiment of interruption — and it is to this interruption that the judgment anxiously responds. The attribution of bastardy inscribed on the mirror adverts to her defection from a paternal order of culture. In the same way, her effacement of the mirror-function is put on display — it no longer gives Sara her identity. Just as Sara Thornton's mirror does not reflect her as a feminine image to herself, so Sara Thornton herself is viewed in law as a woman who does not reflect man's image of her. Her mirror lacks the tain that would grant her the femininity given her by the masculine, by the law, by marriage. In its place is a depth of aggression. In marriage, we find a violently mimetic relation in which two rivals struggle for dominance. I have argued elsewhere that law regards marriage as inevitably but unproblematically violent by virtue of its mimetic structure (Young, 1994). Yet, here we see, the interruption of marital mimesis being legally prohibited in the name of the feminine. Within the legal text is a condemnation of Sara Thornton *as woman*: her tools of femininity (mirror, lipstick) are but devices in a masquerade of all that is feminine for law. The legal response to the interruption that this anecdote puts on display is thus to efface it by representing it as the latent violence of the feminine. Beneath her superficial conformity to the norms of femininity lies violence and aggression.

The writing of the lipsticked message also operates within the legal narrative as evidence of a developing aggressiveness in Sara's behaviour: this is compounded by the next set of details which describe her as staying later in the pub than her stepson (no doubt inappropriate behaviour for a married woman) and being described by the taxi driver who brought her home as 'quarrelsome and arrogant' (*Thornton* at 310). Sara Thornton is being constructed as a potentially violent actor, in this lead-up to the homicide, which occurred a short time after her return home. Malcolm Thornton, in contrast, is described as 'still sound asleep on the couch' (at 310); that is, harmless — which is to say, it is a sleep which prefigures the sleep of the dead. The details of the homicide are recounted as follows. Sara Thornton had changed into her nightclothes. Malcolm was lying on the sofa. The report states: 'the appellant went up to her bedroom and changed into her nightclothes. She then went down, according to her, to try to persuade the deceased to come to bed' (*Thornton* at 310).

The insertion of the phrase 'according to her', for the first time in the narrative, acknowledges Sara Thornton's subjectivity in the event; yet at the very moment of doing so, it insinuates doubt as to the purpose of Sara Thornton's behaviour at a crucial indexical point for the formal doctrines of law. A charge of murder requires the prosecution to prove that the defendant had intention to kill or cause really serious injury.[16] The moment of doubt allowed by the narrative as to her intention in going downstairs acts as the culmination of the construction of her behaviour as potentially violent. It permits, indeed requires, the consideration of her intention as violent. Such a requirement builds upon the impression created by the judgment's interpretation of Sara Thornton's remark to Mrs Thomas and inflects the rest of the scene, which relates the exchange between Malcolm and Sara Thornton: 'he refused [to come to bed], called her 'a whore' and said that she had been selling her body: she was not going to get any money from him and he would kill her if she had been with other men. She said that she had only been trying to raise money for their business. She was hurt and wounded by his remarks ...' (*Thornton* at 310). Note that the report leaves an ambiguity as to whether Sara Thornton meant that she had *not* been 'selling her body' or that she was selling her body to raise money for their business.[17]

At this point, having been abused verbally, having recently been threatened by him, having been assaulted by him in the past, she goes to the kitchen and finds a knife. This is for protection if he attacks her. Returning to the sitting room, a further exchange takes place: 'she again asked him to come up to bed but he refused and again made wounding remarks to her saying that he would kill her when she was asleep. She then sat on the edge of the couch by his chest and said: 'Come to bed', all the while holding the knife in her 'clenched hand' (*Thornton* at 310). We have been told that Sara Thornton was 'hurt and wounded by his remarks' which he then repeats. The judgment, however, is not preparing to establish provocation in the form of Malcolm Thornton's 'wounding remarks'. On the contrary, through emphasising that

Sara Thornton was 'wounded', the report compounds its construction of her coming response to his remarks as disproportionate. He wounds; she kills.[18] Later in the narrative, a further exchange is mentioned: 'She had said words to the effect: "If you don't come to bed, I'll kill you. Come on, this is enough. I'll kill you before you get a chance to kill me." He said: "Oh yeah, go on then. Oh yeah, go on," saying it very sarcastically' (*Thornton* at 311). The narrative here builds throughout this scene on its earlier establishment of Sara Thornton as masquerading a surface of femininity over her violent potential: she invites him to bed *while* holding a knife. Dressed in a nightgown *yet* wielding a knife, she is an icon of femininity as death; a man who accedes to her invitation to the marriage bed might find himself castrated or killed.[19] The judgment sees the knife as puncturing her charade of femininity. Compare the case of Georgina Gee,[20] who stabbed to death her abusive husband. The 68-year-old woman had married a man described as 'a heavy drinker, prone to bullying, argumentative, abusive and sometimes violent behaviour'. He had made insulting remarks about Mrs Gee's disabled son from her first marriage; Mrs Gee responded by picking up a knife. Her husband is reported to have said: 'Go on, stick it in me', adding, 'You haven't got the bottle'. Mrs Gee stabbed him twice. Her plea of guilty to manslaughter by reason of diminished responsibility was accepted by Mr Justice Sedley, who said, while sentencing her to three months' probation: 'You were in a state of such anxiety and confusion that you could not have formed any intention to kill your husband. I think you should be allowed to live your days in peace, as much peace as you can find'. Sara Thornton is represented in a very different way. The judicial narrative builds her violence into its account of the *mise-en-scène*: she sits down by his chest (and thus is at a position of advantage to stab him, since he lies below her on the sofa); she speaks violence (in her directly reported threats which elicit Malcolm's response of 'go on'; Malcolm's original threats to kill Sara in her sleep are not reported directly: direct speech attributes facticity; by omitting to quote his threats directly, the imputation of implausibility is effected); in her seeking out the knife (she arms herself, she anticipates a violent act, she seeks to ensure the outcome of his death). After the third exchange, she 'stood up in front of him holding the knife in her clenched hand. She then brought [the knife] down towards him thinking he would ward it off. He did not and the knife entered his stomach' (*Thornton* at 311). The first statement, which underlines her dominant and aggressive position (now standing *over* him and *clenching* the knife) sits oddly with the second sentence which includes her supposition that he would defend himself and describes the 'stabbing' with a notable lack of agency (*the knife entered his stomach*, as if of its own accord). The overwhelming impression is of a woman looming horrifically over a prostrate masculinity: the trial judge told the jury to consider the reasonableness of her '[stabbing] her husband as he lay defenceless on that settee deep into his stomach' (*Thornton* at 312).

The history that is Sara Thornton's personal past (her previous relationships, her school days, her behaviour, her lovers, her emotions) is inscribed in the legal narrative as a violent history. The narrative carefully represents the event and its history as incidental to the collision between victim (Malcolm Thornton) and violent actor (Sara Thornton). The violence exists in Sara Thornton's state of mind, her erratic behaviour, her developing intention to kill, her supposed reluctance to take the legal way out (divorce, separation), her wayward actions (alone in a pub, quarrelsome in a taxi), her failure as a wife (a previous failed marriage, her separate bedroom). Her artifice of femininity, the lipstick, allows her to inscribe her violence upon a mirror in the matrimonial home. Her femininity, however, is perceived as a device, since her violence bursts through in its writing ('Bastard Thornton. I hate you'). Her pretence at maternal concern (seeking to protect her daughter from her husband's violence) is revealed as masquerade by the improper force of its expression ('you touch my daughter, you bastard, and I'll kill you'). Her charade of wifely invitation (asking Malcolm Thornton to come to bed with her) is unmasked by the irresistible violence of her desires which lead her to get a knife, to position herself, to state her lethal intent and slowly sink the knife into Malcolm Thornton's stomach.

In *Ahluwalia*, however, the defendant and her act of homicide are constructed in an entirely different manner: Thornton's narrative is one which emphasises the extraordinariness of her action (to stab, instead of to walk out of the room), while Ahluwalia's describes the mundane and everyday nature of the situation. Kiranjit Ahluwalia, we are told, 'visited her mother-in-law on the afternoon of 8 May' (the homicide took place during the night between 8 and 9 May 1989). She was also looking after her younger son 'who was unwell'. Ahluwalia is immediately represented as caring towards her children and dutiful in her attention to familial relationships. Deepak Ahluwalia had been having an affair (known to his wife: 'he had taunted her with this relationship') and had told his girlfriend that his wife 'was going to pack and leave that evening' (*Ahluwalia* at 892). The subsequent events were gleaned from police interviews with Kiranjit Ahluwalia which were not 'wholly consistent': no adverse inference is drawn from this, whereas Thornton's conflicting statements to the police ('I loved him' and 'he deserved to die') are construed as evidence of her mendacity. The court summarised the facts as follows:

It seems she put her son to bed and gave the deceased his dinner. He then tried to mend a television set. The appellant tried to talk to him about their relationship, but he refused, indicating that it was over. He demanded money from her to pay a telephone bill and, according to her, threatened to beat her if she did not give him £200 the next morning. He then began to iron some clothes and threatened to burn the appellant's face with a hot iron if she did not leave him alone.

(Ahluwalia at 892–3)

As in *Thornton*, the Court repeats an insertion of subjectivity with the phrase 'according to her'. Here, however, it does not introduce doubt; on the contrary, it serves to underline Ahluwalia's version of what happened later as true, dispelling any possible doubt with the next sentence ('he then ...'). With Thornton, the phrase provides for a sceptical response to her story: the next sentence directly quotes Malcolm Thornton ('he ... called her "a whore"'), attributing facticity to his perspective and partiality to hers. The husband and wife are also positioned as actors in a typical domestic scene, involving food, minor repairs, bills. Sara Thornton had been drinking alone in a pub, a less obviously matrimonial event. The judgment goes on to elaborate the details of Deepak Ahluwalia's death:

The appellant went to bed about midnight. She was unable to sleep and brooded upon the deceased's refusal to speak to her and his threat to beat her the next morning. She had bought some caustic soda a few days earlier with a view to using it upon the deceased. She had also bought a can of petrol and put it in the lean-to outside the house. Her mind turned to these substances and some time after 2.30 am she got up, went downstairs, poured about two pints of the petrol into a bucket (to make it easier to throw), lit a candle on the gas cooker and carried these things upstairs. She also took an oven glove for self-protection and a stick. She went to the deceased's bedroom and threw in some petrol, lit the stick from the candle and threw it in the room. She then went to dress her son.

(Ahluwalia at 893)

Domesticity and familial responsibility figure in the description of the homicide. The means of killing are elaborated within the familiar and familial kitchen equipment (oven glove, gas cooker, bucket, candle). Ahluwalia's first thought after setting fire to her husband is to dress her son. Despite the violence of her action, the narrative still elects to represent her as a product of familial relationships and as a creature of the home. The passage is also astonishing for its glossing over several important aspects of the legal basis of moral responsibility for murder. Kiranjit Ahluwalia, we are told, had bought petrol and caustic soda *with the purpose of or 'view to using' them on her husband*.[21] The judgment employs a neutral phrase, 'using it on', instead of the more aggressive possibilities such as 'burning to death'. Compare *Thornton*, where the trial judge is approvingly quoted as asking the jury to consider whether it was reasonable for a wife 'to fatally stab' her husband instead of walking out of the room (*Thornton* at 312). Ahluwalia also had to walk downstairs and outside of the house to get the caustic soda and petrol, during which time the court might have felt that she should have reflected on the nature of that which she was about to do (even without the formal requirements for provocation, which incorporate specifications about 'cooling-off' and reflection on the nature of the act). In contrast to the displacement of Thornton's emotional disorder by the legal chronology and its return as an excessive violence, in this judgment Ahluwahlia's mental disorder is incorporated into law from the outset. The judgment passes over her actions without adverse comment, allowing instead that her actions appear *as if* in a dream or fiction, as if by a sleepwalker. This is not to say that Thornton's actions do not appear as if in a dream, on a stage. In fact, one of the crucial ingredients of the legal scene of conjugal homicide is the dissociated actions of the woman, the irreality in which the woman is imagined as moving. In *Thornton*, the knife just enters the body of the victim; in *Ahluwahlia* the *tone* of the description creates the impression of Ahluwahlia moving from one action to the next, from one short sentence to the next, as if in a trance.[22]

The irreality of Ahluwalia's actions is compounded in the Court's description of the response subsequent to the attack on her husband. Her husband, having tried unsuccessfully to douse the fire in the bath,[23] has rushed from the house, on fire, and is being assisted by neighbours. Meanwhile:

> Other neighbours rushed to the house. They found the door locked and saw the appellant standing at a ground-floor window clutching her son, just staring and looking calm. They shouted at her to get out of the house [it is now ablaze]. She opened a window and said, 'I am waiting for my husband,' and closed the window again. She was prevailed upon to hand the child out and later emerged herself. She stood staring at the blazing window with a glazed expression.
>
> (*Ahluwalia* at 893)

Having been persuaded to leave the burning house, Ahluwalia was arrested and, from prison, wrote to her mother-in-law that Deepak Ahluwalia had committed so many sins that she 'gave him a fire bath to wash away his sins' (*Ahluwalia* at 893). Within the Court's description of Ahluwalia's actions, there are many points at which the formation and existence of an intention to kill or cause really serious injury are put on display (her purchase of the petrol and caustic soda for the purpose of doing some injury to her husband; the lapse of time between their last interaction and her response; the preparations she had to go through in order to carry out the act). At the trial, however, counsel for Ahluwalia (who did not give evidence at trial)[24] argued that she had no intention to kill or inflict serious injury, only to inflict some pain on him (*Ahluwalia* at 893). The argument failed. The care in purchasing and preparing the materials for the act was no doubt an obstacle; using a bucket to make the petrol easier to throw and by protecting herself with an oven glove indicated that she was engaged on a dangerous plan. In using gloves, there is an acknowledgment of the risk of harm to herself, and an awareness of the vastly increased risk of serious harm to the person on whom she would throw the petrol. While the narrow focus on such acts preceding the killing is a convention of murder trials in which intention is disputed and there is no confession, the secondary line of defence in *Ahluwahlia* expands the circumstances on which responsibility for the death can be restaged. The defence of provocation relied upon the whole history of the marriage and Deepak Ahluwalia's ten-year abuse of her, culminating in the evening of 8 May 1989. This secondary defence also failed. Ahluwalia was convicted of murder.

At her appeal, three grounds of appeal were presented. The first related to the trial judge's direction to the jury on provocation. This followed closely the classic doctrinal statement in *R v Duffy* (as amended by the *Homicide Act* 1957): 'Provocation is some act, or series of acts, done [or words spoken] ... which would cause in any reasonable person, and actually causes in the accused, a sudden and temporary loss of self-control, rendering the accused so subject to passion as to make him or her for the moment not master of his mind' (*R v Duffy* [1949] 1 ER 932 at 932). The trial judge in *Ahluwalia* added: 'Bear in mind, it is a sudden and temporary loss of self-control for which you are looking, not a thought-out plan how to punish him for his wickedness'.[25] He also stated that such a 'sudden and temporary loss of self-control' would have to be considered in the 'context of the facts as described by the appellant herself' (*Ahluwalia* at 894). In *Thornton*, no comparable direction is given to the jury; they are invited instead to consider, given that 'there are ... many unhappy, indeed miserable, husbands and wives. It is a fact of life. It has to be faced, members of the jury. But on the whole it is hardly reasonable, you may think, to stab them fatally when there are other alternatives available, like walking out or going upstairs' (*Thornton* at 312).

The direction's appeal to the circumstances surrounding and preceding the death functions to legally foreclose the experience of the abused woman. The direction in *Ahluwahlia*, however, it is that experience which is registered — yet, as will be argued, on condition that the abuse is suffered by a woman who can be represented as abiding by the marital and maternal norms of familial femininity.

In doctrinal terms, much of Ahluwalia's appeal was focused upon the notion of a 'sudden and temporary loss of self-control', since that expression had been construed many times to mean that a lapse of time between the provocative act or words could prove fatal to a plea of provocation (*R v Ibrams* (1981) 74 Cr App R 154; *R v Whitfield* (1976) 63 Cr App R 39; *Thornton*). The several hours that had lapsed between Deepak Ahluwalia's threat to beat her and burn her face with a hot iron and Kiranjit Ahluwalia's getting out of bed to find the petrol, may well have been seen as inconsistent with the notion of a 'sudden and temporary loss of self-control'. This is so particularly given that, in *Thornton*, a lapse of time of only several minutes had been considered ample as a 'cooling-off period' and had been seen as crucial in destroying her defence of provocation. It is vital to note that the Court in *Thornton* is only able to emphasise a lapse of time between provocative act and homicidal response by means of a particular timeframe. The Court starts this time frame before Sara Thornton goes into the kitchen to find a knife (which, she argued, had been for her protection against a possible attack) and after Malcolm Thornton's first insulting remarks. As such, the time spent in the kitchen is deemed to be time which was and should have been spent reflecting on the desire to kill and deciding against it. However, if Sara Thornton were thinking only at this point about the possible risk of harm to herself, then such a period of cooling-down could not occur. The Court construes Sara Thornton as emerging from the kitchen, with the knife, as armed and dangerous, intending to cause serious injury. The judgment is thus able to discount the second exchange with Malcolm Thornton as involving no provocative conduct. If, however, the time-frame were to begin at that point, then Sara Thornton's response could be viewed as almost instantaneous, involving no lapse of time. It is in the judicial narrative of the facts as self-evident and unequivocal that conviction occurs.[26]

The appeal court in *Ahluwalia*, while refusing to challenge the doctrinal definition of provocation, went so far as to state that a delay in response did not in itself mean that provocation could not succeed as a defence, as long as the loss of self-control, when it finally occurred, had been sudden and temporary (*Ahluwalia* at 896). This appeared to take into account the submissions of Ahluwalia's lawyers that abused women may experience a 'slow burn' in losing control rather than an immediate reaction (*Ahluwalia* at 896).[27] Ahluwalia's loss of self-control would have had to have been seen as very slow-burning, due to her purchase of the petrol and caustic soda several days before using them. Her second ground of appeal, which also failed, related to the trial judge's direction to the jury as to the characteristics that were to be taken into account. This relied on the statement in *R v Camplin* that:

[The judge] should then explain to [the jury] that the reasonable man ... is a person having the power of self-control to be expected of an ordinary person of the sex and age of the accused, but in other respects sharing the accused's characteristics as they think would affect the gravity of the provocation to him, and that the question is not merely whether such a person would in like circumstances be provoked to lose his self-control but also would react to the provocation as the accused did. (*R v Camplin* [1987] 2 All ER 168 at 175)

At her trial, the judge's direction to the jury was as follows:

The only characteristics of the defendant about which you know specifically that might be relevant are that she is an Asian woman, married, incidentally, to an Asian man, the deceased living in this country. You may think she is an educated woman, she has a university degree. If you find these characteristics relevant to your considerations, of course you will bear that in mind. (*Ahluwalia* at 897)

Ahluwalia was claiming that the ten years of violence that she had endured should have been taken into account here, by means of a direction to the jury to consider whether she was not just an educated, married, Asian woman, but a *battered woman*. Her argument was that she was suffering from 'battered woman syndrome' and was in a state of 'learnt helplessness' (*Ahluwalia* at 897).[28] The Court acknowledges that English cases have tended to concentrate on physical characteristics: 'Thus age, sex, colour, race and any physical abnormality have been considered' (*Ahluwalia* at 898). However, any mental characteristic would have to be demonstrably permanent in its effect on the defendant's identity; here, however, the court refused to accept that being battered might wreak long-lasting change on a woman's psyche. Lord Taylor states: 'True, there was much evidence that the appellant had suffered grievous ill-treatment; but nothing to suggest that the effect of it was to make her "a different person from the ordinary run [of women]", or to show that she was

"marked off or distinguished from the ordinary [woman] of the community"'
(*Ahluwalia* at 898).[29] Lord Taylor sees Ahluwalia's condition after 10 years
of physical and emotional violence as within the boundaries of what could
normally be expected of an ordinary woman. I will go on to show that, in the
end, it is the narrative of Ahluwalia's situation *as ordinary* that enables her
conviction to be quashed.

The judgment concedes that had certain medical and psychiatric evidence
been made available to the court at trial, the verdict on provocation might
well have been different. However, this is not to imply that the court then
allows this evidence to influence the Court's view of provocation: rather, it is
held to be relevant to diminished responsibility, 'an issue not raised at all at
the trial' (*Ahluwalia* at 899). A doctor's report, available before trial, stated
that Ahluwalia was suffering from 'endogenous depression at the material
time', this being 'a major depressive disorder' (*Ahluwalia* at 900). Somehow
this report had been overlooked at the time of the trial; the Court of Appeal
felt that it would have supported a plea of diminished responsibility. The
judgment states that the court also took into account 'the appellant's *strange*
behaviour after lighting the fire as witnessed by neighbours' (*Ahluwalia* at
900).[30] This overlooked evidence provides the court with a frame in which to
re-interpret the problematic behaviour of Ahluwalia, before and after her act
of homicide. As noted above, many aspects of the case allowed the jury to
infer intention to kill: her purchase of the petrol and caustic soda, her elaborate
preparations for setting fire to her husband, her remaining in the house
afterwards (initially with her son), her comments to neighbours that she was
waiting for her husband, her glazed expression. Thanks to the medical
evidence, the Court is now able to collapse — but not without enfolding
them — in the juridical narrative of diminished responsibility. Following
section 2 of the *Homicide Act* 1957 (5 & 6 Eliz. II c. 11), diminished
responsibility can only apply to an individual who is suffering from an
'abnormality of mind' (as opposed to a 'defect of reason' arising out of a
'disease of the mind' in insanity) such that their responsibility for the crime
should be reduced. Whereas provocation appeals to the experiences and
awareness of the reasonable man (with certain characteristics of the accused),
diminished responsibility feeds off but is not reducible to reason.[31] If
Ahluwalia had been convicted of manslaughter on the grounds of provocation,
her actions would have been considered as identical to those of the reasonable
man with her characteristics: she would have been held to have behaved
with the normality of the normal. As it is, Ahluwalia's conviction for
manslaughter on the grounds of diminished responsibility means that her

situation and mental state must be viewed as belonging in part to some territory of experience which is not touched by reason: her behaviour is only the normality of the abnormal.[32] But more than this, it is at this point in the judicial narrative that Ahluwalia is classified as a *woman* both ordinary and strange. Previously, the report sought to confirm the everyday nature of her situation, by referring continually to her familial bonds, by locating her in familiar settings and associating her with the household and home. She was held up as an ordinary wife and mother, responsive to the duties of those roles. Now the report starts to suggest that she is 'strange', or *unfamiliar*. In her act of homicide, she kills her husband, the *pater familias*, the man to whom her parents gave her in marriage. Her act challenges the primacy of the familial. But in calling her 'strange' and in attributing that 'strangeness' to a mental disorder brought about by years of abuse, Ahluwalia's normality is re-asserted. The law is able to decide that it is her husband's violence which caused her strangeness and hence her act of violence. Without that history, she would have continued to live as a dutiful wife and mother. Her abnormality is merely the abnormality of the normal in the ideality of Woman, as relational, familial and self-sacrificial. Ahluwalia mistook the object of sacrifice: according to the desires of the law, she should have persisted to sacrifice herself. Her 'mistake', in sacrificing her abuser, can be overlooked as it is the act of a woman suffering a mental disorder whose main aim was to preserve her marriage.

The ordinary strangeness of femininity is not to be made available to Sara Thornton. At trial, her counsel attempted to argue that she was suffering from diminished responsibility; but since the reports from psychiatrists disagreed as to the effect had on her act of killing by the 'personality disorder' that the court mentions in its judgment, the defence did not succeed. Her defence of provocation failed, as described above, due to the emphasis put upon the so-called lapse of time during which she should have reflected upon her situation, when she went into the kitchen to get a knife. Beyond this, however, it is not clear how much success could have been available to Sara Thornton: the discursive construction of an aggressive, arrogant, cold-hearted killer dominates the judgment. While Ahluwalia's strangeness was held to be the ordinariness of femininity, Thornton's actions are the strangeness of the extraordinary: the criminal. In pleading provocation, her actions would have had to have been measured against those of the reasonable man with her characteristics. While a man might well be permitted to have the characteristics attributed to Sara Thornton,[33] she could not be permitted to retain them *as a woman*. In *R v Camplin*, Lord Diplock stated: 'A reasonable woman with her sex eliminated is altogether too abstract a notion for my comprehension, or I am confident, for that of any jury.... It hardly makes sense to say ... that a normal woman must be notionally stripped of her femininity before she qualifies as a reasonable woman' (*R v Camplin* [1987] 2 All ER 168 at 180). Allen comments that this statement betrays the fundamental contradiction at the heart of legal discourse, which enjoins a discounting of gender from legal interpretation and yet simultaneously invites an allowance for the very centrality of gender in judgment (H. Allen, 1987, 31). Sara Thornton was stripped of her identity and given instead the legal persona of the unfeminine woman.[34] Judged according to femininity, Thornton was condemned and thus had to be convicted of murder.[35]

Femininity as Marginalia

In each of these two cases there exists a narrative, which concerns the elucidation of aspects of the formal legal doctrines of provocation, murder, diminished responsibility, and manslaughter. In *Ahluwalia*, the headnote lists the key words of the reported judgment as:

> Criminal law - Murder - Provocation - Acts constituting provocation - Domestic violence - Wife killing husband following history of domestic violence and assaults - No sudden and temporary loss of self-control - Whether history of domestic violence amounting to provocation. Criminal law - Murder - Provocation - Self-control of reasonable man - Characteristics of accused - Whether characteristics relating to mental state or personality of accused can be taken into account in determining whether reasonable person having characteristics of accused would have lost self-control. (*Ahluwalia* at 889)

In *Thornton*, the list is as follows:

> Criminal law - Murder - Provocation - Acts constituting provocation - Domestic violence - Wife killing husband following history of domestic violence and assaults - No sudden and temporary loss of self-control - Whether history of domestic violence amounting to provocation. (*Thornton* at 306)

These doctrinal telegrammes are merged with the factual details of the defendant's situation to constitute the textuality of the judgment. In the reading of the reports, however, an entirely separate narrative emerges: this relates to the legal construction of sexual difference. This narrative is located in the margins of the judgment, in the performance of reportage which institutes judgment. Here, the accused will have been judged in terms of propriety of gender and familial relationships.

The battered woman who kills her abuser is judged according to a tension between margin and centre: that is, she is assessed according to whether her act is recuperable as non-threatening to the order of sexual difference. Sara Thornton's actions positioned her on the margins of appropriate femininity; through her drinking, the allegations of sexual impropriety made by the deceased, her perceived aggressiveness, she was represented as an unfeminine woman. Killing her husband was simply the most obvious feature of her lack of femininity: what condemns her is the combination of homicide and a range of symptoms which the court diagnoses as marginal to her sex. The legal symptomatology of sexual difference hinges on definitions of womanhood which are *oppositional*: Sara Thornton is judged according to her failed relationships with men, her problems at school and as a teenager in her family, her ambitiousness, her whispers to a friend which could be read as murderous intent, her lack of fidelity to her husband (alleged by him, symbolised by her drinking alone), her supposed aggressiveness with others (the taxi driver), her lack of affect when calling for help (the emergency call and her comments to police officers). Essential to her condemnation is her unauthentic relationship to the feminine self: as a woman she is held to betray her femininity, presenting a mimesis without reality, a surface covering traitorous depths. Her treason must be punished; the act of homicide is then represented as murder and no defence deemed applicable.[36]

Kiranjit Ahluwalia's situation is articulated and narrated very differently. Inspiring the report is an assessment of Ahluwalia as an authentic woman, true to her feminine identity and to her role as wife and mother. As remarked at various points above, the case report comments on Ahluwalia's strong relational ties: she wishes to remain with such a violent man 'partly because of her sense of duty as a wife and partly for the sake of the children' (*Ahluwalia* at 892); she abandons her legal studies due to family pressure to marry; she goes to family weddings and visits her mother-in-law (and writes to her from prison); she cares for her children and husband, cooking dinner for him even as he announces that he is ending their relationship. She is described as 'abject' and 'slight' (*Ahluwalia* at 892). In her situation, the act of homicide is portrayed as the act of a woman pushed into behaviour that is alien to her by a series of circumstances that she would have otherwise resisted; that is, she displays the frailty of femininity, and it is to this frailty that the judgment extends compassion. Whereas Thornton is viewed as having an aggressive nature, Ahluwalia's unfeminine act of violence is recuperated as an act of femininity. She kills out of her struggle to remain a true and good wife and mother. She kills out of her husband's actions, not as a result of her own will. Thornton's story is represented as one of agency and will: she spoke her homicidal desire to a friend, she took action, she followed her own desires. Ahluwalia's story is characterised as one of passivity: 'her mind turned' to the petrol and caustic soda (as if without any will on her part); she experiences pressures from family and is 'pushed' and assaulted in 'intense' violence by her husband (*Ahluwalia* at 892). Such a lack of voluntariness is held to represent authentic femininity. The judgment of Ahluwalia confirms her place in the register of sexual difference and brings her experiences in from the margin to the centre. Sara Thornton, thanks to her masquerade of womanhood, is compelled to remain on the margins, a border figure whose experiences are discounted and dismissed by the court.

At the margins of the criminal law, then, we find structures of familial responsibility, the proprieties of sexual difference and the orders of matrimony. In this analysis of two cases, I have argued that the case reports tells stories about the situations of both women. Those stories embody law: law not only concerning the necessary state of mind to prove murder or the definitions of reasonableness, but also, at their own margins, laws which testify to and enframe the relationship between criminal justice and the family. Ostensibly two separate bodies of law, criminal law and family law, meet in the story of the battered woman who kills her abuser. In the court, there ensues a struggle over jurisdiction: is the homicide to be understood as the desperate act of a woman forced to kill and failed by the civil system? Or is the act committed by a woman who abandoned her duties of love and responsibility and gave into a criminally lethal desire? *Ahluwalia* demonstrates that when civil law can be blamed, the woman can be exculpated. *Thornton* tells us that the simple yet tragic fact of being battered does not matter in the determination of culpability. In comparing the two judgments, it is inevitable that we opt for one or the other. What has however emerged is that guilt is a confession of law: guilt is a question of letting the law speak (*jurisdicere*) and making visible (*evidere*) the structures of responsibility in and of every narrative. Thornton's responsibility was deemed to be transparent, in plain view. Ahluwalia was at first seen as plainly guilty; however, the Court of Appeal found that beneath her *apparent* responsibility lay more than met the eye. As the fire illuminated the violent house of Kiranjit and Deepak Ahluwalia, so the law cast light on the lost medical evidence and the location of real responsibility (in the violence of her husband, her abnormal mental state and the lack of options available to her). Standing by the blazing window — poised in that dream-like state between the law of violence and the violence of law — she seemed to hesitate between two orders of authority (her probable death, had she remained, and her judgment in law, were she to leave the house). Her liminality and hesitancy to join the law are re-read by the court as mental instability and so she can be allowed to re-enter the community, guilty only of manslaughter. While Thornton repeatedly invited the law to investigate her house and provide some remedy for her plight, the law ignored her. As she stood in the kitchen and selected a knife, so she was forced into a border from which no law would condone her actions. And as she signed her message in lipstick upon the bedroom mirror, so the law signed a warrant to read those words as the guilt of a woman — and which the judgment executed.

Notes

1. Without the conversation on matters criminal with Peter Rush, this essay would have been done for.
2. Hereafter referred to as *Thornton* and *Ahluwahlia* respectively.
3. While it is somewhat conventional to begin with and presuppose that criminal law distinguishes between law and morals, the questioning of morality and the questioning of ethics display a different relation to law. As Kristeva has remarked, 'if contemporary ethics is no longer seen as being the same as morality, if ethics amounts to not avoiding the embarrassing and inevitable problematics of the law but giving it flesh, language and jouissance — in that case its reformulation demands the contribution of women...' (Kristeva, 1977, 49; and more generally, Moi, 1986, 206ff). For a conspectus of ethical questioning in contemporary legal scholarship, see Cornell, 1992.
4. Media interest in these two events has been extensive, launching the judgment of law as a spectacle. There have been television documentaries — for example Network First's programme for Granada, 'Women Who Kill' (11 January 1994) and The Heart of the Matter's programme for BBC1, 'Murder They Said' (3 November 1991). There have been magazine articles such as Thornton's 'Why I Killed My Husband' (Thornton, 1992). And the saga of conjugal homicide has been a staple of newspaper coverage since Thornton's case — not only that which concerned Kiranjit Ahluwahlia but also subsequent ones such as that of Judith Gardiner (whose sentence for manslaughter was reduced from five years' imprisonment to two years' probation in October 1992) and Sandra Fleming (whose case followed Ahluwalia's in permitting evidence to be introduced as to her suffering 'battered women's syndrome'). The concern of this paper is not with the media spectacle of conjugal homicide, but with the judgment of the event. No doubt the judgments take place bathed in the light of this spectacle, and thus respond to it. But more than this, the judgment is just as much a report as the reportage of the media — a staple diet of case reports. My concern is thus with the legal judgment as narrated. This is first and foremost neither a narrative of the event, nor of the trial. What is narrated is the process of judgment. It is here that the facts take on their import: the facts in the case report take place within a second trial — the trial of judgment. In short, the concern of this essay is with the way in which the facts institute a trial of judgment, put judgment on trial.
5. See the newspaper coverage of Eboli's story in the Montreal newspaper, *The Gazette*, 31

March 1992.
6.   The Bobbitt's situation has been widely covered in the media. For example, see Masters, 1993, 116; McNamara, 1993, 46; 'Cleared but Insane: Wife with the Knife', 1994; and 'Your Penis or Your Life', 1994.
7.   Compare, for example, Goodrich, 1990. In the latter, there is a fascinating reading of the factual landscape of legal judgment as the repressed site of common law emotion (Goodrich, 1990, 230–59).
8.   Reference should be made to the paradigmatic work of L. Walker, 1979; 1987.
9.   All recount instances of battered women who married their batterers with the (mistaken) belief that they could influence the men to resist violence or stop drinking.
10.   Incorporated within the judicial doubt as to whether Thornton intended to take her own life is the implication that she could, in the event being considered, have intended to take another person's life.
11.   See Nadel, 1993, for a fuller account of Thornton's life prior to the homicide.
12.   See, *inter alia*, Lacey et al., 1990; and Edwards, 1989. Note that violence by parents against children has never been called 'domestic abuse'; but rather 'child abuse', which itself now contains a reference to the sexual. There have been strong arguments put forward for renaming 'domestic violence' — that is, violence by men against their intimate female partners — 'woman battering' or 'woman abuse'. This argument was played out recently in London, Ontario (Canada), when the Committee for the Study of Family Violence voted to change its long-standing name to the Committee to End Woman Abuse.
13.   Compare *R v Hancock & Shankland* ([1986] AC 455), where the appellants' well-known disapproval of a miner continuing to work during the miners' strike and an alleged earlier assault do not add up to the *mens rea* for murder, despite subsequent events (involving dropping a concrete block off a parapet above the road along which the miner was travelling in a taxi; the driver was killed).
14.   Nadel reports that Mrs Thomas knew that Sara Thornton had reluctantly made an appointment to see a solicitor about obtaining a divorce (Nadel, 1993, 126).
15.   See Nadel for a description of how Helen Thomas was encouraged by the prosecution to describe Sara Thornton's drinking habits (which Mrs Thomas felt were excessive) and alleged marijuana use: 'By getting Helen Thomas to reveal her views on too much drink and illegal drugs, the prosecution had subtly provided the jury with a "respectable" comparison against which to measure Sara — a softly-spoken, gentle, conservative woman who would never do the things the accused did' (Nadel, 1993, 115).
16.   See the infamous cases on intention: *Hyam v DPP* [1974] 2 All ER 41; *R v Moloney* [1985] 1 All ER 1025; *R v Hancock & Shankland* [1986] AC 455; *R v Nedrick* [1986] 1 WLR 1025. It is perhaps no accident that a high proportion of the reports on the indirect doctrine of intention are concerned with deaths in a familial and romantic setting and/or burning houses.
17.   Nadel recounts the emphasis placed on Sara Thornton's sexuality during the trial: she was asked by the prosecutor if she had 'had a little fling with one or two young men who were [at the conference]' (Nadel, 1993, 124); and a lawyer is overheard to say that 'she's not just promiscuous, she's aggressively sexual. She goes about seducing all classes of people ... a very undesirable lady' (Nadel, 1993, 135). In the context of this judgment, it remains to note that Malcolm's accusation of 'whore' is a mirror-image of Sara's accusation of bastardy discussed above. On both occasions, the spectre of defection or interruption is raised and in both instances they are set to work against Sara Thornton. This is the function of the ambiguity or equivocation here — to turn the accusation of whore away from its maker and towards its object.
18.   Proportionality of the response by the accused to the actions of the victim is crucial in legal doctrine. In *R v Newell* (1980) 71 Cr App R 331, it was held that when a friend made insulting remarks about an ex-girlfriend of Newell's, it was out of proportion to the

provocation to respond by smashing a heavy ashtray on the friend's head, thus killing him. Compare *R v Camplin* (1980) Cr App R 331, where insulting remarks made by the victim after having buggered the defendant led to Camplin's hitting the victim with a chapatti pan. This response was not held to be disproportionate to the provocative statement. In the context of conjugal homicide, see also *R v Donachie* (1982) Cr App R 378 in which a battered woman, with an injunction against her husband, who told him to 'fuck off' and spat in his face, was held to have provoked him to stab her innumerable times. He had taken the knife with him when looking for her. The court, despite comments about the seriousness of Donachie's offence (manslaughter on grounds of provocation), reduced his sentence.

19. See the analysis of lethal female sexuality in Theweleit, 1987, which recounts the way in which the female opponents of the Nazi state are depicted as waiting to seduce its *freikorpsmen* into having sex with them, whereupon the women would kill the soldier with the gun or knife she had secreted under her skirts. Similarly, in Thornton's situation, the judgment allows the incongruous juxtaposition of knife and nightdress to insinuate the possibilities of castration or death.

20. Unreported but discussed in 'Woman Who Knifed to Death Jeering Husband Released', 1992. Subsequent details and quotations are taken from this discussion.

21. Notions of 'purpose' or 'aim' provide the mythical foundation of both the subjective and objective right to punish in criminal law, and are elaborated through the doctrine of intention as the law of murder. This myth and its elaboration responds to the defence formula: 'I didn't intend or mean to kill, but I only wanted to frighten'. It is the hierarchy of the disjunctive 'but' which the doctrine of oblique or indirect intention seeks to undo and rearticulate as purpose or aim. The judgment in Ahluwalia would seem to have conceded that Kiranjit Ahluwalia did have an intention to cause harm to her husband. Given the judicial attitude to cases involving fire (*inter alia, R v Nedrick* [1986] 1 WLR 1025; *Hyam v DPP* [1974] 2 All ER 41), it is hard to see how they would not conclude in this case that Ahluwalia intended that her husband should suffer really serious harm.

22. A final example: it was reported that a woman who killed her husband after he hit her told the police that 'it [the knife] just went in and then he suddenly said there was a pain' (*The Guardian*, 17 December 1994).

23. In this respect, Deepak Ahluwalia's description of what his wife did to him differs from hers: in his account (given in hospital) she threw caustic soda over him as he lay in bed; then, as he rushed into the bathroom to assuage the burning of the caustic soda, threw 'something else' (*Ahluwalia* at 893) over him. Police officers did find 'a bucket still smelling of petrol on the landing outside the bedroom, also a saucepan in the bathroom basin with caustic soda in the bottom. Later, the effects of caustic soda [presumably, corrosive burning] were found on the bathroom floor' (*Ahluwalia* at 893). This would seem to support the claim that she threw something on her husband twice (facilitating perhaps the jury's inference that she had intention to kill or cause really serious injury). The saucepan of caustic soda is not mentioned in the court's account of her actions.

24. Kennedy notes the importance of demeanour and deference of defendants at trial and when giving evidence: Thornton was viewed negatively by the court and jury because she appeared 'too feisty' and assertive. Ahluwalia at her appeal, as remarked above, is described by the court as 'slight' (Kennedy, 1992, 215).

25. Since the jury convicted, presumably they decided that the evidence demonstrated that Ahluwalia was engaged in a plan to punish wickedness: certainly the letter written to her husband's mother could be construed as creating a portrait of an avenging angel.

26. Jackson reverses the priority of law-construction over fact-construction in the jurisprudence of law, and provides some of the most interesting insights into the pragmatics of legal judgment (B. Jackson, 1988).

27. This, while rather an unfortunate metaphor given the details of this particular homicide,

derives from research done, particularly in the United States, on the responses of abused women (L. Walker, 1979; 1987; Browne, 1987).

28. For a detailed explanation of this term, see Walker, 1979; 1987, and see my critique of it in Young, 1993a.

29. Lord Taylor is quoting from *R v McGregor* ([1962] NZLR 1069 at 1081–2). Lord Taylor translates 'ordinary run of mankind' into 'ordinary [run of women]' and 'ordinary man of the community' into 'ordinary [woman] of the community'. Such a transposition, as has been repeated often enough, assumes that men and women and masculine and feminine start off the positions of equality. The transposition thus neutralises while maintaining the hierarchy. Sexual difference remains as an unassimilable element interior to law. Allen illuminates this dynamic not simply as a matter of logic but as a failure of the legal imagination (H. Allen, 1987, ch. 2). On 'ordinary womanhood', see Young, 1993b; and on the ideological realism of 'community' and its displacement of the real, see Rush and Young, 1994.

30. Emphasis added.

31. What was once excluded as 'moral insanity' or 'partial insanity' by the M'Naghten doctrine of insanity is now embedded in the doctrine of diminished responsibility. As such, diminished responsibility — as legal doctrine — is the site where psychiatric and juridical categories exchange places, where the moral and the reasonable are inseparable in and as law. On the genealogy of psychiatric and juridical relations, see Johnstone's essay in the present book. It is this exchange of places which haunts the judgment in Ahluwahlia, and is traced in the relation between provocation and diminished responsibility. The exclusion of provocation not only creates the distinction between the normal and the abnormal, but also maintains their inseparability. As such, the judgment faces the prospect that it cannot tell the difference between the normal and the abnormal.

32. This should not be taken as opposing the presentation of evidence of battered women's syndrome because it inevitably leads to representing women as abnormal. Rather, I am noting that in Ahluwahlia the presentation does lead to a representation of the abused woman as abnormal, albeit normally abnormal. For other cases where evidence of battered women's syndrome was presented yet which did not result in the representation of women as abnormal, see *R v Lavallee*, (1990) 55 CCC (3d) in Canada on self-defence and battered women's syndrome, and *Runjanjic & Kontinnen* (1991) 63 A Crim R 362 in Australia on duress and battered women's syndrome. Walker's accounts of her work as expert witness for battered women who kill also testify to the wide range of uses that evidence as to this syndrome could and should have (L. Walker, 1979; 1987).

33. See for example *R v Donachie* (1982) 4 Cr App R 78.

34. Cf Barthes: 'Periodically, some trial, and not necessarily fictitious like the one in Camus's *The Outsider*, comes to remind you that the Law is always prepared to lend you a spare brain in order to condemn you without remorse, and that, like Corneille, it depicts you as you should be, and not as you are' (Barthes, 1972, 44).

35. I noted earlier that the juridical scene of judgment is marked by the irreality of women. It seems to me that the narrative of law interrupts that irreality by reinscribing it in the binary opposition of active and passive, ordinary and strange, masculine and feminine. In *Thornton*, this is done by transferring the malice of the victim onto the accused; in *Ahluwahlia*, it is by returning the malice of the victim to the victim — and retaining the intention of the accused with justifying or excusing conditions. In this way, the distinctiveness of diminished responsibility in and for this judgment emerges: it functions to disjoin and conjoin active and passive, ordinary and strange, malice and intention — by assigning them to the discrete positions of accused and victim, masculine and feminine.

36. Sara Thornton was sentenced to imprisonment for life. Her attempts to have her case reconsidered failed repeatedly: she went on a hunger-strike while in prison, she appealed to the Home Secretary to consider fresh evidence, and she also asked for a pardon to be granted. Whereas groups such as Justice For Women have had success in the results of

the cases of, for example, Gardiner, Emery and Fleming (unreported), Thornton's situation appears far more difficult. Thornton was eventually released in 1995 pending a retrial. At the retrial, she was found guilty of manslaughter and in June 1996 sentenced to five years' imprisonment — a period she had already served for the initial conviction of murder. It is not insignificant that, in sentencing Thornton the second-time round, the retrial judge took account of the difficulties of living with an alcoholic and remarked that killing her husband was diminished by the abnormality of her mind (*R v Thornton (No. 2)* [1996] 2 All ER 1023). At present, some 70 other women are serving prison sentences in England for killing their male spouses.

7 Eloquence and Imagery: Corporate Criminal Capacity and Law's Anthropomorphic Imagination

LESLIE J. MORAN

Introduction[1]

Recent incidents have once again focused attention upon and generated debate about the ability or inability of the criminal law to regulate the activities of incorporated companies (Wells, 1988; 1989; 1990; 1993).[2] Demands that companies be subject to the criminal law and attempts to use the law to meet these demands have a long history (Laski, 1921a; 1921b; W.J. Brown, 1905; Cranfield, 1914; Winn, 1929; Welsh, 1946).[3] In general it is a history of the concept of corporate personality that is concerned with the legal capacities, liabilities, privileges, disabilities and responsibilities of the corporation. In particular it is a history of the imbrication of corporate personality and criminal law: of the criminal law's attempt to negotiate and manage the troublesome perplexities of corporate personality. This essay will explore the nature of the legal practice that works to transcribe corporate personality into the criminal law and thereby invent corporate criminal liability. It will provide a description of that legal practice and consider the problems that are intrinsic to that practice. Given that there are many legal practices and many criminal practices, the primary emphasis of the essay will be upon English jurisprudence and academic commentaries.

Corporate Criminal Incapacity

An observation made in 1700 provides a concise example of a relationship between the legal capacity of the corporation and criminal law that has had considerable currency in English law. Holt CJ declared: 'A corporation is not indictable but the particular members of it are' (*Anon.* (1700) 12 Mod. 559). Here, the corporation as a subject in law was allotted a particular position within the criminal law. It had no autonomous criminal capacity. Thereby the corporation in itself was placed outside the domain of criminal responsibility. However, acts performed in the context of corporate activities might be subject to criminal law but liability would be imposed in a particular way. It would fall only upon the shoulders of the members who had come together to form the corporation.[4] Holt's observation draws our attention to the fact that for a considerable period of time criminal capacity and liability was a quality peculiar to a particular type of legal subject; the natural legal subject.

This example is illustrative of the tradition in English Common Law that takes the natural legal subject as a representation of the fullness of legal capacity. The corporation appears in its shadow as a relatively impoverished juridical subject. Blackstone, writing later in the eighteenth century, describes this impoverishment. It is evidenced in a series of privileges and disabilities that mark the boundaries of the juridical status of the corporate legal subject (Blackstone, 1979, vol. 1, ch. 18). One example refers to the fact that the corporation could not appear before the law in person. This characteristic of the corporate legal subject is explained by reference to the invisibility of the corporation; a reference that is repeated in many of the instances that illustrate corporate juridical disqualification. For example it informs Blackstone's observation that a corporation could not take the oath as it could neither appear in person nor swear. It operates in the conclusion that the corporation was incapable of particular categories of wrong. Thus the corporation could not be made defendant to any action for battery or such like personal violence, as it could neither beat nor be beaten. In addition the attribution of invisibility to the corporation rendered particular punishments problematic. A corporation could not in law commit treason or felony as, up until and including the time when Blackstone wrote, upon conviction the punishment was death; a corporation could not be executed. Other penalties (such as attainder, forfeiture or corruption of blood) presupposed a juridical subject with a physical presence and thereby they were rendered inapplicable to the corporation. For similar reasons a corporation could not be outlawed, for outlawry supposed a precedent right of arrest: an invisible entity could not be seized and incarcerated. In all of these examples the disqualification of the corporate subject draws attention to the fact that in part the corporation was a non-viable legal subject (Butler, 1991). More specifically they draw attention to the importance of absence and invisibility in the production of this juridical state. Here the corporate legal subject, with all its limitations, stands in stark contrast to the plenitude of the natural legal subject. While the absence and invisibility of the corporate body are overcome in the qualified presence of the corporate legal subject, the natural legal subject represents full presence made manifest in the immediate physical body of the human individual.

Blackstone's examples have both direct and indirect significance for the development of an understanding of the criminal capacity of a corporation. For example in criminal proceedings before the Assizes and in the Sessions Court the Common Law required that a defendant charged with a criminal offence appear in person. As a general rule proceedings could not be brought against the corporation in these courts as a corporation could not satisfy this requirement. Furthermore, officers of the company, such as the directors of the company, could not appear for the defendant company as they were not the defendant. Likewise an attorney could not appear at the Assize or Sessions Court as the law required the defendant to appear in person.[5] Finally, Blackstone's examples demonstrate that the criminal capacity of the corporation was limited as the corporation was excluded from whole categories of criminal wrongs and forms of punishment. In the final instance, Blackstone concluded, the corporation could not commit a crime.

The limited criminal capacity of the corporate legal subject is not merely of remote historical interest. More recent cases draw attention to the fact that many aspects of corporate criminal incapacity have had considerable durability in the English Common Law tradition. For example, in 1922 the Court of Criminal Appeal was still able to quash a conviction against the defendant, Daily Mirror Newspapers Limited, on the basis that the corporation was beyond the criminal law (*R v Daily Mirror Ltd* [1922] 2 KB 530). In general the decision relied upon an argument that the necessary procedural prerequisites could not be applied to an incorporated company. Under the *Grand Juries (Suspension) Act* 1917 (7 & 8 Geo. V c. 4) the validity of the indictment rested on compliance with a statutory requirement: the person, against whom it was sought to present the indictment, must have been committed for trial. According to this procedure the warrant of commitment contained a command to the constables to take the defendant to His Majesty's prison and to deliver the defendant and the warrant to the Governor. The warrant then directed the Governor to retain the defendant in custody and to deliver the same to the next Assize. The argument for the company was that the command could not be physically carried out as a corporation could not be imprisoned. The court agreed. As no proper commitment for trial had been carried out the indictment and conviction were quashed (*Criminal Justice Act* (1925)

15 & 16 Geo. V c. 86, s. 33; *Magistrates Courts Act* 1980, s. 46).

Difficulties also persisted in the context of criminal penalties. In the case of *Hawke v E. Hulton & Co. Ltd* ([1909] 2 KB 93), the company was charged under s. 41 of the *Lotteries Act* 1823 (4 Geo. IV c. 60) which made it an offence for any person to publish a proposal or scheme for the sale of chances in a lottery, not authorised by Act of Parliament. The Act declared that a person found guilty of the offence should be deemed a rogue and vagabond and was to be punished for the first offence by imprisonment and for a second offence by imprisonment and whipping. The court concluded that an incorporated company could not be convicted under s. 41 as the words rogue and vagabond were said to be wholly inappropriate to a company and as such the words suggested that the use of 'person', in the section, did not include the corporate person. Thereby the corporate person was placed beyond the jurisdiction of the criminal law.[6]

The application of the basic doctrinal requirement of *mens rea* to the corporate person has been the most persistent difficulty for corporate criminal capacity. The judiciary have regularly concluded that 'offences, certainly offences of commission, are offences of individuals, not of corporations. A corporation cannot have *mens rea*' (*Pharmaceutical Society v London & Provincial Supply Assn Ltd* [1880] 5 QB 310 at 313). A recent incident suggests that the application of *mens rea* to the corporation continues to trouble English law. In *P&O European Ferries (Dover) Ltd.* ((1991) Cr App R 72)[7] the court had to decide whether a charge of manslaughter could be brought against a corporation. Having reviewed the case law, Turner J concluded that it might be possible for an incorporated company to be guilty of an act of manslaughter. In the first instance this marks an important development in English law; the ability to initiate proceedings for manslaughter against a corporation and more specifically the attribution of an appropriate *mens rea* to the corporate person. However, before hearing the evidence for the defence, the trial collapsed due to difficulties in satisfying the specific requirements of *mens rea* imposed by the court. It would appear that the ultimate stumbling block in this case was the specific test developed to evidence the mind of the corporation.[8] Corporate liability will arise, the court concluded, only in those situations where the prohibited act and guilty mind of the corporation can be evidenced in the act and mind of a single individual who is the embodiment of the corporation. The imposition of this test appears to have played a significant role in the collapse of the trial and in the decision in subsequent cases not to proceed with criminal proceedings based upon manslaughter.[9] These recent developments would suggest that the difficulties relating particularly to the attribution of a mind to the corporation, and more generally to the criminal capacity of the corporation, will persist into at least the immediate future.[10]

Metaphor and the Anthropomorphic Imagination of Law[11]

While it would appear from Blackstone's observations and from the more recent examples of corporate criminal incapacity that the attribution of absence and invisibility to the corporation has played a key role in limiting its criminal capacity, it would be wrong to conclude that this has generated difficulties that were unique to criminal law.[12] For the Common Law the corporation is ideal, *in abstracto* (*The Case of Sutton's Hospital* 10 Co Rep. 23a at 32b). This refers to the general attribution of absence to the corporation. Blackstone plots its general effects in his catalogue of corporate privileges and disabilities. The list includes examples that relate to both civil and criminal corporate capacity.[13]

However, despite the general applicability of absence, the history of corporate capacity suggests that the law's response to the absence and invisibility of the corporation has produced different effects in different contexts. In general the history of corporate capacity in English law is a history of corporate civil capacity and criminal incapacity. This section of the essay will be concerned with a consideration of the nature of the legal practices that produce corporate capacity. Particular attention will be paid to one example of corporate civil capacity; namely contractual capacity. The success of the law in producing corporate contractual capacity and liability provides an example of the way the Common Law managed the absence and invisibility of the corporation in the fabrication of legal capacity.

By the end of the eighteenth century Blackstone was able to conclude that the corporation had considerable contractual autonomy. It had the ability to enter into contracts in its own right. It had the power to sue and be sued, to implead and be impleaded, to grant and to receive in its own right. It had the capacity to own property and to alienate property. In stark contrast to his observations on the criminal capacity of the corporation, where he could merely catalogue the impossibility of capacity, in the context of contractual capacity he concluded that the corporate legal subject could in its own right do 'all acts as natural persons may' (Blackstone, 1979, vol. 1, 463).

The corporation is thus attributed with civil capacity. The question that needs to be addressed then is, given the overwhelming criminal incapacity of corporations by virtue of its invisible absence, how is the contrary outcome produced in civil law while retaining and asserting the invisible absence of corporations. Coke provides a general insight into the nature of the relationship between legal practice and corporate capacity. The corporation, he observed, 'exists only in intendment and consideration of law' (Blackstone, 1979, vol. 1, 463).[14] That is first and foremost capacity is an effect of the law; all the other issues are secondary and take place within this initial attribution. Thus in order to understand the (contractual) capacity of the corporation it is essential to pay particular attention to legal practice. Blackstone provides an example that may be used to demonstrate the nature of that legal practice:

> When a corporation is erected, a name must be given to it; and by that name alone it must sue and be sued, and do all legal acts; .... the name is the knot of its combination, without which it could not perform its corporate function. The name of incorporation, says Sir Edward Coke, is a proper name, or name of baptism; and therefore when a private founder gives his college or hospital a name, he does it only as godfather; and by that same name the king baptizes the incorporation.
>
> (Blackstone, 1979, 462–3)[15]

This draws attention to various aspects of the legal practice that produces corporate capacity. Firstly, the law overcomes the absence of the corporation and the invisibility of the corporate body by formal means. The legal requirement of a name is a device through which the corporation is made to appear in law. The name is a mark that may signify the presence of a subject in law. As such the rule works to erect the corporate person as a possible tangible legal reality.

To end our analysis at the legal rule would be premature. Blackstone's example draws our attention to another dimension of legal practice. This is to be found in his reference to the corporate name as a proper name and a baptismal name given both by the founder (as godfather) and by the king (as law and priest). The proper and the baptismal are important in several respects. First, both seek to attribute particular characteristics to the name and to naming. For example the reference to the legal name as a proper name directs our attention to the fact that the name performs a particular function. It suggests that the name stands for the thing itself in its totality. It expresses the uniqueness of the subject that it designates. Here the name is a mark that is taken as a representation of the full presence of the (individual, human) subject. Secondly, the reference to the name as a proper and a baptismal name draws attention to another aspect of legal practice; the use of metonymy. In metonymy an idea or collection of ideas associated with a detail become detached from one idiosyncratic context and are represented as expressive of qualities associated with a general term. Thus as metonyms the proper and the baptismal are words that refer to particular characteristics and practices of naming that are read as words expressing general characteristics of naming. For example the reference to baptism is a reference to one specific practice associated with naming human individuals within a particular cultural tradition. As a metonym baptism works to associate attributes specific to that particular set of practices to naming in general. Like the reference to the name as the proper name, baptism emphasises the name as a mark of the full presence of the individual human subject. Furthermore, baptism draws attention to naming as an initiatory rite, a ritual of purification and an expression of divine agency and divine presence.

In their application to the corporation the proper and the baptismal also function in another way; as metaphors. Metaphor works in a particular way. It suggests similarity and connection between two points. Here the association is between the natural subject and the corporate subject. Metaphor is put to work to transmit attributes from one place to another. The metaphorical use of the proper and the baptismal provides a vehicle through which particular practices of naming the human (natural) subject might be transferred to other rituals of naming, in particular the legal rule that requires the corporate name. This transfers particular attributes associated with baptismal naming — such as the conjunction of full human presence and divine presence — to the corporate subject. The task of metaphor is not to insist upon a literal similarity but to exploit a common denominator: the name.

Blackstone's example draws attention to the fact that the legal practice that produces corporate capacity does not end in the declaration of a legal rule. It is also a practice of reading the rule. The rule of naming is to be read by way of metonymy and metaphor. The legal practice of reading that produces corporate capacity proceeds by way of a very specific set of metonyms and metaphors. They are anthropomorphic.[16] Particular qualities and attributes associated with the human subject (full presence) are made proximate to and carried over to the absent, invisible subject that is the corporation, enabling it to be represented in law in each of its capacities as (full) presence. Finally, while these reading practices produce proximity it must be noted that metaphor also depends upon distance or dissimilarity as a pre-requisite of connection. Thus in order for practices associated with the human subject to operate as metaphor in this context the human subject must be that which is also separate and apart from the corporate subject. In proximity there is always already distance.

The use of anthropomorphic metonyms and metaphors in the production of contractual capacity is not unique to a reading of the legal rules relating to the name of the corporation. Blackstone provides another instance of this practice in the production of corporate contractual capacity. He notes that the law required the corporation to act by way of a corporate seal. The legal requirement is explained in the following terms: 'a corporation, being an invisible body, cannot manifest its intentions by any personal act or oral discourse: it therefore acts and speaks only by its common seal'.[17]

Here the gloss on the legal rule resorts to both metonymy and metaphor. 'Act' and 'speak' operate as metonyms. As specific gestures of the human subject, each gesture is read not as some idiosyncratic and isolated aspect of the human subject but as a sign of some general quality; a sign for the fullness of that subject. Blackstone's gloss also draws attention to a second dimension of the reading of these terms. In their application to the corporation, they are transposed to produce meaning in a different context. They are read as anthropomorphic metaphors of full presence transferring attributes from the natural legal subject to the corporate legal subject. They produce a particular reading of the legal rule that requires the application of a seal as evidence of the presence of the natural legal subject to the corporate subject.[18] Through anthropomorphic metonyms and metaphors the corporation might be said to mimic the natural legal subject; to produce contractual capacity in particular or legal capacity more generally.

Finally, it is important to recognise that the use of anthropomorphic metonyms and metaphors is not of unique concern to questions of contractual capacity in particular or to civil capacity in general. These reading practices are central to all corporate matters. In general the corporeal refers to the body. The corporate body is always-already metaphor. In the first instance that body is the body of the individual subject. The corporate and the corporation refer to a second, collective, body (Kantorowicz, 1957; Gierke, 1900; 1958; Barker, 1958). This second body is a thing that is different and apart from the individual body but through metaphor and metonymy is made in the image of that body. Again the connection is not the physical resemblance (the corporate body tends to be made up of many human individuals) but particular qualities such as a name, actions, social effects. Through these points of connection attributes associated with the individual body are transmitted to another place in order to represent them as qualities of another thing, for example as God's image and agent, as a thing of many parts interconnected and interdependent, as naturalness, unity, singularity, individuality. Through metonym and metaphor these qualities not only are transmitted from the individual subject to the other subject made up of many individuals but the collectivity appears as the image of the human subject.[19]

As Blackstone noted, absence as marked by the invisibility of the corporation is at the heart of the juridical disqualification of the corporate legal subject. Legal practice is a response to this state of affairs. As such the legal practice that produces corporate capacity is a practice concerned with the fabrication of presence (visibility). Blackstone demonstrates that this legal practice is a textual practice; of writing and reading rules, of anthropomorphism, metaphor and metonymy. Furthermore that textuality is a matter of production. The effect is the production of a corporate presence in the image of the natural legal subject. Thereby the corporation may act and be acted upon in its own right.[20]

Anthropomorphic Metaphors and Criminal Capacity

Having drawn attention to some of the main features of the legal practice that produces corporate civil capacity this section of the essay will return to the issue of the criminal capacity of the corporation. Particular attention will be paid to the legal rules and the practice of reading that works to produce both corporate criminal capacity and the privilege of corporate criminal incapacity.

As has already been demonstrated the history of the English Common Law provides many examples of the durability of corporate criminal incapacity. Various attempts have been made to change this state of legal affairs. From time to time Parliament has introduced statutory rules to create corporate criminal capacity. These initiatives have taken various forms. For example, statutes have been used to create specific corporations as legal subjects with criminal capacity.[21] Laws have been enacted to create new offences which, by virtue of interpretation sections, could be committed by corporations.[22] Finally, a more radical statutory initiative that had an impact upon the question of corporate criminal capacity was the creation of a new type of criminal wrong; the strict liability offence.

These legislative interventions were relatively successful. Some of the earliest instances of corporate criminal capacity arise in the context of statutory corporations. For example in 1842 in the case of *R v Birmingham & Gloucester Railway Co.* ([1842] 3 QB 222) the criminal capacity of a corporation was established in the context of nonfeasance (a failure to carry out a statutory duty). In 1846 in the case of *R v Great North of England Railway Co.* ((1846) 9 QB 316) criminal capacity was established in the context of misfeasance (the commission of an act that is unlawful). Corporate criminal capacity through strict liability was a much later development. In 1902 in *Perkes,*

Gunson & Tee Ltd v Ward ([1902] 2 KB 1) the court concluded that a corporation was capable of being guilty of a strict liability offence.

While statute was central to the creation of criminal capacity in these cases, the disputes and their resolution engage with the legal practice of anthropomorphic metaphor and metonymy. For example in *R v Birmingham & Gloucester Railway Co.* ((1846) 9 QB 316), counsel for the defence argued that the statutory rule ought to be read by way of the extant tradition of corporate criminal disqualification. His argument proceeds by way of drawing the court's attention to the many examples of corporate criminal incapacity: a corporation could not satisfy the procedural requirement that it appear in person; no punishment could be enforced against the corporation as it could not be taken; only the members of the corporation could be proceeded against. All of these references seek to frame the legal rule in such a way as to limit the reading of the subject of that rule to the natural legal subject. As such the argument seeks to limit the availability of anthropomorphic metaphor and metonymy. Counsel for the prosecution sought to persuade the court that other practices of reading were required. Having asserted that there was no direct precedent in favour of criminal capacity he argued that the rule ought to be read by way of an emerging tradition of capacity. As such his argument refers (indirectly) to those practices of metonymy and metaphor that are central to the fabrication of corporate capacity. In particular he resorted to developments in *Yarborough v Bank of England* ((1812) 16 East 16) which related to civil capacity. In that case the court noted the development of corporate civil capacity and concluded that, where rights and powers had been created by the rules and practices of the law, liabilities might also be generated. Translating that into a criminal context, where a statute created a corporation with specific powers it might also create the same corporation with duties enforceable through the criminal law. As such the legal subject might be read as a reference to the corporate legal subject alone or a reference to both the natural and corporate subject.[23] The decision had direct significance in *R v Great North of England Railway Co.* The court applied the *R v Birmingham & Gloucester Railway* ([1842] 3 QB 222) case by way of the following argument. Nonfeasance, they concluded, was one species of wrong. Misfeasance was merely another species of the same general category of wrong. If a corporation could be capable in law of the former it could also be capable of the latter.[24] Finally, in *Perkes v Ward* liability was produced through a reading of 'person' as metaphor. Person, the court concluded, was a reference to both the natural and the artificial (corporate) juridical subject.[25]

Each of these instances of corporate criminal capacity occurred in the context of statutory initiatives that had, in their different ways, limited significance. A legislative strategy that had the potential to have a more widespread impact upon the question of corporate criminal capacity was the enactment of criminal capacity by way of a general rule of interpretation. The first example of this practice is to be found in legislation of 1827: 'An Act for Further Improving the Administration of Justice in Criminal Cases in England'. Parliament declared that:

> wherever this or any other Statute relating to any Offence, whether punishable upon Indictment or summary Conviction, in describing or referring to the Offence or the Subject Matter on or with respect to which it shall be committed, or the Offender or the party affected or intended to be affected by the Offence, hath used or shall use Words importing the Singular Number or the Masculine Gender only, yet the Statute shall be understood to include several Matters as well as One Matter, and several persons as well as One Person, and Females as well as Males, and Bodies Corporate as well as Individuals, unless it be otherwise specially provided, or there be something in the Subject or Context repugnant to such Construction...
> (*Criminal Law Act* (1827) 7 & 8 Geo. IV c. 28, s 14)[26]

Little judicial consideration appears to have been given to this Act and no significance was given to it in the early cases dealing with the criminal capacity of statutory corporations. The first extensive judicial consideration of the meaning and effect of the 1827 Act is to be found in a case dealing with corporate civil capacity: *The Pharmaceutical Society v London & Provincial Supply Assn Ltd* ([1897] 4 QB 313). The case is of significance here as not only does it provide an example of the legal practices that make up the judicial responses to this particular type of legislative initiative to create corporate capacity but the case also had specific significance for the question of criminal capacity.

The case arose out of a dispute relating to a provision in the *Pharmacy Act* 1868 which declared that:

> [i]t shall be unlawful for any person to sell or keep open shop for retailing or dispensing or compounding poisons, or to assume or use the title chemist ... unless such a person shall be a pharmaceutical chemist ... within the meaning of this Act, or be registered under this Act. (*Pharmacy Act* (1868) 31 & 32 Vict. c. 121, s. 1)

Following the procedures laid down in an earlier Act (*An Act for Regulating the Qualifications of Pharmaceutical Chemists* (1852) 15 & 16 Vict.

c. 56, ss. 12–14), breaches of the law were to be dealt with before the County Court. The matter initially came before the High Court as proceedings had been brought against a company, London and Provincial Supply Association, incorporated under the *Companies Acts* 1862 (25 & 26 Vict. c. 89) and 1863 (26 & 27 Vict. c. 118). The court was asked to determine whether the statutory provision applied to an incorporated company; did 'person' include a corporation?

In order to resolve the point the Act of 1827 was referred to by counsel for both parties. On behalf of the plaintiff, the Attorney-General used the Act to demonstrate the existence of a general rule of interpretation; person included a body corporate (*Pharmaceutical Society* [1897] 4 QB 313 at 317). Counsel for the defendant argued that the existence of an Act of Parliament that brought an incorporated body under the law evidenced a general rule of exclusion; the word person did not *prima facie* include a corporation (*Pharmaceutical Society* [1897] 4 QB 313 at 314). A corporation might only be brought under the law by way of a specific enactment.

In the High Court the Attorney-General's specific argument was rejected. Cockburn CJ concluded that the Act of 1827 did not establish a rule of general significance. The Act was expressly limited to criminal matters. As such the Act applied neither directly nor indirectly to the civil matter before the court (*Pharmaceutical Society* [1897] 4 QB 313 at 317). However the High Court proceeded to resolve the matter in favour of the plaintiff. Having adopted a general rule of exclusion, the Court found that the *Pharmacy Act* itself required that 'person' included a corporation. On appeal to the Court of Appeal the decision of the High Court was overturned (*Pharmaceutical Society* [1897] 4 QB 313 at 313) and on a further appeal to the House of Lords the decision of the Court of Appeal was confirmed (*Pharmaceutical Society v London & Provincial Supply Assn Ltd* [1880] AC 857).

As a preliminary point it is important to recognise that the general interpretation rule seeks to impose a particular practice of reading the law. As an attempt to promote the idea of the criminal capacity of a corporation the statute seeks to institutionalise the use of established legal practices of anthropomorphic metonymy and metaphor that generate capacity in a different context. But at the same time, the statute seeks to preserve certain boundaries to those legal practices. Thereby it seeks to preserve, to a degree, the *status quo ante* and with it practices of reading through which the corporate person might remain a relatively disqualified legal subject. As such the statute enacts inclusion and exclusion. The reports of *Pharmaceutical Society v London & Provincial Supply Assn Ltd* demonstrate that inclusion and exclusion takes place in a play between the general and the particular.[27] Given that there is play, the interpretation of a statutory rule is potentially openended, both in terms of the outcomes of decision and in terms of the context of the decisions (criminal or civil). In their judgments the judges inhabit this openness and (re)draw the boundaries of certain legal practices of reading by way of an alwaysalready established complex collection of reading practices. The decisions demonstrate that, in the face of a requirement to comply with a particular practice of reading to produce specific outcomes, at the same time the law enables the agents of legal practice to retain the capacity to produce a rich and contradictory set of different outcomes.

The case also illustrates the way that a dispute over one metaphor may generate other disputes. For example in the *Pharmaceutical Society* case in the first instance the battle over reading practices takes place in the context of the metaphorical reading of person; does person include both the natural and corporate person? However, this does not exhaust the dispute. The dispute shifts from one centred upon a direct reading of 'person' as metaphor to a more indirect analysis of the metaphorical potential of 'person' by way of a series of arguments centred upon other words in the legislation: 'examination', 'certification', and 'registration'. These words are rendered significant in the context of the dispute over 'person' as they are read metonymically; each specific requirement of the law is read as a reference to specific characteristics that inform the general word 'person'.

Lord Selborne LC provides an example of this line of argument (*Pharmaceutical Society* [1880] AC 857 at 863-4). In general he proceeds to read three different statutory requirements (registration, election and examination) as metonyms of the general juridical subject (person) of the legislation. All are read in a similar manner. Registration will be considered in more detail to illustrate the practice. Registration, he concluded, required the making of a claim by notice in writing, signed by the person. These observations seek to read 'registration' as a term that implies a physical practice.[28] As a metonym of the juridical subject it names that subject as one that must have an immediate physical presence; the natural legal subject. When conjoined to a reading of 'person' Lord Selborne's reading strategy produces 'person' as a reference to the natural legal subject and precludes the possibility of reading 'person' as a reference to the corporation. As such he precludes the possibility of reading person as metaphor. In turn this reading practice is applied to the other statutory professional requirements of election and examination. Together the reading practices deployed in these arguments deny the possibility of reading the general term of the legislation, 'person', as metaphor.[29]

The denial of metaphor also occurs at a more general level. Both Lord Selborne and Lord Blackburn seek to explain the restriction of metaphor by way of a distinction between on the one hand, legal language as the popular, ordinary, natural or common use of language and, on the other hand, legal language as the technical use of language. Within this binary scheme metaphor is associated not with the positive term, the natural use of language in law, but with the negative term, the unnatural use of language in law.

However, while this binary opposition takes the natural as the dominant (preferred) term this does not exhaust the matter as the binary retains the possibility of metaphor in law as a specialist or exceptional use of language. As such it retains the possibility of a metaphorical reading of 'person'. In this context legal practice is concerned with a search for authority to engage in this unnatural practice. For the judges in the *Pharmaceutical Society* case the justification for this unnatural practice is to be found not in judicial practice itself, which is thereby associated with the natural use of language, but outwith judicial practice. The authority must come from the legislation itself. More specifically, it depends upon the object and the policy of the Act. Legal practice then becomes a search for what was 'understood by the Legislature', for 'what the Legislature was thinking', or for 'what the Legislature was not thinking'. The judges explain that their search is for 'the intention of the statute', or for what the Act 'says', for what is 'upon the face of the Act' (*Pharmaceutical Society* [1880] AC 857 at 871).

At this point it might be useful to reflect more generally upon the nature of the legal practice that denies corporate capacity. It has interesting characteristics. Whilst it is a search for the authority to resort to the unnatural practice of metaphor it is always-already an unnatural practice of metaphor. Examples are to be found in the many references to the mind, the thoughts and the intention of the Legislature, the physiognomy of an absent, metaphysical thing.[30] This is particularly ironic in two respects. First the conclusion that the Act does not authorise the use of metaphor depends upon the use of metaphor. Secondly, at that moment in time when the judiciary are denying the juridical subjectivity of the corporation on the basis that '[t]he metaphysical entity ... the corporation, cannot possibly have competent knowledge' (*Pharmaceutical Society* [1880] AC 857 at 870), the judiciary are also declaring that '[t]he Legislature was not thinking of a corporation at that moment, but said in the preamble that henceforth ...' (*Pharmaceutical Society* [1880] AC 857 at 870). As such the denial of the possibility of the capacity of one metaphysical entity in law (the corporation) depends upon the attribute of comparable capacities to another metaphysical entity (the

Legislature). The judicial practice that polices the availability of metaphor and thereby limits the availability of juridical capacity to the corporation resorts to contradiction. The use of metaphor in law may depend upon the denial of its usage as a necessary aspect of legal practice and its displacement into the realms of the exceptional.

While the issue of corporate criminal capacity was not the direct object of concern in this case it did have some significance in the proceedings. In particular it appeared in the Court of Appeal in the judgment of Bramwell LJ (*Pharmaceutical Society* [1880] 5 QB 310 at 313–4, 315–6).[31] Having declared that as a general rule person may include corporation, Bramwell LJ introduced the word 'offence' to negate such a reading. First he noted that ss. 1 and 15 of the *Pharmacy Act* created a wrong and provided for its punishment. While any breaches of the Act were to be dealt with by the County Court, and as such were civil matters, the statute that dealt with the enforcement mechanisms used the language of criminal wrongs, 'offence' and 'offender', and the 'penalty' was at the disposition of the Crown. As such the statute talked about these wrongs as if they were criminal matters. Bramwell LJ resorts to the word 'offence' to read 'person'. More specifically he noted that an offence required *mens rea*. Only human subjects, he concluded, were capable of such a state of mind and therefore only the natural legal subject had the capacity to commit offences. Therefore the subject of the legislation, 'person', must refer to the natural legal subject and thereby excluded the corporation.

Again the argument has interesting characteristics. For example, the enforcement of the breach of the statute through the civil courts draws attention to the fact that in the statute 'offence' is not used as a reference to a criminal wrong (which might be described as a literal use of the term). In its use in a civil context 'offence' is used metaphorically. Bramwell LJ's resort to the term exploits this metaphorical use of 'offence'. However, in the act of exploiting this metaphorical usage and extending it by way of a reference to *mens rea*, Bramwell LJ seeks to deny the use of metaphor and seeks to exploit its literal meaning. As such he resorts to 'offence' as a mere reference to the criminal law (its literal meaning). Likewise the emphasis on *mens rea* and the mind are invoked as references to the specific requirements of criminal law. They have significance as they are taken as signs of the specific subject of criminal law which seems to require an immediate physical presence that is peculiar to the natural legal subject. As such *mens rea* and the mind are presented in order to deny the operation of 'offence' as metaphor. Through the use and denial of metaphor Bramwell LJ seeks to deny a metaphorical reading of 'person' and thereby confirm the disqualification of the corporate subject.

The judgments of the *Pharmaceutical Society* case demonstrate that in the past while *Interpretation Acts* might have attempted to enact the extension of corporate criminal capacity they also enacted a certain ambivalence towards that objective. This ambivalence had particular significance. It created a space within law whereby legal practice might be used to both expand corporate capacity and to further restrict its development. One effect of the first legislative initiative appears to have been that it created the opportunity for the judiciary to reaffirm the criminal incapacity of the corporate legal subject.[32] In the next section I go on to consider the articulation of such incapacity with the formal doctrine of *mens rea*.

The Corporate Mind

The most recent debates around corporate criminal capacity and *mens rea* arising out of the P&O ferry disaster have drawn attention to the difficulties that the judiciary have had in imagining a corporate criminal mind. However, while the difficulties associated with the attribution of *mens rea* to the corporation might suggest that the mind of the corporation was beyond the anthropomorphic imagination of the judiciary, such a conclusion would not be correct. The history of the Common Law in England demonstrates a certain ambivalence with regard to the question of the mind of the corporation.

Prior to Bramwell LJ's observations in 1880 the English judiciary had already demonstrated a capacity to invent the corporate mind. The issue of the corporate mind had been addressed not in the criminal law but in the context of civil law. It arose specifically in actions against incorporated companies for malicious libel, malicious prosecution, and malicious obstruction. In all of these civil wrongs malice was taken to refer to a specific state of mind. Those against liability argued that the absent and invisible corporation did not have a mind. A person without a mind was incapable of malice and could not be sued for such wrongs.[33] The judiciary rejected such arguments and through the production of a corporate mind imposed civil liability upon the corporation. These outcomes were achieved in various ways. One response is demonstrated in *Whitfield v South Eastern Railway Co.* ((1858) EL BL and EL 115) where an action of malicious libel[34] was brought against the corporation. The court was able to establish corporate liability by means of a particular strategy of interpretation. It took the form of a distinction between substance and form; between malice in fact and malice in law. The court concluded that the wrong was concerned not with malice in fact but malice in law. Liability might arise in the latter case where the defendant was proved to have complied with certain formal requirements; malice in law was established when the defendant was shown to have merely ordered publication of the libel. Beyond this, specific evidence of motive and thereby the mind was not required. When applied to a corporation malice might be proved by evidence of publication. Thus the mind of the corporation might be produced as an effect of a particular reading of a legal rule creating the wrong. Through this limited enquiry liability was imposed upon both the natural and the corporate legal subject.[35]

The judiciary responded in a slightly different way to the issue of the corporate mind the following year. In *Green v London General Omnibus Co.* ((1859) 7 C.B. (N.S.) 289) an action was brought against the company for wrongfully and maliciously obstructing the plaintiff in his business. It was alleged that the defendant used its omnibuses to obstruct the omnibuses driven by the servants of the plaintiff, and hindered, threatened and prevented persons from becoming passengers of the plaintiff. Again the legal argument was primarily concerned with the ability of the corporation to be malicious. In this case the resolution of the riddle of the mind of the corporation focused not so much upon the statutory language but upon the identity of the subject that performed the action. Was the subject of the action merely the human subject, (the servant), or was the act of the human subject the act of another (absent) subject, the corporation?

In responding to this issue the court looked to the purpose of the action. They concluded that the actions complained of were all connected with driving vehicles and that these actions related to the objects of the company; the company was incorporated for the purpose of driving vehicles, as specified in its constitutional documents (the memorandum of association). As all of the actions were done within the scope and objects of the company, the subject of the acts, even though performed by the servants of the defendant, was the company. Therefore liability could fall on the shoulders of the company.

The company was presenced in the acts of its servants by virtue of the fact that the servant's act fell within the objects of the company. Here the rules of agency, developed in the context of two human subjects with the attributes of full presence (master and servant), take on a metaphorical dimension in their application to an analogous situation — the relationship between a corporate (absent) master and the human servant. This use of the agency rule has further significance. Not only was the mere presence of the corporation evidenced through the act of the individual. As Erle J. noted, 'an action for a wrong will lie against a corporation, where the thing that is complained of is a thing done within the scope of their incorporation, and is one which would constitute an actionable wrong *if committed by an individual'* (*Green* at 303).[36] When applied in the context of malice all those qualities and characteristics attributable to the natural person (both as a state of mind and as a physical act) might, through agency, become characteristics (the mind and act) of the corporation. As such this development might allow the corporation, when presenced in the human subject, to take on all of the characteristics associated with the act of the human individual concerned.

The approach to the corporate mind developed in this case resorts to both metaphor and metonymy. Metaphor is at work in the application of the agency rule to a new context; to corporate masters. Metonymy is at work in the production of the act of the servant as the act of the corporation. Here one human subject connected with the company stands for the whole corporate subject. Furthermore through metonymy the characteristics that the law attributes to that natural legal subject are read as the attributes of the corporate legal subject.[37]

The production of presence by way of the mind of the corporation led the court to the conclusion that the corporation was liable for the intentional acts of misfeasance of its servants, provided they were sufficiently connected with the scope and objects of incorporation. However, it is important to note that these developments did not produce uniform effects in law nor did they remain unchallenged in the specific context in which they were originally formulated. For example Lord Selborne in the House of Lords considered the legal relationship between master and servant (rule of agency), and the corporate mind in *Holdsworth v City of Glasgow Bank Liquidator* ([1880] 5 AC 317 at 328). While he accepted the application of the rule of agency to corporations (that the master was liable in civil law for the acts of the servant, the agent), this did not, in the context of wrongs involving deceit or malice, necessarily lead to the conclusion that the mind of the servant was taken to be the mind of the corporation. A more serious challenge to this development of a corporate mind is to be found in *Abrath v North Eastern Railway Co.* ([1886] 11 AC 247). Lord Bramwell, in addressing the question of malice, took the opportunity to condemn the jurisprudence dealing with the mind of the corporation. He declared:

> I take this opportunity of saying as directly and peremptorily as I possibly can; and I think the reasoning is demonstrative. To maintain an action for a malicious prosecution it must be shown that there was an absence of reasonable and probable cause, and that there was malice or some indirect and illegitimate motive in the prosecutor. A corporation is incapable of malice or of motive.
>
> (*Abrath v North Eastern Railway Co.* at 251)[38]

For Lord Bramwell the legal practice that purported to erect in law a corporation without a mind was the end of the matter and as such beyond judicial modification, substitution or abandonment. The novelty, justified in *Green v London General Omnibus Co.* by the exigencies of modern times (*Green* at 833) and the need to submit incorporated companies to the rigour of the law where they had intentionally done a wrongful act, was condemned by Lord Bramwell as no more than naked opportunism:

> [E]very one, or every counsel and solicitor listening to me, knows that the only reason why a railway company is selected for an action of this sort is that a jury would be more likely to give a verdict against a company than against an individual.
> (*Abrath v North Eastern Railway Co.* at 252)

Lord Bramwell's judgment attempted to deny the legitimacy of these practices and to repress their possibility.

Not only did these arguments have a difficult passage in the context of civil capacity, they had little contemporary currency within the realms of criminal legal practice. Not only did Lord Bramwell personify a certain judicial hostility to the mind of the corporation in a civil context but as has already been noted he also personified direct judicial hostility to the corporate mind in a criminal context. When sitting in the Court of Appeal in *The Pharmaceutical Society* case he denied the possibility of corporate *mens rea*. Various additional factors worked to prohibit the spread of these civil law practices to the criminal law. First, in criminal law, the rule of agency, whereby the master might be responsible for the acts of the servant, in general did not apply (L.H. Leigh, 1982; Holmes, 1891; Wigmore, 1894; Sayre, 1930). Secondly, while it might be possible to argue that a corporation might have capacity and therefore be liable for civil wrongs done in connection with the lawful objects of a company, it was argued that the corporation had neither capacity nor competence to perform acts that might give rise to criminal liability (Goodhart, 1925; Warren, 1925; L.H. Leigh, 1969, ch. 2). In order to understand how these difficulties were overcome it is necessary to return to developments within the context of civil capacity.

The seeds of the criminal mind of the corporation developed out of changes in the legal practice relating to the metaphor of master and servant in a civil law context. In order for these civil law developments to be applicable in a criminal context the agency relationship had to disappear. Perhaps the clearest example of this development within the context of civil capacity is to be found in the judgment of Lord Haldane in *Lennards Carrying Co. Ltd v*

Asiatic Petroleum Co. Ltd ([1915] AC 705). He observed that:

> a corporation is an abstraction. It has no mind of its own; its active and directing will must consequently be sought in the person of somebody who for some purpose may be called an agent *but who is really the directing mind and will of the corporation, the very ego and centre of the personality of the corporation...*
> (*Lennards Carrying Co. Ltd* at 713)[39]

The technique Viscount Haldane demonstrates here has particularly interesting characteristics. First, he resorts to a metaphorical reading of the agency rule to represent the link between the corporation and a natural legal subject. Thereafter he transcends the agency relationship. The human subject becomes the ego of the corporation; the corporate conscious, the corporate thinking subject, the corporate juridical 'I' (*The Compact Oxford Dictionary*, 1991).[40] As such the natural legal subject in itself disappears in order to reappear as the corporate legal subject personified. Thus the mind of the human subject becomes the mind of the corporation. Agency disappears through the emphasis on metonymy; the individual (as the part) is read as the whole, the corporation. This produces important effects. The separate entity of the servant disappears. Viscount Haldane notes this transformation when he points to the inadequacy of the term 'agent'. Out of the device of agency the law has invented a new relationship where only the corporation exists.

Evidence of the use of this practice in a criminal context follows in *DPP v Kent & Sussex Contractors Ltd* ([1944] 1 KB 146). Having asserted that there was no direct precedent in favour of criminal capacity Viscount Caldecote CJ noted that:

> although the directors or general manager of a company are its agents, they are something more. A company is incapable of acting or speaking even of thinking except in so far as its officers have acted, spoken or thought ... it is *unnecessary*, in my view, to inquire whether it is proved that the company's officers acted *on its behalf*. The officers *are* the company for this purpose.
> (*DPP v Kent & Sussex Contractors* at 155)[41]

A more recent example is to be found in the case of *Tesco Supermarkets Ltd v Nattrass* ([1972] AC 153) where Lord Reid observed that:

> [a] living person has a mind which can have knowledge or intention or be negligent and he has hands to carry out his intentions. A corporation has none of these: it

must act through living persons, though not always one or the same person. Then the person who acts is not speaking or acting for the company. He is acting as the company and his mind which directs his acts is the mind of the company. There is no question of the company being vicariously liable. He is not acting as a servant representative, agent or delegate. He is an embodiment of the company, or one could say, he hears and speaks through the person of the company, within his appropriate sphere and his mind is the mind of the company. If it is a guilty mind then that guilt is the guilt of the company. It must be a question of law whether, once the facts have been ascertained, a person in doing particular things is to be regarded as the company or merely as the company's servant or agent. (*Tesco v Nattrass* at 170D)

In this extended analysis of the development of the corporate mind Lord Reid demonstrated the nature of the legal practice that produces the presence of the corporate subject in the natural subject. Not only is it a reading of the natural subject as a metonym of the corporate subject but it is a reading of the natural subject as a metaphor of corporate capacity.

The success of this line of development was demonstrated in the more recent case of *P&O European Ferries (Dover) Ltd* ((1991) 93 Cr App R 72). Charting the development of corporate criminal capacity in general and the invention of the corporate mind in both civil and criminal law in particular, Turner J was able to declare that 'there is no conceptual difficulty in attributing a criminal state of mind to a corporation' (*P&O European Ferries* at 73). He concluded that 'where a corporation through the controlling mind of one of its agents, does an act which fulfils the prerequisites of the crime of manslaughter, it is properly indictable for the crime of manslaughter' (*P&O European Ferries* at 84). However, the application of this conclusion to the corporation and the events in question was far from unproblematic. In particular the sinking of the ferry was the outcome of a multiplicity of decisions and actions performed by several individuals within the context of a complex hierarchical bureaucracy. In applying the anthropomorphic metonyms and metaphors of corporate capacity to this situation Turner J concluded that corporate liability might arise where 'a person who is the embodiment of a corporation and acting for the purposes of the corporation is doing the act or omission which caused the death ...' (*P&O European Ferries* at 89). This conclusion was one of the factors that brought the proceedings to a premature close. It proved to be impossible in the context of a large and complex bureaucracy to embody in one individual both the mind function and the hand function of the corporation.

This failure has interesting characteristics. In particular it is a failure that suggests that at least the judge and the lawyers for the prosecution misunderstood the nature of the legal practice that made corporate liability possible. The conclusion that the hand and mind come together in the same individual is to read embodiment as a reference to those characteristics of the natural legal subject, rather than to read embodiment as a metaphor of the subject. As such it misrecognises a fundamental characteristic of the legal practice that creates corporate capacity.

Conclusion

This essay has been concerned with the development of an analysis of a set of juristic practices. These practices have a particular importance as they have been the medium through which a particular set of agents of the law — legal academic writers, practitioners and the judges — have responded to questions of corporate accountability and responsibility within the context of a domain of the law that continues to play a central role in the production of social order. It is trite to observe that in this respect the common law has developed on a case by case basis.[42] The concern of this essay has been to take a closer look at the nature of the legal practices that inform this hesitant process of change.

In general this legal practice is a practice of rule making and a practice of reading the law that takes place in a specific context; the point where the unthinkable and the unnameable is constituted as a viable subject in law. Juristic practices occupy the gap that separate the unintelligible from the intelligible in law. As such they are concerned not only with the production of the corporate person as a legal subject through a certain intelligibility of presence in the law, but they are also concerned with the production of the unintelligibility of the corporation as a legal subject, as absence in law. Here subjectification is partial, contingent, inconsistent and contradictory. Here subjectification is shown to be an effect rather than a cause. Finally, it is a practice that often operates in ignorance of itself, frequently misrecognises itself and regularly seeks to deny the nature of the practice.

Notes

1. Special thanks are due to Peter Rush who initially promoted my interest in this particular domain of criminal law. His unflagging and tenacious commentary on the various drafts has been an essential part of the gestation of this essay. Thanks are also due to Michael Salter, Piyel Haldar, Marinos Diamantidis and Elena Loizidou for their patience, support and insights all of which have enriched the analysis.
2. See also Blom-Cooper, 1990; Field and Jorg, 1991; Kelly, 1991; McIntosh, 1991; and Zander, 1990.
3. For more recent examples see Box, 1983; and Bernard, 1984. The most thorough

analysis of corporate criminal capacity to be conducted within recent English scholarship is L.H. Leigh, 1969. Celia Wells has recently drawn attention to the impoverishment of English legal writing on the corporation. With a few notable exceptions (Hart, 1954; Ireland et al., 1987; and more recently, Norrie, 1993) there is little recent writing within English academic scholarship that attempts to theorise the jurisprudence of corporate personality. In part this essay is an attempt to respond to this impoverishment. Cf Wells, 1988, 85. In the United States there is much recent work that seeks to develop a critical analysis of the corporation. For example see Hager, 1989; Horowitz, 1985; Millon, 1990; Schane, 1987; and Winter, 1989.

4.   The claim that only the members might be the object of the criminal law's concern is perhaps too simplistic. Liability might also fall upon the officers of the company, though as natural legal subjects and not as agents of or as the personification of the corporation. For example see *R v Medley*, where an action was brought, 'against the chairman, deputy chairman and others of the board of directors as several persons employed by them ...' (*R v Medley* (1834) 6 Car. & P. 292 at 292). In addition the Common Law recognised the possibility of corporate criminal liability of municipal corporations. For a general discussion on the point see L.H. Leigh, 1969, especially ch. 2.

5.   While a corporation could not appear in person before the Assize Court an action might proceed by way of certiorari. The matter would then be dealt with by the High Court. In that court a corporation could plead by attorney. See *R v Birmingham and Gloucester Railway* [1842] 3 QB 222 at 222–3.

6.   For a more recent example of disqualification based upon the impossibility of the offence, see *R v Cory Brothers & Co. Ltd* [1927] 1 KB 810.

7.   Also *R v HM Coroner for East Kent, ex parte Spooner and Others, R v HM Coroner for East Kent, ex parte De Rohan and another* (1989) 88 Cr App R 10. The collapse of the trial appears to have arisen due to a number of factors. In addition to those specifically relating to the legal capacity of the corporate person which are the object of consideration in this paper, there was a separate but related problem dealing with the components of the substantive requirement of the concept of gross negligence and its application to the corporate entity. See also Department of Transport, 1987.

8.   '[A] person who is the embodiment of a corporation and acting for the purposes of the corporation is doing the act or omission which caused the death, the corporation as well as the person may also be found guilty of **manslaughter**' (*P&O European Ferries (Dover) Ltd* (1991) Cr App R 72 at 88–9, per Turner J). **For an analysis** of the decision, see Moran, 1992.

9.   For example see Bergman, 1990; Hargreaves, 1991; P. Allen, 1992; and Slapper, 1992.

10.   For example see Brown and Rankin, 1990; Snider, 1991; Fisse, 1983; and Kraakman, 1984.

11.   On metaphor and the corporation see Millon, 1990. On anthropomorphism and the corporation see Carr, 1905, ch. 10.

12.   For example see *Harman v Tappenden* (1801) 1 East 555; *Yarborough v Bank of England* (1812) 16 East 6; *Murray v East India Co.* (1821) 5 B. Ald. 204; *Maund v Monmouthshire Canal Co.* (1842) 4 Man. & G. 453; *Eastern Counties Railway Co. v Broom* (1851) 6 Ex. 314; and *Stevens v Midland Railway Co. & Lander* (1854) 10 Ex. 352.

13.   For example a corporation cannot be an executor, administrator or trustee (Blackstone, 1979, vol. 1, 464).

14.   Blackstone echoes comments made by Sir Edward Coke in *The Case of Sutton's Hospital* 10 Co. Rep. 23 at 32b.

15.   The reference to Coke is to his comments in *The Case of Sutton's Hospital* 10 Co. Rep. 23a at 28b.

16.   The place of metaphor and anthropomorphism within law is discussed in Douzinas et al., 1991.

17.   For another example of this metonymy/metaphor in operation see *Church v Imperial Gas, Light & Coke Co.* (1838) 6 AD & E 845. While the requirement of the corporate seal resolved problems of presence in a contractual context, this did not exclude the possibility of controversy. This arose in the context of simple contracts. See *Tilson v Town of Warwick Gas Light Co.* (1825) 4 B. & C. 962; *Beverley v Lincoln Gas Light & Coke Co.* (1837) 6 AD & E 829; and *Church v Imperial Gas Light & Coke Co.* The seal also had significance for questions of capacity in tort. See for example *Smith v Birmingham & Staffordshire Gas Light Co.* (1834) 1 AD & E 527.

18.   The application of the rule that requires the imprint of a seal developed in the context of relations of two natural legal subjects and was transferred to a corporate context, where at least one of the parties is an artificial legal subject. The application itself might be a reading of the rule by way of metaphor.

19.   While metaphor brings the individual and the association of persons together as a body, the language that is used to refer to that body marks that body as both the same as but separate from the body natural: body politic, body corporate, corporation aggregate. It is important to note that the binary relation between the body natural and the body politic is always a violent hierarchy in which the body natural is the preferred term. The hierarchy is imprinted on all binary forms relating to these two bodies. See Moran, 1992.

20.   The production of corporate presence by way of a name has significance beyond contractual capacity. Through the name, other powers, rights, and duties might be ascribed to the corporate subject as an individual in itself, separate and apart from the several natural persons that come together to form the corporation. See Blackstone, 1979, vol. 1, 462–3.

21.   The criminal capacity of statutory corporations tends to be found in the context of those corporations that fulfil a quasi-public role, for example municipal corporations — for example *R v The Mayor etc of Liverpool* (1802) 3 East 86 and *R v The Mayor, Alderman and Burgess of the Borough of Stratford-upon-Avon*, (1811) 14 East 348 — and utilities corporations as in the example of *R v Birmingham & Gloucester Railway* [1842] 3 QB 222.

22.   For examples, see L.H. Leigh, 1969, 20–1.

23.   For example see *R v The Mayor etc of the City of Liverpool* (1802) 3 East 86 and *R v The Mayor etc of Stratford-upon-Avon* (1811) 14 East 348. Other arguments presented on behalf of the prosecution noted the availability of the procedure of certiorari that would enable the courts to circumvent some of the procedural obstacles that might preclude the possibility of criminal proceedings.

24.   In addition Lord Denman CJ in support of liability argued that it was not always possible to decide whether the wrong was the cause of an act or an omission. It would be wrong, he concluded, to exclude liability by way of technical rules which would merely add to the complexity of the law (*R v Great North of England Railway Co.* (1846) 9 QB 316 at 325–6).

25.   The argument here is similar to the relationship between nonfeasance and misfeasance, a relationship between particular and general.

26.   A second Parliamentary intervention relating to the general criminal capacity of corporations is to be found in the 1889 *Interpretation Act* (52 & 53 Vict. c. 63) which declares that with respect to penal provisions 'the expression "person" shall, unless the contrary intention appears, include a body corporate' (s. 2). This section has now been superceded by the *Interpretation Act* 1978. This Act consolidates the Act of 1889 with other subsequent *Interpretation Acts*. Section 5, Schedule 1, declares that 'person' includes a body of persons corporate or unincorporate. Schedule 24 (6)

declares that the definition of a 'person', so far as it includes bodies corporate, applies to any provision of an Act whenever passed relating to an offence punishable on indictment or on summary conviction. As the Act of 1978 merely consolidates the earlier legislation it is to be assumed that the caveat, 'unless the contrary intention appears' still applies.

27.   In the House of Lords, Lord Selbourne LC and Lord Blackwell adopted a slightly different approach. Greater emphasis was placed upon the existence of a settled general rule that 'person' included not only the natural individual but also the corporate subject. However both concluded that the corporation was not to be subject to the terms of sections 1 and 15 of the *Pharmacy Act*. They arrived at this conclusion on the basis that the Act itself specifically excluded the possibility of its application to a corporation.

28.   This ought to be contrasted with the earlier discussion of Blackstone's metaphor of the seal as sign of the corporation. There the metaphor was read as a symbol of presence. Here, with 'registration', the metaphor is read literally or 'technically'.

29.   This particular practice of reading is repeated in the context of election and examination. In proceeding with the various examples the legal argument produces a series of resemblances; between registration and election, between election and examination. Thereby one instance functions as a metaphor of the other. All function as metonomys of general capacity.

30.   In their application to language natural/unnatural are already operating as metaphors.

31.   See Lord Blackburn's comments on criminal capacity (*Pharmaceutical Society v London & Provincial Supply Assn Ltd* (1880) 5 AC 857 at 869–70).

32.   As 'person' is a general term of art in legislation creating criminal wrongs the case had general significance. In addition the case retained a certain currency after the second *Interpretation Act* of 1889 (52 & 53 Vict. c. 63). See *Perkes v Ward* [1902] 2 KB 1, and *DPP v Kent and Sussex Contractors* [1944] 1 KB 146.

33.   For example see *Green v London General Omnibus Co.* (1859) 7 C.B. (N.S.) 289 at 294.

34.   Libel was one exception to the general rule of criminal incapacity.

35.   In giving judgment Lord Campbell CJ went further. Drawing attention to the then recent cases of *R v Birmingham and Gloucester Railway* [1842] 3 QB 222, and *R v Great North of England Railway* (1846) 9 QB 316, he suggested that as a corporation had been found to be capable of and criminally liable for an act of omission and an act of commission these decisions might be interpreted as supporting a general conclusion that a corporation was capable of malice in fact or express malice.

36.   Emphasis added.

37.   See also *Barwick v English Joint Stock Bank* (1867) 2 Exch. 259 and *Holdsworth v City of Glasgow Bank Liquidator* [1880] 5 AC 317. The different arguments producing the mind of the corporation in the context of civil law in these cases were not necessarily used in isolation but were also used in conjunction with each other. For example, see *Edwards v Midland Railway Co.* [1880] 6 QBD 287.

38.   Cf Lord Fitzgerald at 255.

39.   Emphasis added.

40.   Academic commentaries upon this development persistently misread *ego* as *alter ego*. For example see Wells, 1993. Alter ego suggests a second self, an agent, or a representative. Lord Haldane's innovation suggests ego rather than a second self. A consequence of this misreading of Lord Haldane's innovation is the suggestion that Lord Reid's exposition of the corporate mind differs from that of Lord Haldane. This conclusion is wrong. There is no difference between what has been misnamed the alter ego doctrine and the identification doctrine.

41.   For direct discussion of the interface between tortious and criminal liability, see at 157.

42.   For example see *P&O European Ferries (Dover) Ltd* (1991) 93 Cr App R 72 at 84, per Turner J, and Bernard, 1984.

8 Cutting Our Losses: Criminal Legal Doctrine

SHAUN MCVEIGH AND PETER RUSH

To common apprehension, the laws of inheritance are absolutely unrelated to the criminal law, yet, in fact, they repose upon it. Thus the law is that the eldest son is heir-at-law to his father.
(J.F. Stephen, 1863, 1)

*All law
criminal in
one sense*

(J.F. Stephen, 1863, 1)

That a text can have several interpretations is warning enough that there is violence dwelling in the house.　(Jabes, 1993, 42)

How is doctrine currently represented? In many respects, our modern understanding of doctrine is perceived as being in trouble; its status and aspirations, its topics and its promises, are seemingly besieged on all sides by legal practitioners, sociologists, economists, philosophers, not to mention all those others who are uncomfortable with the disciplinary boundaries of the legal academy.[1] The prospect of a legal science no longer seems capable of admiration, let alone affords consolation. Reason and its substitutes seem incapable (if they ever were) of supplying foundational principles. The possibility that legal doctrine could be understood as a social science seems attractive only to the extent that social science shares in the same problem of order and location. The quest for a language that both encompasses its subject matter, directs its action and performs as an organiser of facts, is precisely a staging of a juridical order of social science (van de Kerchove and Ost, 1994).[2] Even the common law tradition of experience has declined in the presence of a technological reason which has excluded experience itself from thought, splitting knowledge from understanding (Murphy, 1991). Such a story of broken promises, failed foundations, lost experiences, shattered dreams, has a certain symbolic burden on our imaginations. Yet to characterise this situation in *solely* negative terms somewhat begs the question of the nature of the dreams, promises, foundations — in short, the nature of doctrine as the subject of law. It is thus necessary to begin by reconstructing the promise or dream of criminal legal doctrine.

Before exchanging the masks of doctrine, we return albeit briefly to the conventional teaching of crime and law. Typically, attempts to understand criminal law proceed through either a philosophical or socio-historical reconstruction of the normative order that is and should be law. On one side, and perhaps the more philosophical and jurisprudential, this has required providing and finding a logic internal to law, a reason or logic that is properly legal. On another side, and perhaps the more philosophical and socio-legal (and apparently more historical), the reconstruction of a normative order has demanded that doctrine provides and finds a logic external to law, a logic of social action and a law which is subordinate to a socio-logic. Representing doctrine in this way is not without its problems. The subject of law is delivered as moral responsibility and/or social action. What is lost in this mode of representation is precisely the subject of law as a mode of representation — namely, the dogmatic tradition with its emphasis on the transmission of the inherited truths of law, and the knowledge of the particular forms of legal reason and action (Goodrich, 1990, ch. 8). Doctrine is excluded as the unnecessary disorder of practice, as the delirium of judgment. Nevertheless, doctrine reappears. In the socio-legal reconstruction, it reappears as nothing more or less than an obstacle in the way of the realisation of good government and plain-speaking. Largely irrelevant, we should stop getting mired in the labyrinthine and reified structures of doctrine. On the other side, doctrine does not fare much better at the hands of the philosophers. While not banished as an obstacle, as somehow being in the way of the real business of law, doctrine is here reduced to little more than a practice on the way to reason, justice and law. Not quite legal, the teachings of the tradition need to be brought to book, to reason, to coherence, to a systematic arrangement. The problem it seems is whether doctrine does or can ever measure up to the requirements of a logic of reason; what is demanded of doctrine is that it become fully legal, fully rational. On either side, then doctrinal order would appear to have been misplaced.

It is tempting to frame this question of loss in relation to a more general demise of ethics and law. In this context two types of explanation have typically been put forward. One is that the loss can be sited and cited in history, and thus we are now living in the aftermath of a disaster. What has been lost in time is the prudence and practice of the tradition, the common law way of life, the common law way of doing things (MacIntyre, 1985; Simmonds, 1984).[3] This account points to the institutional loss of doctrinal argument as a part of legal science and practical reason. A second explanation points to the ethico-political direction and sees the loss as framed from within philosophy. Here, the lack is formulated in terms of a crisis of reason, the irremediable redemption of law and morality, reason and emotion, and form and substance. In the absence of continued attention to the effects of these antinomies, jurisprudence and substantive law are condemned to an oscillation between a *petit* metaphysics of legal order and an unbounded decisionism of the will (G. Rose, 1984, ch. 1; Rush, forthcoming, ch. 1; Dalton, 1985). On this account, questions of the authority of posited laws, the implication of the juridical (descriptive) and the litigious (prescriptive) in law, and the question of the authorship of law cannot be overcome exclusively in terms of knowledge or by resort to action (Douzinas and Warrington, 1994, ch. 4). They remain the irremediable condition of modern thought.[4]

Of course such arguments have not entered the academic domain uncontested. However, they do delineate some of the questions that legal doctrine has been called to answer. Historically it might be thought that failure to respond to these questions has led to the demise of doctrinal thought and a turn to a jurisprudence that simply states that such questions are inappropriate as questions of law. In ethico-political terms it might be thought that the suppression of the doctrinal nature of law is another sort of response — one whose consequences are far from clear.

Such a diagnosis of the conditions of social existence would be the basic precondition of a critique of substantive criminal law. Such a critique would follow those social conditions into law, and indicate the consequences for legal thought. In doing so, the critique responds to two fundamental questions — the question of the transmission and teaching of the social order (in the name of law, justice, the good, or some other honorific); and the question of the genealogical order of law. With differing emphases the essays in this collection have been concerned not so much with the apparent inability of legal doctrine to deliver on the promise that it makes; they are concerned that legal doctrine delivers the lesson of law and its order all-too-well. While we are sympathetic to (and hence inevitably share) such a critique, this book is not only concerned with pursuing a critique of substantive criminal law. The question of doctrine (and its possible loss) is also a question of the modes of representation of law. This question cannot be bypassed, at least not without repressing the workplace of doctrine. Here we turn to investigate the grounds and structures of the representation of law.

In proleptic terms, we will argue that it is still possible to imagine an interiority of law — or at least an enfolded surface — without losing either doctrine or law. Rather than being lost or found once and for all, this folding can only be experienced as interiority second time round. If doctrine is the subject of law, it has a flickering existence. As one aspect of the representation of law, doctrine offers up a view of existing law, of law as already existing in place and in order. Here all the instances of the law are reflected back into themselves to form an image, and specifically an image in which an ideal law appears for us. In recent decades, this extant system and its ideal law has appeared somewhat tarnished by the spate of miscarriages of justice and of extended public protest. Such episodes remind us that the legal system and its specular mirror is beset both by a necessary force and a loss of faith in the ideal it reflects. In saying this, however, it must not be forgotten that the specular mirror of law has an underside, a tain or silver-backing. As a matter of *re*imagining criminal law, doctrine reflects a somewhat different order of images. It is not so much an ideal order of reification or abstraction, but rather a structural and unconscious order. In this other arena, doctrine would have as its concern the processes — or more properly, structures — of identification. In particular, it would be concerned with how we identify and identify with the laws from where we look at ourselves; with how we construct the places from where we receive the message of our law and assume our inheritance. In other words, this other arena of doctrine returns us, once again, to the jurisdiction of law: its sites of enunciation and its transmission, its parts of speech and its reproduction. In this context, doctrine forms a part of the many signifying systems in which (criminal) legal doctrine cannot but take part.[5] In summary terms, the return to doctrine here is a return to a different order of images so as to calculate the possibilities of reimagining law otherwise. In more modest terms, our proposal is to return the question of jurisdiction to the question of the form and idiom of legal doctrine.

Margins

Part of the uncertain status of the doctrinal aspects of law lies precisely in locating the position that doctrine will have to have taken in order to propose the nature of juridical existence as a question of law. Rather than take the image of doctrine as simply a transparent image, we take it as a structure that has misrecognised itself and its other. This requires a reconsideration of the mechanics of projecting such an image or, in traditional terms, a reconsideration of the general elements of the dogmatic order; a reading of the terms of institution, judgment, and address.

Questions of institution are the most common feature of dogmatic thought.

It establishes, or grounds, the meaning of law through creating the grammar or classificatory order of legal actions. Institutional questions can be characterised as answering issues of law in terms of a logic of legal life.[16] Judgment involves law in the task of discrimination or differentiation through history. Judgment as discrimination is here turned not to the founding of law as such, but to governing the propriety of decision through rhetoric and hermeneutics. The troubled relations between questions of institution and judgment are of course the familiar staple of dispute within the schools of jurisprudence. Less familiar, although no less obvious, is the sense that these disputes also effect the image of legal doctrine, and not only the reflected or ideal order of law. Finally, it can be noted that the claim of legal judgment is to establish the appropriate differences within law in the name of doctrine and justice. The third term, address, is less noted today as a characteristic feature of criminal legal doctrine. In part, this is because address is normally assigned the role of setting the scene; address functions as the framing term of doctrine. The knowledge of address is primarily procedural. Address acts as the procedure through which criminal law as doctrine is transmitted. Characteristically this procedure is enacted or represented in terms of a process of questioning or interrogation. Most importantly, questions of address act as the destination of doctrine; a question of address stands in for the end or final judgment of criminal legal scholarship.

To elaborate how these formal aspects of criminal law are currently understood, it is necessary to turn to the judgments of criminal law. Consider *R v Hancock & another* ([1986] 1 All ER 641).[7] The case report contains two judgments: first, the judgment of Lord Lane for the Court of Appeal and, second, the judgment of Lord Scarman for the House of Lords. Two 'miners on strike' were held responsible for the death of a taxi driver whose passenger was a 'miner going to work' (*Hancock* at 647). Hancock and Shankland had accepted that they were guilty of manslaughter, but the Crown was unsatisfied and had insisted on pursuing a murder prosecution. They were convicted of murder by a majority verdict after a trial 'lasting eight working days'. On appeal, the Court of Appeal substituted the verdict of manslaughter and imposed sentences of eight years imprisonment (*Hancock* at 642). The Crown appealed to the House of Lords, where the appeal was dismissed. One obvious context for these judgments is thus the policing of the miner's strike and the more generalised destruction of unions throughout the 1980s. Nevertheless, the report of the judgments is also one in a long and labyrinthine line of reports on the juridical definition of intention and, specifically, indirect or oblique intention. Commentary on these case reports has been extensive. It has largely been concerned to annotate the definition of intention in terms of a series of conjunctions — whether distinctions, oppositions or analogies — between intention and desire, presumption and inference, law and evidence, law and politics, legality and morality. What we find remarkable however is that the judgments and their exegesis dissolve the definition of intention into a problem of the administration of justice. At the same time, this problem of administration is resolved into three issues: the hierarchical relation between trial judge and jury, the relation of submission and obligation between lower and higher courts, and the legitimacy of the modes of serious social speech. Thus, in *R v Moloney* ([1985] 1 All ER 1025), Lord Bridge frames his definition of intention as a direction to the jury. In the interests of having directions which are 'clear to judges and intelligible to juries', Lord Bridge formulates the prohibition on and disavowal of defining intention in normal cases:

> The golden rule should be that, when directing a jury on the mental element necessary in a crime of specific intent, the judge should avoid any elaboration or paraphrase of what is meant by intent, and leave it to the jury's good sense to decide whether the accused acted with the necessary intent, unless the judge is convinced that, on the facts and having regard to the way in which the case has been presented to the jury in evidence and argument, some further explanation or elaboration is strictly necessary to avoid misunderstanding.
>
> (*Moloney* at 1032, 1036–7)[8]

Similarly, Lord Hailsham expresses:

> the pious hope that your Lordships will not again have to decide that foresight and foreseeability are not the same thing as intention although either may give rise to an irresistible inference of such, and that matters which are essentially to be treated as matters of inference for a jury as to a subjective state of mind will not once again be erected into a legal presumption. They should remain what they always should have been, part of the law of evidence and inference to be left to the jury after a proper direction as to their weight, and not part of the substantive law.
>
> (*Moloney* at 1027)

In short, the definition of intention as an administrative problem of criminal law is *framed* in terms of the complex of address, judgment and institution. It is through this complex that the criminal law of intention gets off the ground. And yet, this frame is taken as read, as already established and present. The question of instituting, addressing and judging intention is presented *as if* it were prefatory to the main problems. Lord Scarman is in this respect exemplary. At the outset of his judgment in *Hancock*, he takes time out to frame his response to the certified question of law. These remarks extend for two pages (in an eleven page report, four of which are reporting the judgment of the Court of Appeal) and concern directions to the jury, directions to the lower courts, and directions to the public (*R v Hancock* [1986] 1 All ER 641 at 646–7).[9] Only after this excursus does the judgment settle into a discourse on intention; it is only after two pages that the 'facts' and the 'logic' of intention is broached.

Such a process, whereby the framework of substantive law is effaced in the moment that it is taken up and stated, is not confined to these cases. Rather, what we are remarking here is a more general structure in which doctrine as the complex of institution, judgment and address is lost — or at most, effaced and forgotten — at the outset. And in its place is put a universal or general theory of action and a universal or general theory of moral responsibility. Furthermore, with this substitution, these universal or general theories never settle down and take hold but circulate between law and evidence, motive and intention, law and procedure.

Turning to the textbooks of criminal law, doctrine meets much the same fate: the complex of address, judgment and institution are summarily dispatched in the opening of the book, as if somehow prefatory to the main task of general principles, rules of law and definitions — merely preliminary to dictating the answers to the question, *what is crime?* Hence, questions of the province of criminal law, of the destination or aims of criminal law, and the subjective and objective right to punish, are treated as if they are detachable from both the general elements of criminal law and the particular definitions of particular crimes.[10] The result is that doctrine is first evacuated from the textbooks of criminal law — progressively becoming a term of art, then a term of inconvenience, and finally disappearing. Secondly, and in the same move, this evacuation of doctrine is laminated with a substitute-formation: namely, doctrine as a system of principles and rules, a logic of reasonable actions.[11] In this double move, the evacuation does not get rid of doctrine, does not hollow out an empty space through which we can pass to get to law. Rather, it enfolds doctrine within an economy of law.

Scenography

To examine more closely the working of the double gesture we turn to the circulation of doctrine in the first textbook — in fact, the first book — of criminal law: *A General View of the Criminal Law of England*. In it, James

Fitzjames Stephen announces the transition from the laws of crime to criminal law. In it, it is possible to read the reason for, and the structure of, the use of a substitute-formation that we know as criminal law (J.F. Stephen, 1863).

Stephen begins by announcing a new province of law; namely, the 'province of criminal law'. In fact, this announcement is the project of the book and perhaps of his life's work. How does he go about doing this? First, he sets out somewhat apologetically the subjects of this new province in terms of the reception of criminal law. As he remarks, '[i]t is intended neither for practical use nor for an introduction to professional study. Its object is to give an account of the general scope, tendency, and design of an important part of our institutions....' It would appear to have no discernible audience; it is intended neither for the education of students, nor for legal practitioners. Presumably the province of criminal law and its book addresses some audience. But rather than doing so directly, as the above quotation indicates, Stephen makes a detour and simply moves from a statement of who it is not intended for to a general account of the general subject-matter. The subject thereby becomes a matter of doctrine, subject to the possibility of the generality of the criminal law. In answering the question of address in terms of (an) institution, Stephen evades the possibility of there being no recipient of criminal law, of the message of criminal law getting lost. There is a price to be paid however. Stephen and criminal law perform a reversal of cause and effect (metalepsis): it is not possible to determine from Stephen's account whether the province or its subject come into being first. From the outset, they are enfolded and visibly set in motion, as if they were already receiving an audience before the law.[12] The metalepsis repeats itself in all the major distinctions Stephen seeks to make in determining the province of criminal law and, most notably, his substantial distinction between what he describes as 'the order of thought' and 'the order of time', between logic and history. It is this distinction of orders or genres that Stephen will have deployed in attempting to distinguish between criminal law and criminal procedure. This latter distinction will also have been caught in the question of which comes first, criminal law or criminal procedure?

In chapter 2, Stephen turns to the institution of the province of criminal law as a question of history and logic. In synoptic terms, the history of law becomes its logic.[13] Stephen collapses the disparate traditions of the law of public wrongs and the pleas of the Crown, that is the Institutists and the common lawyers. This sets in train the transition from the 'laws of crime' to 'criminal law'. Such a transition is familiar to us, its inheritors. But what is less familiar is that the transition is a shift in the order of representation. In this transition there is a shift in the nature of law, a shift in the nature of crime and a consequent displacement in the nature of the relation between law and crime. It is a move from crime as a sign of the thing in itself or moral fact, to crime as a sign of an action the traces of which are to be found in the evidence of the senses. The effect of this move is that law is taken out of crime, and what remains is a different law and a different crime. Crime remains as a general theory of action and law is left as a general theory of moral responsibility. This would appear to be the genesis of modern criminal law.

It is of course a momentous feat and Stephen achieves it with remarkable economy. As we have indicated, he begins in the preface of his textbook by asking the question what is the province of criminal law. He asks this as a question of address and gives an answer in terms of the institution of law: not so much *who receives it?*, but *here it is*. Stephen appears to ground the question of address, yet he does so with an ungrounded institution. The institutional question has been left hanging. And, as we will read, when it comes to grounding the institution, a similar torsion recurs: Stephen institutes law as a matter of logic but the answer he gives is in terms of rhetoric — that is, in terms of the domain of judgment and the practice of differentiation.

Between and Within Law

For Stephen, the logic of institution is a matter of the proper definition of criminal law. This takes place throughout but can be seen most clearly in the first three pages of chapter 1 of *A General View*. There, he provides a two-step definition; the first distinguishing *between* law and non-law in terms of crime and non-crime, and the second *within* law distinguishing between criminal and non-criminal law. The first step is the familiar Austinian jurisprudence of law as a command and crime as disobedience of the command backed by punishment. In short, criminal law is the first law. The second step separates the criminal law from the non-criminal law by reserving for criminal law the potential pain of punishment and leaving general sanctions for non-criminal law. Hence he begins his account of the province of criminal law thus:

> The object of this chapter is to show what is the subject-matter to which criminal law relates, and what are the component parts of which by the nature of the case it must consist. First, then, what is a law, what is a crime?

A law is a command enjoining a course of conduct. A command is an intimation from a stronger to a weaker rational being, that if the weaker does or forbears to do some specified thing the stronger will injure or hurt him. A crime is an act of disobedience to a law forbidden under pain of punishment. It follows from these definitions that all laws are in one sense criminal, for by the definitions they must be commands, and any command may be disobeyed. (J.F. Stephen, 1890, 1)

For Stephen, the paradoxical moment lies in the institution of law because, *as a matter of logic or definition*, 'all laws are in one sense criminal'. However, while all law is criminal as a matter of logic, that logic cannot carry us over into the institution of law itself without invoking history. Stephen must already know how to differentiate between a law and a crime, in order to *then* ask: what is a law, what is a crime? In other words, the paradoxical truth of his answer lies in the need to both exclude and include history. The need for history arises in the requirement to ground the sanction or, more properly, to differentiate the legitimate from the illegitimate force of law. Law must be judged as enforceable not just classified.[14]

Why this paradox comes to exist as a paradox of judgment can be seen more clearly by following its displacement into the division of the parts of law: substantive and procedural. Here, the relation between law and crime must again follow the twin gesture of exclusion and reincorporation. The first step in the name of logic excludes history to distinguish between punishments and sanctions, and the second step recalls history to render visible and bind (Hachamovitch, 1994) that distinction in the practice of law: first in terms of punishment, second in terms of the courts of justice and their procedures. This metalepsis, or reversal of cause and effect, is not simply a tautology — and thus a matter of circulation in the order of logic[15] — but actually invokes and inscribes a different generic order. In this economy, questions of history are questions of judgment because their form of differentiation is one of value and effect and not validity. Moreover, Stephen makes this differentiation through the process of lining up in serial form: history, procedure, evidence, and the courts.

At every point in Stephen's system of classification, this moment of history or value is recuperated to the order of logic only to be expelled in the search for particular definitions. One final example will suffice here: namely, the way in which the parts of criminal law are divided and divided into evidence, procedure and substantive law.

What starts as a question of institution posed as a logic of grammar gets answered in terms of judgment. Judgment appears here as a history of legal argument in the courts; that is, a history of rhetoric. The institution of criminal law is described in terms of a grammar and, specifically, a grammar which divides into the laws of crimes and punishments and the law of criminal procedure, each of which have their own subdivisions.[16] History is then subordinated to or brought into relation with this grammar:

> Independently of these broad general divisions, which must apply to every legal system whatever, certain features, peculiar to each particular system, affect the character of every part of it. The skeleton of criminal law, in every country, is on the same general plan; but the shape of the members, their proportionate importance, and general appearance, differ widely; so that there is a corresponding difference in the functions which they are fitted to discharge. (J.F. Stephen, 1863, 8)

Nevertheless, for this subordination to take place, history must already have been detached from the logic of grammar. This detachment becomes evident at the outset of chapter 2. The germ of the criminal procedure of our own times is found by Stephen in the procedure of the itinerant Justices in eyre (*in itinere*). However in order to *show* this germ or originality, he needs to take a step further back, to that which 'preceded its establishment' (J.F. Stephen, 1863, 11). This pre-original original is the domain of evidence: 'If a criminal was taken in the fact; if the murderer was discovered with the knife in his hand; .... the constable, sheriff, or lord of the franchise, might instantly put him to death without further inquiry' (J.F. Stephen, 1863, 11–12). The grammar of legal action is not itself procedure, but rather a 'skeleton'. The logic of this grammar is not itself logical; it needs history as the rhetoric of procedure to make it so. The logic needs an 'execution at the spot' to make it logic.[17]

As with institution in the domain of address, so with judgment in the domain of institution: the judgment of law has been left hanging. It is necessary now to follow the torsion within which judgment is caught. What is asked as a question of judgment gets answered in terms of address. We saw earlier in the analysis of the textbook tradition that criminal law is established as universal or general principles both of moral responsibility and of action. It is at this point that judgment is invoked, judgment as the genre of differentiation is called in aid to move from the universal to the particular. On a first reading this is achieved by distributing criminal law into its component parts of speech: adjectival or evidential laws, adverbial or procedural laws, and nominative or substantive laws. Judgment binds through a classificatory system of types.[18] It enables the universal form of moral responsibility and legal action to be given form and made typical. And it is in relation to these types that particular judgments are made.

However, if the genre of judgment requires us to differentiate solely in terms of legal argument (history and rhetoric), these types of legal speech do not allow us to do so. The operation of the classificatory system is not a matter of pure discrimination. Not only have matters of judgment become inscribed within and through those of institution, the immixture of time and thought. In addition, to be able to differentiate, judgment requires knowledge of the actions of law: its procedures, conduct and manners. This returns us to the question of address begun in our reading of *Hancock*. As we saw there, the judgment was framed by Lord Scarman in terms of the judicial function of directing juries and, specifically, the appellate role in providing guidance to trial judges in exercising their discretion or in directing juries.[19] In that case, it was perhaps understandable, given the fact that the trial judge had followed to the letter the impeccable directions of Lord Bridge in *Moloney*'s case, and yet the jury returns perplexed and in dissent over the precise legal definitions with regard to intent and foreseeable consequences. But such difficulty is not confined to the particular case. In fact, most legal definitions in criminal law are framed as judicial directions to juries. What this indicates is that the difficulty of judgment in modern criminal law is that judges do not simply decide; juries do. The judge addresses herself to the forms of law, and judges whether its topics or promises have been adhered to properly. The question of decision goes to the jury (do we believe your facts or argument?), and the question of interrogation (by what doctrine do you believe?) remains with the judge. At every point, judgment needs something else to make differentiation possible. What is this extra, this excess? To pass judgment, it needs an object to accuse, an accusative object. To pass on judgment, it needs an address. While this address might at some point be justice, in the meantime it is doctrine and, in substitute form, criminal law.

A Double Accusative

How should this circulation of the terms of doctrine as the possibility of jurisdiction be understood? In beginning with J.F. Stephen, we have taken the determination of criminal law as a question of audience address. We have returned to repeat that opening gesture. What has been lost and gained in the process? The earlier discussion of *Hancock*, *Moloney* and the textbook tradition allowed us to see that what is put to one side in criminal law is the complex of address, institution and judgment. What Stephen has here helped us to read is the aporias or non-passages in each of these doctrinal instances.[20] The aporia of address is located in the impossibility of guaranteeing its aims and with what effect; that of institution is established in the necessary impossibility of beginning criminal law in law; and that of judgment is invested in the paradox of differentiation. What we have seen in the case reports and textbook tradition is the attempt to expel these aporias as if they were mere epistemological difficulties and hence accompanied by the complaint that if we could just clear them up, we could then move on. But what Stephen helps us see is their return and circulation. They never settle down; neither evacuated nor ingested but endlessly substituted and enfolded as criminal law. Stephen's starts with address, giving us an answer in terms of institution; then the question of institution is answered in terms of judgment; and finally judgment is answered in terms of address. And so it goes on: you believe you are on one path and it turns out that you are on another. Doctrine circulates *both* as the instances of address, institution and judgment, *and* as the point from which all three instances are put into circulation.

In the process of this particular circulation, Stephen and we have moved from a term of address as a destination, as a potential audience of a product, through to the question of address as a mode of interrogative force. Doctrine, in effect, has been framed in terms of a double accusative. For an account of the shape of a double accusative, let us briefly turn to the work of C.S. Kenny and, in particular, to the *Outlines of Criminal Law* which many have taken as inaugurating modern criminal law (Kenny, 1902).[21]

Whereas J.F. Stephen begins with the question of the province of criminal law, for Kenny the primary question is 'the nature of a crime'.[22] With this it would seem that he does away with many of the difficulties that we found in Stephen. The question of the nature of criminal law in general has simply been put aside. Yet even with Kenny, this negation or disavowal does not manage to expel the problem entirely. As he remarks:

> There is one grave — if not indeed insoluble — difficulty which has to be faced in studying the law of crime. And this difficulty unhappily comes at the very outset of the subject. For it consists of the fundamental problem — *What is a Crime?* Clearly the criminal law is concerned with crimes alone, not with illegal acts in general. But how are we to distinguish those breaches of law which are crimes from those which are merely illegal without being criminal? (Kenny, 1902, 13)[23]

Yet on closer inspection this is not Kenny's first question at all. From its opening sentence the institution of criminal law is posed and answered in terms of the address of criminal law and, specifically, in terms of its importance for its user. On the one hand, there are those who respond to the call of public duty, or the call of professional activity, and on the other, there is 'the plainest private citizen' (Kenny, 1902, 1). This distinction is repeated in the distinction Kenny makes between thoughtful men and ordinary readers. Criminal law is 'rendered attractive to all thoughtful men by its direct bearing on the most urgent social difficulties of our time and on the deepest ethical problems of all times'. On the other hand, ordinary readers or plain citizens, 'whether thoughtful or thoughtless, are fascinated by its dramatic character — the vivid and violent nature of the events which criminal courts notice and repress as well as of those by which they effect the repression' (Kenny, 1902, 2).[24] In these initial pages, what Kenny is circumscribing is the inevitability of law's accusation, one which neither prudence nor moral principles can avert. In turning crime into law, into the law of intention, what is lost is the object and objection of crime, the refractory address and ground of crime. In brief, Kenny is right to make the interrogatory *What is a Crime?* an accusative one, but he is wrong to make the accusative question exclusively one of definition. For, in sticking to the subject of crime, he loses the accusative object of the question: crime. He turns it, in advance, into (the subject-matter of) law. What is lost is that the accusation is doubled. Law is accusative but so too is crime; it also carries with it the force of a question, the force of the knowledge, representation and action of an address. In losing this other accusative, in turning it in advance into law, Kenny represses and compresses the relation between these two founding accusations.

Exergue

In Kenny's ambition to name and seal the fate or character of criminal law, once again, it is possible to see more clearly the generic predicament of criminal legal doctrine. Where once the laws of crime promised a differentiated legal dogmatics, the form of criminal law as elaborated in the tradition inaugurated by Stephen has taken a more occluded structure. In the absence of divine (which is to say, external) certification, questions of law are referred to narratives of moral responsibility and action, answered largely by recourse to biography, whether that be of legislation, judgment, scholarship, criminality, victimage and so on. If this is the form of criminal law, the order of fiction or speech generated therein settles for a system of circulation and deferral. In analytic terms, the order of communication that sets in motion the form of human sociality appears to operate as a repressed element of criminal law. It reappears as doctrine, the other scene that enfolds or generates criminal law.

If we are to give into this genesis, what must be given up? In formal terms, we have seen that in the move from the laws of crime to a general theory of moral responsibility, what is removed is doctrine as the law of crime. We have also seen that, in the move from the laws of crime to a general theory of action, what is removed is doctrine as the crime of law. What would thus be given up (for Kenny) is the space of the double accusative and (for Stephen) the time for thought. The risk might be that, in acceding fully to this generation of criminal law, we would indeed have killed the doctrinal corpus of law: the power to speak in the name of law, the potential of jurisdiction. We would have lost our inheritance and remain as the dead letters of law. Such a sentence does not mean that law is no longer effective; simply following in the footsteps of posited law has the disturbing tendency to give rise to even more virulent juridical action. As the essays in this book attest, the jurisdiction of criminal law is littered with dead bodies and their images, our memories. What this dispersal of bodies and body-parts reminds law is that law cannot tell the difference between criminal law and criminal law: which is the adjective and which is the noun. The anxiety of criminal law is that it tends to confuse semblance and substance, law and order. While its actions might be warranted by law, it cannot judge which interrogatories are accusations and which are questions. After all, what is a crime? what is a law?

It is nevertheless the case that a doctrinal corpus remains and remains as an indelible (if illegible) stain; perhaps scrubbed and fitted up with suit and tie or berobed and bewigged, but not yet cleansed. How then to respond to this material object, this repressed body of law? We have indicated some of the things the response cannot be. It cannot simply be a matter of improving on our philosophical or socio-historical reconstructions of the normative legal order. Nor can it simply be a matter of returning to the common law way of doing things, let alone substituting it with a more efficient administration which is user-friendly. It cannot simply be a matter of producing better or more sensitive statutes, case reports, not to mention textbooks less resistant to theory. Nor can it simply be a question of putting the parts of law back together again; returning process and proof, procedure and evidence, to the substantive criminal law. While such actions might make (criminal) law more respectable and decorous, they once again attempt to bypass the doctrinal corpus of law. As we have seen, however, doctrine is *both* inevitable *and* problematic. In the account given, doctrine re-emerges here and there as the repressed restaging of jurisdiction, of the power and authority to speak in and as law. In analytic terms, the predicament of criminal law is that it only experiences the loss of doctrine second-time round and in the form of injury.

What is thus enfolded in law is a bodily accusation or stain; it is on this condition that doctrine has not yet ceased to be reconstructed and judgment according to law becomes possible, though no less abusive or catachrestic. In restaging the jurisdiction of law, doctrine inevitably returns as the material or bodily stain on the copybook of law. It becomes that which makes analysis possible.

The conclusion that may be drawn from this description is that, *in wanting to be properly legal*, criminal law wants to lose the ability to pose doctrine as the imagination of law and, specifically, doctrine as the way in which it is possible to retain and maintain the subject of law. Criminal law wants to be: a moral philosophy and a government of action. Our concern is that these normative interpretations have delivered criminal law all-too-well, signed their own death warrant and sealed their own fate. Having excised the material site on which to ask the questions of juridical existence, there will have been no introduction to criminal law. The tradition of reason and experience displays a will to pass on nothing but the exclusive teaching of submission, deference and, correlatively, the derision of doctrinal difference. But this is not yet to say that law is incorporeal. If the death warrant has been signed, it has not yet been executed.

Notes

1. We put to one side the barely noticed mutation wrought in the production and reproduction of legal interpretation by the introduction of digital technology (lexis and nexis).
2. See also Constable, 1994, ch. 3 and *passim*. For a sociological expert's experience of this dilemma, see Valverde, 1996.
3. See also White, 1985, ch. 9.
4. At least in so far as the Kantian and Hegelian traditions of legal and social thought are acknowledged; see G. Rose, 1994, xi–xv; Douzinas and Warrington, 1994, ch. 4.
5. Even without considering the multiplicity of contexts in which legal doctrine is put to use, it must be formulated within the domains of legal philosophy, epistemology, legal method, doctrinal classification, and so on.
6. It is this image of doctrine that came to dominate university legal scholarship in the nineteenth century (Sugarman, 1991).
7. Some reports refer to the judgment as *R v Hancock & Shankland*.
8. In posing the definition of intention as a direction to the jury, criminal law draws on the penitential tradition of direction of conscience, and specifically the Jesuitical practice of spiritual exercises. Thus, it is perhaps a historical accident that the judgments on intention have come under pressure as changes are underway in the legal regulation of confession evidence (indirect intention is largely a matter of circumstantial evidence, whereas direct intention is a matter of confessional evidence). More generally, following the passage quoted, Bridge refers to the problem of transferred malice 'which any first year law student could explain to a jury in the simplest of terms' (*Moloney* [1985] 1 All ER 1025 at 1037). Such an evocation of the law student indicates at the very least that the problem of intention

is a question of dogma and doctrine, of the transmission of inherited truths, a question posed by Lord Bridge as a problem of pedagogy.

9. The certified question of law is translated by Lord Scarman at the outset as: the appeal is brought 'to secure a ruling on the refusal of the Court of Appeal to accept as sound the guidelines formulated by this House in a recent case': namely, *Moloney*. But it is not only the Court of Appeal that is refusing to submit to the guidance of the House of Lords. Analogously, Lord Scarman goes on to note that, upon being given an 'impeccable' direction, the jury were 'plainly perplexed' as to the law of murder. However, at the outset, Lord Scarman remarks that 'the appeal is of importance for two reasons. First, of course, there is the need to settle a point of difference between this House and the Court of Appeal'. This point of difference relates to the appellate function of offering general guidance to trial judges on how to direct a jury. The second reason is the 'increase' in crimes of violence 'where the purpose is by open violence to protest, demonstrate, obstruct or frighten'. This reason is also related to the process of directing juries because it expands the range of cases or crimes in which the *Moloney* direction is relevant. But it also involves an address to the public and, in particular, a discourse on the modes of communication: 'Violence is used by some as a means of public communication. Inevitably, there will be casualties; and inevitably death will on occasions result' (*Hancock* [1986] 1 All ER 641 at 648–9).

10. Such detachment is exhibited in a recent report by the Law Commission, where the modern 'philosophical foundations' of consent are first *not* adopted by the Commission (para 2.1) and then included as Appendix C. See Law Commission, 1995. This approach is lamented in the editorial of *Criminal Law Review* (1996, 75–6).

11. On the concept of substitute-formations, see Freud, 1975, vol. 20, 77.

12. As a socio-historical aside, it may be noted that there has been and continues to be a narrow educational margin between universities and legal practice. In constructing doctrine as a general theory of responsibility, academics created a place for themselves from which to address the university. On the other hand, and at the same time, in constructing doctrine as a general theory of action, they created a place for themselves from which to address the practitioner. As such, the narrow margin was more of a non-place which sends the legal writer circulating between practitioner and university. In biographical terms, Stephen was a journalist, barrister, colonial legal adviser, judge, lecturer, and so on.

13. Thus, '[t]he general nature of the commonest and most important crimes is substantially the same under all circumstances, and at every period of history. Disobedience to government, violence, theft and fraud, in different forms and with different aggravations, make up almost all crimes which can be committed' (J.F. Stephen, 1863, 32). Stephen's approach to Bracton's text on homicide is exemplary. After arranging and reducing the text of Bracton into a table or tabular form, he notes: 'The fanciful character of some of these subdivisions sufficiently shows how ill it is fitted for the purposes of a legal definition, for which, in all probability, it was never intended' (J.F. Stephen, 1863, 41).

14. See, for example, his use of the example of the law of inheritance (J.F. Stephen, 1863, 1–2). See also our discussion below of the grounding and differentiation of law in courts.

15. Having noted at the outset that the relation between crime and law in criminal law is 'paradoxical', Stephen concludes: 'Though the notions of law and crime are thus, in reality, correlative and co-extensive, and though the phrase "criminal law" may thus be accused of tautology, it may be and generally is used in a sense definite enough for practical purposes, but much narrower' (J.F. Stephen, 1863, 2).

16. For a condensed example, see J.F. Stephen, 1863, 7–8, where Stephen sets out the arrangement that he will follow in his representation of criminal law.

17. See his remark that, for the Anglo-Saxons, '[i]f the criminal was not taken in the fact, and executed on the spot, his fate depended almost entirely on his character' (J.F. Stephen, 1863, 12). On character as fate, see Benjamin, 1978. This is not the place to go into the extensive history of the skeletal figure of law. Suffice it to note that it is related to the

foundational figures of the grave and the spectacle or theatricality of crime for the plain man that Kenny will use some 40 years later (Kenny, 1902, 3).

18. As Stephen remarks: 'jurisprudence ... is not, strictly speaking, the science of law but the science which classifies and describes the relations with which law has to deal' (J.F. Stephen, 1863, 330). Relatedly, this process of typification is more conventionally experienced as the prevalence of legal *tests* which seemingly allow the move from principles to pragmatism.

19. As Lord Scarman remarks: 'The judicial function exercised *from time to time* by appellate courts of offering guidance either for the benefit of a judge exercising discretion conferred on him by law or as to the assistance which a judge may properly give a jury in reaching a conclusion of fact can be helpful but *does not result in, or establish, though it should reflect, a rule of law*' (*Hancock* [1986] 1 All ER 641 at 647 (emphasis added)). See also Lord Bridge's declaration that his guidelines on directing juries as to intention were not part of the *ratio decidendi* (*Moloney* [1985] 1 All ER 1025 at 1032–3).

20. For an account of the intellectual history of the aporetic mode of judgment, see Caygill, 1989.

21. Hereafter referred to as *Outlines*. We have taken Stephen's 1863 *General View* as the inaugural work of criminal law. The choice of Stephen is not however by virtue of historical appointment, but rather by virtue of the gesture that he initiates. While the gesture was short-lived (the chapter which we have focused on in our reading was reformulated in 1890 in the second edition of *A General View*), its effects have reverberated and still resound in the predicaments of the present.

22. In the first edition of *Outlines*, this is the title and topic of chapter 1 of book 1 on 'general considerations'. Book 2 treats of the definitions of particular crimes, book 3 treats of judicial proof and evidence in general and as relevant to criminal law, and book 4 treats of criminal procedure.

23. Emphasis in original. He then restages the shift from the law of crime to criminal law in terms of a shift from intrinsic to extrinsic definitions of the act of crime. His preferred answer to the question what is a crime is thus 'a crime is a wrong whose sanction is remissible by the Crown, *if remissible at all*' (Kenny, 1902, 15). This preference will be taken up by later academics, of which Williams is perhaps the last to explicitly do so and at length (G. Williams, 1955, 107–30; 1978, ch. 1). For a reading of this tradition against the grain of critical legal studies, see Farmer, 1996.

24. See also the justification for 'another elementary manual of Criminal Law' in terms of its possible audiences, which Kenny provides in the preface to the book. No doubt the theatricality of crime for the plainman is related to the grave difficulty above and the skeleton of law discussed earlier. What these figures — specifically, hypotyposis — make visible is the death drive of law, its lust to kill.

9 Autobiographic Fragments: The Life of Criminal Law

PETER RUSH[1]

[The] object [of this book] is to give an account of the general scope, tendency, and design of an important part of our institutions, of which surely none can have a greater moral significance, or be more closely connected with broad principles of morality and politics, than those by which men rightfully, deliberately, and in cold blood, kill, enslave, and otherwise torment their fellow-creatures.

(J.F. Stephen, 1863, vi)

If, to use a simile, one views the growing work as a funeral pyre, its commentator can be likened to the chemist, its critic to an alchemist. While the former is left with wood and ashes as the sole objects of his analysis, the latter is concerned only with the enigma of the flame itself: the enigma of being alive. Thus the critic inquires about the truth whose living flame goes on burning over the heavy logs of the past and the light ashes of life gone by.   (Benjamin, 1973, 11)[2]

Towards the end of his life, James Fitzjames Stephen intermittently writes what he calls an *Autobiographic Fragment*. It was and remains unpublished. Unlike his other writings, this text is not a matter of reducing and systematising large masses of detail into the several departments of a life. Rather, it is a fragment, a part that takes on significance only by vir-tue of its place in an entire life now lost. And while at least one of his books has been described as 'a self-portrait of unconscious fidelity',[3] this fragment is an autobiography the function of which Stephen describes as dogmatic: namely, to pass on the inherited truths of his life to his children and to 'bury my dead out of sight'.[4]

He is born into a Clapham Sect family in 1829, the son of James Stephen. His father was known as the scourge of the Colonial Office in which he held appointments for upwards of 30 years, before succumbing to illness. As the eldest son, and thus heir-at-law, James Fitzjames Stephen has a strong filial relationship. In the domestic arena, he is variously called 'Gruffian', 'Little Preacher', and he is referred to by his parents as 'little Fitzy'. No doubt the proliferation of nicknames is in response to the difficulty of distinguishing the name of the father from the name of the son. In the most immediate

200

terms, the name of James Fitzjames Stephen is no less than a statement to the effect that the eldest son is the heir-at-law: James the son of James Stephen. Yet, if what makes him distinctive is that he is named son, nevertheless he had many fathers. Initially unimpressed by Bentham and Austin, he turns out to be a zealous descendant of these two great systematisers. Further, his brother Leslie remarks that Henry Sumner Maine's influence on Fitzjames is second only to their father (L. Stephen, 1895, 102). Or again, in an epistle to Lady Grant Duff, he confesses that he possesses 'a little semi-filial feeling' towards Thomas Carlyle.[5] Aside from such cultural patrimony, it was James Stephen that he admires, often accompanying his father on convalescent sojourns. His display of affection and emotion in the presence of his father is muted. After his father died in 1859, however, he defends his reputation in a thoroughgoing public display of filial affection. In response to remarks by Thomas Mozley which called into question his father's professional competence, he solicits Gladstone's support and writes a letter in *The Times* virulently ridiculing Mozley's remarks.[6]

Fitzjames Stephen's schooling was varied; having been begun at an evangelical school in Brighton, it was continued at Eton for three years as a dayboy. His experience of Eton is unbending in the face of verbal and physical abuse, a situation in which he likened himself to a 'sensible grown up woman among a crowd of rough boys'. Moreover, in his own words, he is 'unteachable' (*Fragment*, 24; 37–8). But when he leaves to complete his schooling at King's College London, he had learnt his lesson well: namely, that a man can 'count on nothing in this world except what lies between his hat and his boots' (*Fragment*, 24).[7] His university career is a mirror-image of his Etonian experience. Whereas at Eton he did not fit in with his peers but was rather aloof and disdainful of them, at Cambridge he makes his mark as a member of the Apostles, largely at the instigation of Henry Sumner Maine. Although he manages to befriend his peers amongst the Apostles, he fails to distinguish himself in his studies. He is known as 'the British Lion', a nickname commemorating his rhetorical prowess. Yet if his command of the forms of agonistic speech make him legendary, his exam performances were average and his 'scholastic performance' was 'lacklustre' (K.J.M. Smith, 1988, 5). Aspiring to be an academic, he tries unsuccessfully to obtain a Trinity Fellowship; and it is only on failing — for the second time — to gain the fellowship that he substitutes a legal career for the academic vocation. Yet he does not go to the Inns of Court to study, but rather reads for an LLB at London University and, in 1854, he is called to the Bar. A year later he marries, like his father, into a clerical family.

As if destined to be a misfit, happy neither as an insider nor an outsider, failing to make friends at Eton, failing to gain an academic position at Trinity College, his choice of a legal career did not dissolve his aspirations to write. Although called to the Bar, it is writing and, specifically, journalism which impels him. As he confesses to his wife Mary Cunningham, 'if my body ever had a call to anything by the voices of nature, I have a call to journalism'.[8] While his paternal and cultural patrimony give him a name and mark him out, it is writing that responds to the demands of his body. Working like a Trojan, he becomes a prolific journalist. And working as a barrister, his writing is peripatetic. Not only are his topics diverse — literary criticism, history, philosophy, theology, law, and more generally the political, social and moral currents of his day — but he writes the essays in hotel rooms, railway stations, and courtrooms. In the latter, he meets his fellow barristers, the profession of which he describes as callous, insensitive, brutal, vulgar, bombastic; a profession which required him to be the 'footstool of another's malignity'.[9] Nevertheless, he continues to divide his time between the vocation of writing and the career of barrister. It is this split that sends him on his way. Nine years after being called to the Bar, he publishes the inaugural book of criminal law: *A General View of the Criminal Law of England*. In one brief volume, it demarcates the province of criminal law (as divided between substantive law, criminal procedure, evidence and punishment); the history of that province; the extant definitions of the law of public wrongs and Pleas of the Crown; in addition to copious comparisons of the English legal system with that of the French and the German. In doing so, the truth-content of law has been excised from the knowledge of criminal law, and covering this breach are the various parts of criminal legal speech: the nominative, the adjectival, and the adverbial. Such a grammar devotes its time and labours to the themes of criminal law, yet what interrupts such a devotion to speech is the material site of enunciation: the preface of the *General View* addresses its readers from 4, Paper Buildings, Temple. It is published towards the end of his career as a barrister, yet it subsides in the wake left by his role as colonial legislator and English codifier.

In 1869, Fitzjames Stephen succeeded Maine as the legal member of the Governor-General's Council in India. He stays in this position for little more than two years, during which time he writes an extensive amount of colonial legislation. The most remarkable was the *Indian Evidence Act*, which abolished all previous laws and centred the law of evidence of the Indian sub-continent on a peculiarly English concept of relevance (J.F. Stephen, 1872).[10] This Act, together with the introductory essay which he appends to it, represent a somewhat Herculean attempt to refound the Law of Evidence. Distinguishing and dividing as he goes, Stephen displaces the law onto the *relations between* observable phenomena[11] and excises all that could be irrelevant and foreign. As he remarks, there is as 'much moral cowardice in shrinking from the execution of a murderer as in hesitating to blow out the brains of a foreign invader' (J.F. Stephen, 1864b, 753).[12] If his colonial codification was a success, back in England he signally fails in his attempts to codify the judge-made and statutory law.

Leslie Stephen, biographer and intellectual historian, wrote of his older brother Fitzjames that 'the legal career always represented the substantive, and the literary career the adjective'. By way of a certain ellipsis, Fitzjames's substantive legal career is focused on the adjectival law, not only as a jobbing barrister but also as colonial legislator, and again as an English codifier. On his return, he puts his energies into the 1872 Code of Evidence. In the subsequent year, he writes a Homicide Law Amendment Bill. Both codification projects are frustrated. Regarded 'as something of a self-seeking interloper' by the Home Office and the Lord Chancellor's Office,[13] Fitzjames Stephen returns to writing. Since his return from India, he had worked on and published what will have become his most remembered book: *Liberty, Equality, Fraternity* (1873).[14] It is not a distinctly legal book. Rather like *A General View*, it speaks of the moral significance of social institutions which kill, enslave and otherwise torment their fellow-creatures and thus, by virtue of its subject-matter, is addressed to the general population. His next two books however are products to be consulted and consumed by lawyers, and as such peculiarly legal: namely, *A Digest of the Law of Evidence* (1876), and *A Digest of the Criminal Law* (1877a). They are what he calls 'law-books', and are written out of and predicated upon the failure of codification. Yet, if the books are written to salve the loss of the codes, Stephen is well-aware that writing law-books also exacted their cut. Thus, he remarks that studying law is always undertaken at the reader's peril. Similarly, he described the activity of writing legal digests as a 'killing tedium' and, more generally, writing law-books as 'so horribly dull and laborious that I cannot bring myself to give my whole strength and time to it'.[15] In the early years of barristering, writing is represented as his vocation. Now, in being assimilated to law in the form of codes and books, writing becomes not so much a corporal compulsion but a cognitive burden. Condemned to follow posited law, adjectives begin to weigh heavily.

The practice of judgment according to law would be the same. Stephen was appointed a judge of the Queen's Bench Division in 1879. He finds being a circuit judge 'exceedingly dull and petty'. It involves 'sitting 10 hours a day trying all kinds of abominations', and what is worse 'corrupting' the mind of the judge by inducing him to try long cases in his sleep at night.[16] Of his 13 years on the Bench, what has been remembered is the banality of everyday judgment; a recent portraitist describes them as a relative failure where 'failure lay in being unremarkable, in not being extraordinary' (K.J.M. Smith, 1988, 248).[17] But if the everyday prompted the nightly dream of judgment, that delirium is restaged in the daily practice of judgment. As he confesses to his correspondent, Stephen would distract himself by writing letters from the Bench during trials over which he presided.[18] Such distractions aside, judging would make the dream of writing possible. During the first three years on the Bench, he hopes that the appointment to the Bench had not only secured his future finances, but also would permit him to 'realise some of the dreams of my earlier life as to the writing of books'.[19] This is not a return to the exhila-ration of satisfying the bodily compulsion to write with which he represented his journalism. What appears second time round is the three-volume *A History of the Criminal Law of England* (J.F. Stephen, 1883). Here, the task of differentiation is referred to the history of the forms of legal speech, a history which judgment replays and, in replaying, submits to law. On finishing the *History*, Stephen experiences a profound sense of loss and melancholia. Of such a tragic vision, Fifoot can only remark that it is a 'self-portrait of unconscious fidelity, warts and all' (Fifoot, 1959). On finishing the *History*, the dreams of writing are however interrupted by the demands of judgment. Within a year of the conviction of Florence Maybrick for the murder of her husband, the press begin calling into ques-ion Stephen's professional competence as a judge. He is however unaware of the furore brewing. In fact, he has not long before finished the second edition of the *General View*, re-written and 'which contains in a very moderate compass the essence of what I have learnt during a long and greatly varied experience of 36 years as a barrister, a member of the Indian Council, an author, a draftsman, and a judge' (J.F. Stephen, 1890, vi). His son, Herbert, is approached by the Lord Chancellor but the son refuses to betray the father by encouraging him to resign. Lord Coleridge intervenes, and brings the matter to Stephen's attention. He refuses to resign because of public and legal concern over his incapacity, but he immediately steps down from the Bench for reasons of health. The legal profession gathers to commemorate his retirement and laud his accomplishments at a ceremony held at the beginning of the Easter law sitting. Three years later, in 1894, James Fitzjames Stephen dies of chronic renal failure. His brother Leslie had remarked that writing is to Fitzjames what dram-drinking is to others. What remains is: a death certificate citing 'Blight's disease' as the cause of death; a body of work on criminal law, evidence, and criminal procedure, together with numerous essays; a one-sided correspondence, since he had been in the habit of burning all the letters he received; and an autobiographic fragment which mentions that an earlier journal had been reduced to ashes.

Notes

1. Thanks to Shaun McVeigh for his conversations of life, death and law; and to Alison Young who reminds me that writing in law remains possible.
2. Quoted and translated in the introduction by H. Arendt.
3. The remark is made by Fifoot and the book in question is *A History of the Criminal Law of England* (Fifoot, 1959, 123).
4. *Autobiographic Fragment of James Fitzjames Stephen*, unpublished, written between 1884 and 1887 (hereafter *Fragment*). In addition to the published works of J.F. Stephen, I have derived especial assistance with the details of a life from the following secondary works and hagiographies: L. Stephen, 1895; Radzinowicz, 1957; and K.J.M. Smith, 1988. The latter is perhaps the most thorough and invaluable in reclaiming J.F. Stephen as a 'law and society' scholar; it has provided me with my quotations from Stephen's letters to Lady Grant Duff and from *Fragment*.
5. See J.F. Stephen's letter to Lady Grant Duff, 8 October 1884.
6. The anecdote to which Stephen took objection was contained in the first edition in 1862 of Mozley's *Reminiscences*, and was subsequently excised from the second edition. J.F. Stephen's letter is in *The Times*, 6 July 1882. On the unpopularity of his father, see L. Stephen, 1895, 50ff.
7. See also L. Stephen, 1895, 80.
8. J.F. Stephen, letter to Mary Stephen (née Cunningham), 15 February 1871.
9. See his discussion and remarks in J.F. Stephen, 1864a, 681; 1861, 465.
10. The introduction runs for some 134 pages. The Act remains in force today in India, although section 2 which abolished all prior rules of evidence was itself abolished in 1938. On relevant facts, see sections 6–11 of the Act.
11. The somewhat obvious — though no less curious — effect of this move is that evidence becomes allegorical and the law of evidence becomes a matter of governing the proper methods of referring to the absent other of law. In sociological terms, evidence is reduced to phenomena of observation and inference (the facts) and the real remains in the facts as traces or vestiges of another's life — and death. The dependence of the law on traces of death rather than death as such is elaborated in Stephen's introduction to the *Indian Evidence Act*: 'the general principles of evidence are, perhaps, more clearly displayed in trials for murder, than in any others. Murders are usually concealed with as much care as possible; and, on the other hand, they must, from the nature of the case, leave traces behind them which render it possible to apply the argument from effects to causes with greater force than in most other cases' (J.F. Stephen, 1872, 56). What is put on display here is the anxiety of losing the referent. This anxiety is a commonplace of the emergent nineteenth century hermeneutics of evidence in, amongst others, medicine (and its concern with autopsies), the moral sciences (and its concern with manners), theology (and its concern with providential forces) and law. In respect of law, see for example the notion of murder as predicated on 'vestiges' in the earlier work of Starkie (1842, vol. 1, 558–9, 562). Yet it draws on a longer legal tradition in which the law of murder is structured as response to a

secret killing. The hermeneutic of this secret was couched in national terms as the death of a Frenchman by an Englishman. On this motif, see Hachamovitch's essay in the present book.

12. In this respect, he was involved in defences of both English massacres in India and in the trial of Fenians in England. For a consideration of Stephen in India, see Bhabha, 1994, ch. 7, especially 129–32.

13. This characterisation is found in K.J.M. Smith, 1988, 81.

14. It is a reply to J.S. Mill's *On Liberty*, and it is in this context that Stephen's book is permitted to enter the legal arena, typically in jurisprudential courses, and typically as a sideshow to the Millsian problematic.

15. J.F. Stephen, letter to Lady Grant Duff, 8 October 1884.

16. J.F. Stephen, letters to Lady Grant Duff, 9 November 1882 and 9 May 1886.

17. See also Radzinowicz, 1957, 437–50.

18. J.F. Stephen, letter to Lady Grant Duff, 9 December 1881.

19. J.F. Stephen, letter to Lady Grant Duff, 11 December 1879.

References

Books and Journals

Abraham, N. and Torok, M. (1986) *The Wolf Man's Magic Word: A Cryptonomy*, University of Minnesota Press, Minneapolis.

Alison, A. (1989) The Practice of the Criminal Law of Scotland, orig. 1833, Law Society & Butterworths, Edinburgh.

Allen, H. (1987) *Justice Unbalanced: Gender, Psychiatry and Judicial Decisions*, Open University Press, Milton Keynes.

Allen, P. (1992) 'The New Marchioness Enquiry', *New Law Journal*, vol. 142, pp. 44, 46–7.

Allison, J. (1990) 'In Search of Revolutionary Justice in South Africa', *International Journal of the Sociology of Law*, vol. 18, pp. 409–28.

Anon. (1865) 'The *Summary Procedure (S.) Act* 1864', *Journal of Jurisprudence*, vol. 9, pp. 51–9.

Aquinas, T. (1990) *Summa Theologica*, trans. M.D. Jordan, University of Notre Dame Press, Notre Dame.

Ashworth, A. (1991) *Principles of Criminal Law*, Clarendon Press, Oxford.

Baer, E. (1986) 'The Medical Symptom', in J. Deely et al. (eds), *Frontiers in Semiotics*, Indiana University Press, Bloomington.

Barker, E. (1958) 'Translator's Introduction', in O. Gierke, *Natural Law and the Theory of Society 1500–1800*, Cambridge University Press, Cambridge.

Barthes, R. (1972) 'Dominici, or the Triumph of Literature', in *Mythologies*, trans. A. Lavers, Paladin Press, London.

Barthes, R. (1987) *Michelet*, Hill & Wang, London.

Bartlett, R. (1986) *Trials by Fire and Water: The Medieval Judicial Ordeal*, Blackwell, Oxford.

Bataille, G. (1988) *The Accursed Share*, vol. 1, trans. R. Hurley, Zone Books, New York.

Bataille, G. (1989) *Theory of Religion*, trans. R. Hurley, Zone Books, New York.

Bataille, G. (1991) *Visions of Excess*, ed. and trans. A. Stoekle, University of Minnesota Press, Minneapolis.

Beattie, J. (1986) *Crime and the Courts in England 1660–1800*, Clarendon Press, Oxford.

Bellamy, J. (1973) *Crime and Public Order in England in the Later Middle Ages*, Routledge & Kegan Paul, London.

Benjamin, W. (1973) *Illuminations*, Fontana, Glasgow.

Benjamin, W. (1978) 'Fate and Character', in *Reflections*, Schocken Books, New York.

Bentham, J. (1830) *The Rationale of Punishment*, London.

Beowulf (1980) Penguin, London.

Bergman, D. (1990) 'Manslaughter in the Tunnel?', *New Law Journal*, vol. 141, pp. 1108–9, 1129.

Bernard, T.J. (1984) 'The Historical Development of Corporate Criminal Liability', *Criminology*, vol. 22.

Berques, P. (1962) *The Maghrib Between Two World Wars*, Praeger, New York.

Bhabha, H. (1994) *The Location of Culture*, Routledge, London.

207

Blackstone, W. (1966) *Commentaries on the Laws of England*, vol. 1, orig. 1765, Clarendon Press, Oxford.

Blackstone, W. (1979) *Commentaries on the Laws of England 1765–9*, University of Chicago Press, Chicago.

Bloch, M. (1993) *Feudal Society*, Routledge, London.

Borch-Jacobsen, M. (1990) *Lacan: The Absolute Master*, Stanford University Press, Stanford.

Box, S. (1980) 'Where Have All The Naughty Children Gone?', in National Deviancy Conference (ed.), *Permissiveness and Control: The Fate of the Sixties Legislation*, Macmillan, London.

Box, S. (1983) *Power, Crime and Mystification*, Routledge, London.

Brace, G.L. (1886) *Gesta Christi*, London.

Bracton (1256) *De Legibus et Consuetudinibus Angliae* (Woodbine's edn); trans. *On the Laws and Customs of England* (1968) Harvard University Press, Cambridge, MA.

Brehier, E. (1928) *La Theorie des incorporels dans l'ancient stoicisme*, Librairie Philosophique J. Vrin, Paris.

British Sessional Papers (1866) Royal Commission on Capital Punishment 1864–6, vol. 21.

Brown, H.H. (1895) *The Principles of Summary Criminal Jurisdiction According to the Law of Scotland*, T & T Clark, Edinburgh.

Brown, K. (1986) *Bloodfeud in Scotland 1573–1625*, John Donald, Edinburgh.

Brown, R. and Rankin, M. (1990) 'Persuasion, Penalties and Prosecution: Administrative v Criminal Sanctions', in M.L. Friedland (ed.), *Securing Compliance: Seven Case Studies*, University of Toronto Press, Toronto.

Brown, W.J. (1905) 'The Personality of the Corporation and the State', *Law Quarterly Review*, vol. 21, pp. 365–79.

Browne, A. (1987) *When Battered Women Kill*, Free Press, New York.

Burman, S. and Scharf, W. (1990) 'Creating People's Justice: Street Committees and People's Courts in a South African City', *Law and Society Review*, vol. 24, pp. 695–744.

Burt, C. (1944) *The Young Delinquent*, 4th edn, University of London Press, London.

Butler, J. (1991) 'Imitation and Gender Subordination', in D. Fuss (ed.), *Inside/Out: Lesbian and Gay Theories*, Routledge, New York.

Cameron, Lord (1988) 'The High Court of Justiciary', *Stair Memorial Encyclopaedia*, vol. 6, pp. 336–79, Butterworths & Law Society, Edinburgh.

Carlen, P. (1986) 'Psychiatry in Prisons: Promises, Premises, Practices, and Politics', in P. Miller and N. Rose (eds), *The Power of Psychiatry*, Polity Press, Cambridge.

Carlson, E. and Dain, M. (1962) 'The Meaning of Moral Insanity', *Bulletin of the History of Medicine*, no. 36, pp. 130–40.

Carr, C.T. (1905) *The General Principles of the Law of Corporations*, Cambridge University Press, Cambridge.

Carson, W.G. (1984/5) 'Policing the Periphery: The Development of Scottish Policing 1795–1900', *Australian & New Zealand Journal of Criminology*, vols 17 & 18, pp. 207–32; 3–16.

Carson, W.G. and Idzikowska, H. (1989) 'The Social Production of Scottish Policing 1795–1900', in D. Hay and F. Snyder (eds), *Policing and Prosecution in Britain 1750–1850*, Oxford University Press, Oxford.

Castel, R. (1975) 'The Doctors and Judges', in M. Foucault (ed.), *I, Pierre Rivière*, Pantheon, New York.

Caygill, H. (1989) *The Art of Judgement*, Blackwell, Oxford.

Chambers, R. (1986) *A Course of Lectures on the English Law; delivered at the University of Oxford 1767–1773*, ed. T. Curley, University of Wisconsin Press, Madison.

Cicero (1972) *Of the Nature of the Gods*, trans. H.C.P. McGregor, Penguin, London.

Cockburn, J.S. (1991) 'Patterns of Violence in English Society: Homicide in Kent 1560–1985', *Past and Present*, no. 130, pp. 70–106.

Coke, E. (1853) *Coke Upon Littleton*, Philadelphia.

The Compact Oxford English Dictionary (1991) Oxford University Press, Oxford.

Constable, M. (1994) *The Law of the Other*, University of Chicago Press, Chicago.

Cornell, D. (1992) *The Philosophy of the Limit*, Routledge, New York.

Coulson, M. (1976) *Sanskrit: An Introduction to the Classical Language*, Hodder & Stoughton, Oxford.

Cranfield, G.F. (1914) 'Corporate Responsiblity for Crime', *Columbia Law Review*, vol.14, pp. 469–83.

Crawley, E. (1934) *Oath, Curse, and Blessing*, Watts & Co., London.

Criminal Law Commissioners (1843) *Seventh Report*, Government Printer, Melbourne.

Crompton, R. (1587) *L'office et authoritié de Justices de Peace*, Paris.

Dalton, C. (1985) 'An Essay in the Deconstruction of Contract Doctrine', *Yale Law Journal*, vol. 94, pp. 997–1114.

Davey, Dr (1859) 'On the Relations Between Crime and Insanity', *Journal of Mental Science*, vol. 5, pp. 82–94.

Davies, S.J. (1980) 'The Courts and the Scottish Legal System 1600–1747: The Case of Stirlingshire', in V.A.C. Gattrell et al., *Crime and the Law*, Europa, London.

de Certeau, M. (1985) 'What We Do When We Believe', in M. Blonsky (ed.), *On Signs*, Johns Hopkins University Press, Baltimore.

de Certeau, M. (1986) *Heterologies: Discourse on the Other*, Manchester University Press, Manchester.

de Roover, R. (1974) *Business, Banking, and Economic Thought in Late Medieval and Early Modern Europe*, University of Chicago Press, Chicago.

de Tocqueville, A. (1969) *Democracy in America*, ed. J.P. Mayer, trans. G. Lawrence, Modern Library, New York.

Deleuze, G. (1968) *Différence et répétition*, Presses Universitaires de France, Paris.

Deleuze, G. (1990) *The Logic of Sense*, ed. C.V. Boundas, trans. M. Lester with C. Stivale, Columbia University Press, New York.

Deleuze, G. (1991) *Empiricism and Subjectivity*, Columbia University Press, New York.

Department of Transport (1987) *MV Herald of Free Enterprise*, Report of Court No. 8074 Formal Investigation, HMSO, London.

Derrida, J. (1978) *Edmund Husserl's Origin of Geometry: An Introduction*, Nicolas Hays, New York.

Derrida, J. (1981) 'Freud and the Scene of Writing', in *Writing and Difference*, trans. A. Bass, University of Chicago Press, Chicago.

Derrida, J. (1986) 'The Anglish Words of Nicolas Abraham and Maria Torok', in N. Abraham and M. Torok, *The Wolf Man's Magic Word: A Cryptonomy*, University of Minnesota Press, Minneapolis.

Derrida, J. (1989) *Of Spirit: Heidegger and the Question*, trans. G. Bennington and R. Bowlby, University of Chicago Press, Chicago.

Derrida, J. (1990) 'The Force of Law: The "Mystical Foundation of Authority"', trans. E.D. Litowitz, *Cardozo Law Review*, vol. 11, pp. 919–1045.

Donnelly, M. (1983) *Managing the Mind: A Study of Medical Psychology in Early Nine-teenth-Century Britain*, Tavistock, London.

Douzinas, C. and Warrington, R. (1994) *Justice Miscarried*, Harvester/Wheatsheaf, London.

Douzinas, C. et al. (1991) *Postmodern Jurisprudence*, Routledge, London.

du Bois, P. (1991) *Torture and Truth*, Routledge, New York.

Duff, A. (1990) *Intention, Agency and Criminal Liability*, Blackwell, Oxford.

Duhot, J.-J. (1989) *La Conception stoicienne de la causalité*, Librairie Philosophique J. Vrin, Paris.

Dumezil, G. (1988) *Mitra-Varuna: An Essay on Two Indo-European Representations*, trans. D. Coltman, Zone Books, New York.

Dupont, F. (1989) 'The Emperor-God's Other Body', in *Fragments for a History of the Human Body*, part 3, Zone Books, New York.

Durkeim, E. (1965) *The Elementary Forms of the Religious Life*, trans. J.W. Swain, Free Press, New York.

Eco, U. (1984) *Semiotics and the Philosophy of Language*, Indiana University Press, Bloomington.

Eco, U. (1986) 'On Symbols', in J. Deely et al. (eds), *Frontiers in Semiotics*, Indiana University Press, Bloomington.

'Editorial' (1996) *Criminal Law Review*, pp. 73–6.

Edwards, S. (1989) *Policing 'Domestic Violence'*, Sage, London.

Eggleston, R. (1977) *Evidence, Proof and Probability*, Weidenfeld & Nicolson, London.

Ellis, H. (1910) *Criminal*, 4th edn, orig. 1891, London.

Ellis, H. (1939) 'The Individual and the Race', in *Morals, Manners and Men*, London.

Ewald, F. (1985) 'Droit et histoire', in *Droit, nature, histoire: Études sur la pensée de Nichel Villey*, Presses Universitaires d'Aix, Marseilles.

Ewald, F. (1986) 'Pour un positivisme critique: Michel Foucault et la philosophie du droit', *Droits*, vol. 3, pp. 137–42.

Ewald, F. (1988) 'The Law of Law', in G. Teubner (ed.), *Autopoietic Law*, de Gruyter, Berlin.

Farmer, L. (1992) '"The Genius of Our Law": Criminal Law and the Scottish Legal Tradition', *Modern Law Review*, vol. 55, pp. 25–43.

Farmer, L. (1996) 'The Obsession with Definition: The Nature of Crime and Critical Legal Theory', *Social and Legal Studies*, vol. 5, pp. 57–73.

Field, S. and Jorg, N. (1991) 'Corporate Liability and Manslaughter: Should We Go Dutch?', *Criminal Law Review*, pp. 156–71.

Fifoot, C.H.S. (1959) *Judge and Jurist in the Reign of Victoria*, Stevens & Sons, London.

Fisse, B. (1983) 'Reconstructing Corporate Criminal Law: Deterrence, Retribution, Fault and Sanctions', *Southern California Law Review*, vol. 56, pp. 1141–1246.

Fitzpatrick, P. (1987) 'The Rise and Rise of Informalism', in R. Matthews (ed.), *Informal Justice?*, Sage, London.

Fitzpatrick, P. (1991) *Dangerous Supplements: Resistance and Renewal in Jurisprudence*, Pluto Press, London.

Fitzpatrick, P. (1992a) 'The Impossibility of Popular Justice', *Social and Legal Studies*, vol. 1, pp. 199–216.

Fitzpatrick, P. (1992b) *The Mythology of Modern Law*, Routledge, London.

Forbes, W. (1730) *The Institutes of the Law of Scotland*, vol. 2, Mossman, Edinburgh.

Foucault, M. (1977) *Discipline and Punish: The Birth of the Prison*, trans. A. Sheridan, Peregrine, London.

Foucault, M. (1979) *The History of Sexuality*, trans. R. Hurley, vol, 1, Allen Lane, London.

Foucault, M. (1988) 'The Dangerous Individual', trans. A. Sheridan et al., in L. Kritzman (ed.), *Michel Foucault: Politics, Philosophy and Culture*, Routledge, London.

Foucault, M. (1991) 'Governmentality', in G. Burchell et al. (eds), *The Foucault Effect: Studies in Governmentality*, Harvester/Wheatsheaf, Hemel Hempstead.

Frank, J. (1949) *Courts on Trial: Myth and Reality in American Justice*, Princeton University Press, Princeton.

Freud, S. (1940) *Totem and Taboo*, Penguin, Harmondsworth.

Freud, S. (1950) 'Repression', in *Collected Papers*, IV, trans. A. Strachey, Hogarth Press, London.

Freud, S. (1963) 'The Unconscious', in R. Rieff (ed.), *General Psychological Theory*, Collier Books, New York.

Freud, S. (1975) *Inhibition, Symptoms and Anxiety*, trans. A. Strachey et al., standard edn, no. 20, Hogarth Press, London.

Gardner, J. and Jung, H. (1991) 'Making Sense of *Mens Rea*: Antony Duff's Account', *Oxford Journal of Legal Studies*, vol. 11, pp. 559–88.

Garland, D. (1985) *Punishment and Welfare: A History of Penal Strategies*, Dartmouth, Aldershot.

Garland, D. (1990) *Punishment and Modern Society: A Study in Social Theory*, Oxford University Press, Oxford.

Gattrell, V.A.C. (1980) 'The Decline of Theft and Violence in Victorian and Edwardian England', in V.A.C. Gattrell et al., *Crime and the Law*, Europa, London.

Gattrell, V.A.C. (1990) 'Crime, Authority and the Policeman-State', in F.M.L. Thompson (ed.), *The Cambridge Social History of England 1750–1950*, vol. 3, Cambridge University Press, Cambridge.

Gierke, O. (1900) 'The Idea of Organization', in *Political Theories of the Middle Ages*, Cambridge University Press, Cambridge.

Gierke, O. (1958) *Natural Law and the Theory of Society 1500–1800*, Cambridge University Press, Cambridge.

Ginzburg, C. (1986) *Myths, Emblems, Clues*, Radius, London.

Girard, R. (1976) 'Differentiation and Undifferentiation in Lévi-Strauss and Current Critical Theory', *Contemporary Literature*, vol. 17, pp. 404–29.

Girard, R. (1977) *Violence and the Sacred*, trans. P. Gregory, Johns Hopkins University Press, Baltimore.

Goldman, L. (1964) *The Hidden God: A Study of Tragic Vision in the Works of Pascal and the Tragedies of Racine*, trans. P. Thody, St Martin's Press, New York.

Goldman, L. (1973) *The Structure of the Enlightenment*, trans. H. Mass, London.

Goodhart, A.L. (1925) 'Corporate Liability in Tort and the Doctrine of *Ultra Vires*', *Cambridge Law Journal*, vol. 2, pp. 350–64.

Goodrich, P. (1990) *Languages of Law*, Weidenfeld & Nicolson, London.

Goodrich, P. (1994) 'Oedipus Lex: Slips in Interpretation and Law', *Legal Studies*, vol. 13, pp. 381–95.

Gray, K. (1987) *Elements of Land Law*, Butterworths, London.

Green, T.A. (1985) *Verdict According to Conscience: Perspectives on the English Criminal Trial Jury 1200–1800*, University of Chicago Press, Chicago.

Gundersen, A. (1992) 'Popular Justice in Mozambique: Between State Law and Folk Law', *Social and Legal Studies*, vol. 1, pp. 257–82.

Gunn, J. et al. (1978) *Psychiatric Aspects of Imprisonment*, Butterworth-Heinemann, London.

Hachamovitch, Y. (1994) 'In Emulation of the Clouds: An Essay on the Obscure Object of Judgment', in C. Douzinas et al. (eds), *Politics, Postmodernity and Critical Legal Studies*, Routledge, London.

Hager, M. (1989) 'Bodies Politic: The Progressive History of Organizational "Real Entity" Theory', *University of Pittsburgh Law Review*, vol. 50, pp. 575–64.

Haldar, P. (1994) 'Myth Understood', *Law and Critique*, vol. 5, pp. 113–23.

Hale, M. (1736) *Pleas of the Crown*, vol. 1, London.

Hale, M. (1820) *History of Common Law*, London.

Hale, M. (1880) *History of the Pleas of the Crown*, London.

Hamblin Smith, M. (1922) 'The Offender: His Study and His Treatment', *Howard Journal*, vol. 1.

Hanham, H.J. (1965) 'The Creation of the Scottish Office 1881–7', *Juridical Review*, pp. 205–44.

Harding, C. and Wilkin, L. (1988) 'The Dream of a Benevolent Mind: The Late Victorian Response to the Problem of Inebriety', *Criminal Justice History*, vol. 9, pp. 189–207.

Hargreaves, D. (1991) 'Piper Alpha Prosecution Ruled Out', *Financial Times*, 25 July.

Harrison, B. (1971) *Drink and the Victorians: The Temperance Question in England 1815–1872*, Ryburn, London.

Hart, H.L.A. (1954) 'Definition and Theory in Jurisprudence', *Law Quarterly Review*, vol. 70, pp. 37–60.

Hart, H.L.A. (1968) *Punishment and Responsibility*, Clarendon Press, Oxford.

Haynes, S. (1864/5) 'Clinical Cases Illustrative of Insanity', *Journal of Mental Science*, vol. 10, pp. 533–49.

Hegel, G. (1952) *Philosophy of Right*, trans. T.M. Knox, Clarendon Press, Oxford.

Holdsworth, W.S. (1956) *A History of English Law*, vols 1–2, orig. 1909, St Martin's Press, New York.

Holmes, O.W. (1891) 'Agency', *Harvard Law Review*, vols 4 & 5, pp. 343–64; 5.

Honderich, T. (1971) *Punishment: The Supposed Justifications*, Penguin, Harmondsworth.

Horkheimer, M. and Adorno, T.W. (1973) *The Dialectic of Enlightenment*, trans. J. Cumming, Verso, London.

Horowitz, M. (1985) 'Santa Clara Revisited', *West Virginia Law Review*, vol. 88, pp. 173–224.

Horton, J. and Mendus, S. (1994) 'Alasdair MacIntyre: *After Virtue* and After', in J. Horton and S. Mendus (eds), *After MacIntyre*, University of Notre Dame Press, Notre Dame.

Hume, D. (1986) *Commentaries on the Law of Scotland Respecting Crimes*, vol. 2, 4th edn, orig. 1844, Law Society of Scotland, Edinburgh.

Hume, D. (1888) *A Treatise on Human Nature*, Clarendon Press, Oxford.

Ireland, P. et al. (1987) 'The Conceptual Foundations of Modern Company Law', *Journal of Law and Society*, vol. 14, pp. 149–65.

Irvine Smith, J. (1958) 'Criminal Procedure', in *An Introduction to Scottish Legal History*, vol. 20, Stair Society, Edinburgh.

Jabes, E. (1993) *The Book of Margins*, University of Chicago Press, Chicago.

Jackson, B. (1988) *Law, Fact and Narrative Coherence*, Deborah Charles, Liverpool.

Jackson, J.D. (1988) 'Two Methods of Proof in Criminal Procedure', *Modern Law Review*, vol. 51, pp. 549–68.

Jacob, G. (1725) *The Student Companion*.

Johnstone, G. (1988) 'The Psychiatric Approach to Crime', *Economy & Society*, vol. 17, 315–73.

Johnstone, G. (1990) 'Medical Concepts and Penal Policy', unpublished Ph.D. dissertation, University of Edinburgh.

Kantorowicz, E.H. (1957) *The King's Two Bodies*, Princeton University Press, Princeton.

Kaye, J.M. (1967) 'Early History of Murder and Manslaughter', *Law Quarterly Review*, vol. 83, pp. 365–95, 569–601.

Kaye, J.M. (ed. & trans.) (1966) *Placita Corone*, Selden Society, London.

Kelly, I. (1991) 'Corporate Manslaughter and U.K. Common Law: Lessons to be Learned from Our Experience', *Oil and Gas Taxation Review*, p. 148.

Kennedy, H. (1992) *Eve Was Framed*, Chatto & Windus, London.

Kenny, C.S. (1902) *Outlines of Criminal Law*, Cambridge University Press, Cambridge.

Kraakman, R.H. (1984) 'Corporate Liability Strategies and the Cost of Legal Control', *Yale Law Journal*, vol. 93, pp. 857–98.

Kramer, M. (1994), 'False Conclusions from True Premises: Warnings to Legal Theorists', *Oxford Journal of Legal Studies*, vol. 14, pp. 111–20.

Kristeva, J. (1977) 'Heretique de l'amour', *Tel Quel*, vol. 74, pp. 30–49.

Lacan, J. (1966) *Ecrits*, Editions du Seuil, Paris.

Lacan, J. (1968) *The Languages of the Self*, trans. A. Wilden, Johns Hopkins University Press, Baltimore.

Lacan, J. (1986) *Four Fundamental Concepts of Psychoanalysis*, trans. A. Sheridan, Penguin, Harmondsworth.

Lacan, J. (1990) 'Of Structure as an Inmixing of an Otherness Prerequisite to any Subject Whatsoever', trans. J. Mehlman, in E. Roudinesco (ed.), *Lacan & Co.*, University of Chicago Press, Chicago.

Lacey, N. (1993) 'A Clear Concept of Intention: Elusive or Illusory?', *Modern Law Review*, vol. 56, pp. 621–42.

Lacey, N. et al. (1990) *Reconstructing Criminal Law*, Weidenfield & Nicolson, London.

Lacoue-Labarthe, P. (1993) 'The Fable', in T. Trezie (trans. and intro.), *The Subject of Philosophy*, University of Minnesota Press, Minneapolis.

Ladner, G. (1983) 'Roman Attitudes Towards Barbarians', in *Images and Ideas in the Middle Ages*, vol. 2, Edizioni di Storia e Letteratura, Rome.

Lamy, B. (1986) 'The Art of Speaking', in J. Harwood (ed.), *The Rhetorics of Hobbes and Bernard Lamy*, Southern Illinois University Press, Carbondale.

Laplanche, J. (1976) *Life and Death in Psychoanalysis*, trans. J. Mehlman, Johns Hopkins University Press, Baltimore.

Laplanche, J. and Pontalis, J-B. (1986) 'Fantasy and the Origin of Sexuality', in V. Burgin (ed.), *Formations of Fantasy*, Methuen, New York.

Laski, H.J. (1921a) 'The Basis of Vicarious Liability', in *Foundations of Sovereignty*, George Allen & Unwin, London.

Laski, H.J. (1921b) 'The Personality of Associations', in *Foundations of Sovereignty*, George Allen & Unwin, London.

Law Commission (1995) *Consent in the Criminal Law*, Consultation Paper No. 139, HMSO, London.

Laycock, T. (1862) 'The Antagonism of Law and Medicine in Insanity, and its Consequences. An Introductory Lecture', *Journal of Mental Science*, vol. 8, pp. 593–7.

Laycock, T. (1869) 'Suggestions for Rendering Medico-Mental Disease Available to the Better Administration of Justice and the More Effectual Prevention of Lunacy and Crime', *Journal of Mental Science*, vol. 14, p. 334.

Le Goff, J. (1980) 'The Symbolic Ritual of Vassalage', in *Time, Work and Culture in the Middle Ages*, trans. A. Goldhammer, University of Chicago Press, Chicago.

Lea, H.C. (1971) *Superstitions and Force*, MSG House, Berkeley.

Legendre, P. (1982) Paroles poetique échappées du text: leçons sur la communication industrielle, Editions du Seuil, Paris.

Legendre, P. (1988) *Le Désir politique de Dieu*, Fayard, Paris.

Legendre, P. (1989) *Le Crime du Caporal Lortie*, Fayard, Paris.

Legendre, P. (1990) 'The Lost Temporality of Law', *Law and Critique*, vol. 1, pp. 13–25.

Leigh, D. (1961) *The Historical Development of British Psychiatry*, vol. 1, Pergamon, London.

Leigh, L.H. (1969) *The Criminal Liability of Corporations in English Law*, Weidenfield & Nicolson, London.

Leigh, L.H. (1982) *Strict and Vicarious Liability*, Sweet & Maxwell, London.

Lenman, B. (1981) *Integration, Enlightenment and Industrialisation: Scotland 1746–1832*, Edward Arnold, London.

Luard, H. (ed.) (1872–83) *Matthei Parisienis, Monachi Sancti Albani: Chronica Majora*, Longman, London.

MacIntyre, A. (1985) *After Virtue*, Duckworth, London.

MacIntyre, A. (1988) *Whose Justice? Which Rationality?*, University of Notre Dame Press, Notre Dame.

MacIntyre, A. (1990) *Three Rival Versions of Moral Enquiry: Encyclopedia, Genealogy, Tradition*, University of Notre Dame Press, Notre Dame.

MacLeod, R. (1967) 'The Edge of Hope: Social Policy and Chronic Alcoholism 1879–1900', *Journal of the History of Medicine*, July, pp. 214–45.

Maitland, F. (1989) *The Forms of Action at Common Law*, Cambridge University Press, Cambridge.

Maitland, F.W. (ed.) (1903) 'Introduction', in *Year Books of Edward II*, vol. 1, Selden Society, London.

Manchester, A.H. (1980) *A Modern Legal History of England and Wales 1750–1950*, Butterworths, London.

Manetti, A. di T. (1970) *The Life of Brunelleschi*, trans. C. Enggaass, Pennsylvania State University Press, Pennsylvania.

Masters, B. (1993) 'A Night to Dismember: Sex, Lies, and an 8-inch Carving Knife', *Vanity Fair*, November.

Maudsley, H. (1973) *Responsibility in Mental Disease*, orig. 1874, Greenwood Press, London.

Mauss, M. (1967) *The Gift*, trans. I. Cunnison, W.W. Norton, New York.

McBarnet, D. (1981) *Conviction! Law, the State and the Construction of Justice*, Macmillan, London.

McConville, M. (1981) *A History of English Prison Administration*, vol. 1, Routledge, London.

McConville, M. et al. (1991) *The Case for the Prosecution: Police Suspects and the Construction of Criminality*, Routledge, London.

McIntosh, D.A. (1991) *The Myth of Corporate Manslaughter — The Background*, Davies Arnold Cooper (Solicitors), London.

McNamara, L. (1993) 'Cut and Run', *Elle*, November.

McNeill, P.G.B. (1984) 'Discours Particulier D'Escosse 1559–60', in W.D.H. Sellar (ed.), *Miscellany*, vol. 35, Stair Society, Edinburgh.

Menninger, K. (1977) *The Crime of Punishment*, Penguin, Harmondsworth.

Merry, S.E. and Milner, A. (1993) *The Possibility of Popular Justice*, University of Michigan Press, Ann Arbor.

Millon, D. (1990) 'Theories of the Corporation', *Duke Law Journal*, pp. 201–62.

Milsom, S.F.C. (1976) *The Legal Framework of English Feudalism*, Clarendon Press, Oxford.

Milsom, S.F.C. (1981) *Historical Foundations of the Common Law*, 2nd edn, Butterworths, Toronto.

Milsom, S.F.C. (1985a) 'Inheritance by Women', in *Studies in the History of the Common Law*, Hambledon Press, London.

Milsom, S.F.C. (1985b) 'Law and Fact in Legal Development', in *Studies in the History of the Common Law*, Hambledon Press, London.

Milsom, S.F.C. (1985c) 'The Past and Future of Judge-Made Law', in *Studies in the History of the Common Law*, Hambledon Press, London.

Moi, T. (ed.) (1986) *The Kristeva Reader*, Blackwell, Oxford.

Moncrieff, H. (1877) *A Treatise on the Law of Review in Criminal Cases*, W. Green, Edinburgh.

Moore, M.S. (1984) *Law and Psychiatry: Rethinking the Relationship*, Cambridge University Press, Cambridge.

Moran, L.J. (1992) 'Corporate Criminal Capacity: Nostalgia for Representation', *Social and Legal Studies*, vol. 1, pp. 371–91.

Morris, T. (1989) *Crime and Criminal Justice since 1945*, Blackwell, Oxford.

Murphy, T. (1991) 'The Oldest Social Science: The Epistemic Qualities of the Common Law Tradition', *Modern Law Review*, vol. 54, pp. 182–215.

Murphy, T. (1994) 'As If: Camera Juridica', in C. Douzinas et al. (eds), *Politics, Postmodernity and Critical Legal Studies*, Routledge, London.

Nadel, J. (1993) *Sara Thornton: The Story of a Woman Who Killed*, Gollancz, London.

Nietzsche, F. (1909) 'The Genealogy of Morals', in *The Complete Works of Friedrich Nietzsche*, vol. 13, ed. O. Levy, trans. H.B. Samuel, Gordon, London.

Norrie, A. (1989) 'Oblique Intention and Legal Politics', *Criminal Law Review*, pp. 793–807.

Norrie, A. (1991) *Law, Ideology and Punishment*, Dordrecht, Kluwer.

Norrie, A. (1992) 'Subjectivism, Objectivism and the Limits of Criminal Recklessness', *Oxford Journal of Legal Studies*, vol. 12, pp. 45–58.

Norrie, A. (1993) *Crime, Reason and History: A Critical Introduction to Criminal Law*, Weidenfield & Nicolson, London.

Nye, R. (1984) *Crime, Madness and Politics in Modern France*, Princeton University Press, Princeton.

Ong, W. (1958) *Ramus and the Decay of Dialogue*, Harvard University Press, Cambridge, MA.

The Oxford Dictionary of English Etymology (1966) Oxford University Press, Oxford.

Parliamentary Papers (1840) Appendix to 4th Report of H.M. Law Commissioners.

Parliamentary Papers (1872) Report of the Select Committee on Habitual Drunkards.

Parliamentary Papers (1895) Appendix to the Report from the Departmental Committee on Habitual Offenders, Vagrants, Beggars, Inebriates and Juvenile Delinquents.

Parliamentary Papers (1900) Statistics for 1898.

Parliamentary Papers (1908) Report of the Royal Commission on the Care and Control of the Feeble-minded.

Peirce, C.S. (1931–5) 'The Logic of Continuity', in *Collected Papers of Charles Sanders Peirce*, Indiana University Press, Indianopolis.

Pettit, P.H. (1989) *Equity and the Law of Trusts*, Butterworths, London.

Phillipson, N. (1990) *The Scottish Whigs and the Reform of the Court of Session 1785–1850*, Stair Society, Edinburgh.

Plucknett, T.F.T. (1949) *Legislation of Edward I*, Clarendon Press, Oxford.

Plucknett, T.F.T. (1956) *A Concise History of the Common Law*, Little Brown, Boston.

216 Criminal Legal Doctrine

Price, G. (1993) *Byrne and Churchill's Comprehensive French Grammar*, 4th edn, rev. and rewritten, Blackwell, Oxford.

Prichard, J. (1833) *A Treatise on Insanity and Other Disorders Affecting the Mind*, Carey & Hart, Philadelphia.

Prichard, J. (1847) *On the Different Forms of Insanity in Relation to Jurisprudence*, London.

Prins, H. (1986) *Dangerous Behaviour: The Law and Mental Disorder*, Routledge, Chapman & Hall, London.

Radzinowicz, L. (1957) *Sir James Fitzjames Stephen (1829–1894) and his Contribution to the Development of Criminal Law*, Selden Society, London.

Radzinowicz, L. and Hood, R. (1985) *A History of the English Criminal Law and Its Adminis- tration from 1750*, vol. 5, Stevens & Sons, London.

Radzinowicz, L. and Hood, R. (1990) *The Emergence of Penal Policy in Victorian and Ed- wardian England*, Clarendon Press, Oxford.

Ramon, S. (1986) 'The Category of Psychopathy: Its Professional and Social Context in Britain', in P. Miller and N. Rose (eds.), *The Power of Psychiatry*, Polity Press, Cambridge.

Renton, R.W. (1908) 'The Summary Jurisdiction (Scotland) Bill', *Scottish Law Review*, vol. 24, pp. 219–22.

Robertson, C. (1860) 'A Case of Homicidal Mania, Without Disorder of the Intellect', *Journal of Mental Science*, vol. 6, pp. 395–98.

Rose, G. (1984) *Dialectics of Nihilism*, Blackwell, Oxford.

Rose, G. (1994) *The Broken Middle*, Blackwell, Oxford.

Rose, N. (1985) *The Psychological Complex: Psychology, Politics and Society in England 1869–1939*, Routledge & Kegan Paul, London.

Rush, P. (forthcoming) *Trials of Sex*, Routledge, London.

Rush, P. and Young, A. (1994) 'The Law of Victimage in Urbane Realism', in D. Nelken (ed.), *The Futures of Criminology*, Sage, London.

Sachs, A. and Welch, G. (1990) *Liberating the Law*, Zed Books, London.

Sartre, J.-P. (1976) *Critique of Dialectical Reason*, trans. A. Sheridan-Smith, New Left Books, London.

Sayre, F.B. (1930) 'Criminal Responsibility for the Acts of Another', *Harvard Law Review*, vol. 43, pp. 689–723.

Schane, S.A. (1987) 'The Corporation is a Person: The Language of a Legal Fiction', *Tulane Law Review*, vol. 61, pp. 563–609.

Scharf, W. and Ngcokoto, B. (1990) 'Images of Punishment in the People's Courts of Cape Town 1985–1987: From Prefigurative Justice to Populist Violence', in C. Manganyi and A. du Toit (eds), *Political Violence and the Struggle in South Africa*, St Martin's Press, New York.

Scots Magazine (1747).

Sebeok, T. (1986) 'The Doctrine of Signs', in J. Deely et al. (eds), *Frontiers in Semiotics*, Indiana University Press, Bloomington.

Selden Society (ed.) (1963) *Novae Narrationes*, Selden Society, London.

Selden Society (ed.) (1978) *The Reports of John Spelman*, vol. 2, Selden Society, London.

Sellar, W.D. (1989) 'Forethocht Felony, Malice Aforethought and the Classification of Homicide', in W.M. Gordon and T.D. Fergus (eds), *Legal History in the Making*, Hambledon Press, London.

Sereny, G. (1995) *The Case of Mary Bell*, Pimlico, London.

Shapiro, B. J. (1983) *Probability and Certainty in Seventeenth-Century England: A Study of the Relationships between Natural Science, Religion, History, Law, and Literature*, Princeton University Press, Princeton.

Sim, J. (1990) *Medical Power in Prisons*, Open University Press, Milton Keynes.

Simmonds, N.E. (1984) *The Decline of Juridical Reason*, Manchester University Press, Manchester.

Skultans, V. (1975) *Madness and Morals: Ideas on Insanity in the Nineteenth Century*, Routledge & Kegan Paul, London.

Slapper, G. (1992) 'Crime Without Conviction', *New Law Journal*, vol. 142, pp. 192–3.

Smith, D.J. (1995) *The Sleep of Reason*, Century, London.

Smith, J. and Hogan, B. (1990) *Criminal Law: Cases and Materials*, Butterworths, London.

Smith, J. and Hogan, B. (1992) *Criminal Law*, Butterworths, London.

Smith, J.C. (1989) *Justification and Excuse in the Criminal Law*, Butterworths, London.

Smith, K.J.M. (1988) *James Fitzjames Stephen: Portrait of Victorian Rationalist*, Cambridge University Press, Cambridge.

Smith, R. (1981) *Trial By Medicine: Insanity and Responsibility in Victorian Trials*, Edinburgh University Press, Edinburgh.

Smith, R. (1989) 'Mad or Bad? Victorian Studies of the Criminally Insane', *LSE Quarterly*, vol. 3, pp. 1–20.

Snider, L. (1991) 'The Regulatory Dance: Understanding Reform Processes in Corporate Crime', *International Journal of the Sociology of Law*, vol. 19, pp. 209–36.

Sousa Santos, B. (1987) 'Law: A Map of Misreading. Toward a Postmodern Conception of Law', *Journal of Law and Society*, vol. 14, pp. 279–302.

Spens, W.C. (1875) *Jurisdiction and Punishments of Summary Criminal Courts (with special reference to the Lash)*, T & T Clark, Edinburgh.

Spitzer, S. (1982) 'The Dialectics of Formal and Informal Control', in R. Abel (ed.), *The Politics of Informal Justice*, vol. 1, Academic Press, London.

Stafford, B. (1991) *Body Criticisms: Imaging the Unseen in Enlightenment Art and Medicine*, MIT Press, London.

Stafford-Clark, D. (1963) *Psychiatry To-day*, 2nd edn, Penguin, Harmondsworth.

Starkie, T. (1842) *A Practical Treatise on the Law of Evidence*, 3rd edn, V. & R. Stevens & G.S. Norton, London.

Stephen, J.F. (1861) 'The Morality of Advocacy', *Cornhill Magazine*, vol. 3, p. 447.

Stephen, J.F. (1863) *A General View of the Criminal Law of England*, Macmillan, London and Cambridge.

Stephen, J.F. (1864a) 'Bars of France and England', *Cornhill Magazine*, vol. 10, p. 672.

Stephen, J.F. (1864b) 'Capital Punishment', *Fraser's Magazine*, vol. 69, p. 753.

Stephen, J.F. (1872) *The Indian Evidence Act (1. of 1872), with an Introduction on the Principles of Judicial Evidence*, Thacker, Spink & Co., Calcutta.

Stephen, J.F. (1873) *Liberty, Equality, Fraternity*, Macmillan, London.

Stephen, J.F. (1876) *A Digest of the Law of Evidence*, Macmillan, London.

Stephen, J.F. (1877a) *A Digest of the Criminal Law*, Macmillan, London.

Stephen, J.F. (1877b) 'Suggestions as to the Reform of the Criminal Law', *Nineteenth Century*, no. 2, pp. 739–59.

Stephen, J.F. (1882) Letter, *The Times*, 6 July.

Stephen, J.F. (1883) *A History of the Criminal Law of England*, 3 vols, Macmillan, London.

Stephen, J.F.(1884–7) 'Autobiographic Fragment of James Fitzjames Stephen', unpublished.

Stephen, J.F. (1890) *A General View of the Criminal Law of England*, 2nd edn, Macmillan, London.

Stephen, L. (1895) *The Life of Sir James Fitzjames Stephen: A Judge of the High Court of Justice*, 2nd edn, Smith, Elder & Co., London.

Storch, R. (1976) 'The Policeman as Domestic Missionary: Urban Discipline and Popular Culture in Northern England, 1850–80', *Journal of Social History*, vol. 9, pp. 481–509.

Sugarman, D. (1991) 'A Hatred of Disorder: Legal Science, Liberalism and Imperialism', in P. Fitzpatrick (ed.), *Dangerous Supplements: Resistance and Renewal in Jurisprudence*, Pluto Press, London.

Symonds, J. (1864/5) 'Remarks on Criminal Responsibility in Relation to Insanity', *Journal of Mental Science*, vol. 10, pp. 273–5.

Thayer, J.B. (1898) *A Preliminary Treatise on Evidence at Common Law*, Little Brown, Boston.

Theweleit, K. (1987) *Male Fantasies*, vol. 1, Polity Press, Cambridge.

Thomas, D. (ed.) (1972) *State Trials: The Public Conscience*, vol. 2, Routledge & Kegan Paul, London.

Thomas, T. (1972) *Dictionarium Linguae Latinum et Anglicanae*, orig. 1587, Scolar Press, Menston.

Thompson, E.P. (1991) *Customs in Common*, New Press, London.

Thompson, F. (1981) 'Social Control in Victorian Britain', *Economic History Review*, 2nd series, vol. 34, pp. 189–208.

Thomson, J. (1870) 'The Hereditary Nature of Crime', *Journal of Mental Science*, vol. 15, pp. 487–98.

Thomson, J. (1871) 'The Psychology of Criminals', *Journal of Mental Science*, vol. 16, pp. 321–50.

Thornton, S. (1992) 'Why I Killed My Husband', *Woman's Journal*, April, pp. 101–5.

Tierney, B. (1988) *Origins of Papal Infallibility, 1150–1350*, Brill, Leiden.

Trotter, T. (1909) *The Summary Jurisdiction (Scotland) Act 1908*, William Hodge, Edinburgh.

Twining, W. (1985) *Theories of Evidence: Bentham and Wigmore*, Weidenfeld & Nicolson, London.

Ulmer, G.L. (1985) *Applied Grammatology: Post(e)-pedagogy from Jacques Derrida to Joseph Beuys*, Johns Hopkins University Press, Baltimore.

Vaihinger, H. (1924) *The Philosophy of the 'As-If': A System of the Theoretical, Practical and Religious Fictions of Mankind*, trans. C.K. Ogden, Routledge & Kegan Paul, London.

Valery, P. (1964) 'Some Simple Reflections on the Body', in *Aesthetics*, trans. R. Manheim, Bollinger Foundation, New York.

Valverde, M. (1996) 'Social Facticity and the Law: A Social Expert's Eyewitness Account of Law', *Social and Legal Studies*, vol. 5, pp. 201–17.

van de Kerchove, M. and Ost, F. (1994) *Legal System: Between Order and Disorder*, trans. I. Stewart, Oxford University Press, Oxford.

Walker, L. (1979) *The Battered Woman*, Harper & Row, New York.

Walker, L. (1987) *Terrifying Love*, Harper & Row, New York.

Walker, N. (1968) *Crime and Insanity in England*, vol. 1, Edinburgh University Press, Edinburgh.

Walker, N. and McCabe, S. (1973) *Crime and Insanity in England*, vol. 2, Edinburgh University Press, Edinburgh.

Warren, E.H. (1925) 'Torts by Corporations in *Ultra Vires* Undertakings', *Cambridge Law Journal*, vol. 2, pp. 180–91.

Wells, C. (1988) 'The Decline and Rise of English Murder: Corporate Crime and Individual Responsibility,' *Criminal Law Review*, pp. 788–801.

Wells, C. (1989) 'Manslaughter and Corporate Crime', *New Law Journal*, no. 139, pp. 931–4.

Wells, C. (1990) 'Inquests, Inquiries and Indictments: The Official Reception of Death by Disaster', *Legal Studies*, vol. 11, pp. 71–84.

Wells, C. (1993) *Corporations and Criminal Responsibility*, Oxford University Press, Oxford.

Welsh, R.S. (1946) 'The Criminal Liability of Corporations', *Law Quarterly Review*, vol. 62, pp. 345–65.

Whetstone, A. (1981) *Scottish County Government in the Eighteenth and Nineteenth Centuries*, John Donald, Edinburgh.

White, J.B. (1985) *Heracles' Bow*, University of Wisconsin Press, Madison.

Wiener, M. (1990) *Reconstructing the Criminal: Culture, Law and Policy in England, 1830–1914*, Cambridge University Press, Cambridge.

Wigmore, J.H. (1894) 'Responsibility for Tortious Acts: Its History. II', *Harvard Law Review*, vol. 7, pp. 315–37, 383–405, 441–63.

Williams, G. (1955) 'The Definition of Crime', *Current Legal Problems*, vol. 8, pp. 107–30.

Williams, G. (1978) *Textbook of Criminal Law*, Stevens & Sons, London.

Williams, G. (1987) 'Oblique Intention', *Cambridge Law Journal*, vol. 46, pp. 417–38.

Williams, K. (1981) *From Pauperism to Poverty*, Routledge & Kegan Paul, London.

Winn, C.R.N. (1929) 'The Criminal Responsibility of Corporations', *Cambridge Law Journal*, vol. 3, pp. 398–415.

Winter, S.L. (1989) 'Transcendental Nonsense, Metaphoric Reasoning, and the Cognitive Stakes for Law', *University of Pennsylvania Law Review*, vol. 137, pp. 1105–237.

Young, A. (1993a) 'Conjugal Homicide and Legal Violence: A Comparative Analysis', *Osgoode Hall Law Journal*, vol. 31, pp. 761–808.

Young, A. (1993b) 'Femininity on Trial', in A. Sarat and S. Silbey (eds), *Studies in Law, Politics and Society*, vol. 13, JAI Press, Greenwich, CT.

Young, A. (1994) '*Caveat sponsa*: Violence and the Body in Law', in J. Brettle and S. Rice (eds), *Public Bodies, Private States*, Manchester University Press, Manchester.

Young, A. (1996) *Imagining Crime*, Sage, London.

Young, P. (forthcoming) *Punishment, Money and Legal Order*, Edinburgh University Press, Edinburgh.

Zander, M. (1990) 'How Judgment of Risk Sank the Zeebrugge Case', *Independent on Sunday*, 21 October.

Cases and Statutes
United Kingdom

Abolition of Heritable Juridictions Act (1747) 20 Geo. II. c. 43.

Abrath v North Eastern Railway Co. [1886] 11 AC 247.

Anon. (1700) 12 Mod. 559.

Ashford v Thornton (1818) 1 B. & Ald. 405.

Bank Notes Act (1828) 9 Geo. IV c. 23.

Barwick v English Joint Stock Bank (1867) II Exch. 259.

Beverley v Lincoln Gas Light & Coke Co. (1837) 6 AD & E 829.

Burgh Police (S.) Act (1833) 3 & 4 Wm. IV c. 46.

Burgh Police (S.) Act (1892) 55 & 56 Vict. c. 55.

Burgh Police Act (1847) 10 & 11 Vict. c. 39.

Bute v Moore (1870) 1 Coup. 495.

Byrnes v Dick (1853) 1 Irv. 151.
C (a Minor) v DPP [1995] 2 WLR 383.
C v DPP [1994] 3 WLR 888.
The Case of Sutton's Hospital 10 Co. Rep. 23a.
Church v Imperial Gas Light & Coke Co. (1838) 6 AD & E 845.
Circuit Cts (S.) Act (1828) 9 Geo. IV c. 29.
Claim of Right 1689.
Clark & Bendall v Stuart (1886) 1 White 191.
Colliers (S.) Act (1799) 39 Geo. III c. 56.
Company Act (1862) 25 & 26 Vict. c. 89.
Company Act (1863) 26 & 27 Vict. c. 118.
Court of Chancery of Lancaster Act (1850) 13 & 14 Vict c. 43.
Court of Session Act (1830) 11 Geo. IV & 1 Wm. IV c. 69.
Criminal Justice Act (1925) 15 & 16 Geo. V c. 86.
Criminal Law (S.) Act (1830) 11 Geo. IV & 1 Wm. IV c. 37.
Criminal Law Act (1827) 7 & 8 Geo. IV c. 28.
Criminal Procedure (S.) Act (1887) 50 & 51 Vict. c. 35.
Daniel v Camplin (1845) 7 Man. & G. 172.
DPP v Caldwell [1982] AC 341.
DPP v Kent & Sussex Contractors [1944] 1 KB 146.
DPP v Smith [1961] AC 290.
Earl of Arundel's Case (1500) 99 SS 64.
Eastern Counties Railway Co. v Broom (1851) 6 Ex. 314.
Edwards v Midland Railway Co. [1880] 6 QBD 287.
Elliott v C (a minor) [1983] 1 WLR 939.
Exchequer Court Act (1856) 19 & 20 Vict. c. 48.
General Police and Improvement (S.) Act (1862) 25 & 26 Vict. c. 101.
Grand Juries (Suspension) Act (1917) 7 & 8 Geo. V c. 4.
Great Yarmouth Haven & Pier Repairs (duties) (1681) 1 Ja. II c. 16.
Green v London General Omnibus Co. (1859) 7 C.B. (N.S.) 289.
Harman v Tappenden (1801) 1 East 555.
Hawke v E. Hulton & Co. Ltd [1909] 2 KB 93.
Holdsworth v City of Glasgow Bank Liquidator [1880] 5 AC 317.
Homicide Act (1957) 5 & 6 Eliz. II c. 11.
Hyam v DPP [1974] QB 99; [1974] 2 All ER 41.
In Re Ellenborough Park [1956] Ch. 131.
Interpretation Act (1889) 52 & 53 Vict. c. 63.
Interpretation Act 1978.
King's Presentation to Benefice (1390) 13 Rich. II c. 1.
Lamb v Threshie (1892) 3 White 261.
Lennards Carrying Co. Ltd v Asiatic Petroleum Co. Ltd [1915] AC 705.
Lincs. Rolls, 1381–1396.
Magistrates Courts Act 1980.
Maund v Monmouthshire Canal Co. (1842) 4 Man. & G. 453.
McPherson v Boyd (1907) 5 Adam 247.
Mental Deficiency Act (1913) 2 & 3 Geo. V c. 28.
Murray v East India Co. (1821) 5 B. Ald. 204.
P&O Ferries (Dover) Ltd. (1991) 93 Cr App R 72.

Parliamentary Papers (1826–7) Act of Adjournal of the High Court 1827, XIX, 689.

Paton v Neilson (1903) (J.) 5 F. 107.

Perkes, Gunson & Tee Ltd v Ward [1902] 2 KB 1.

Pharmaceutical Society v London & Provincial Supply Assn Ltd [1880] 5 QB 310; (1880) 5 AC 857.

Pharmaceutical Society v London & Provincial Supply Assn Ltd [1897] 4 QB 313.

Pharmacy Act (1868) 31 & 32 Vict. c. 121.

Police (S.) Act (1850) 13 & 14 Vict. c. 33.

R v Ahlers [1915] 1 KB 616.

R v Ahluwalia [1992] 4 All ER 889.

R v Birmingham & Gloucester Railway [1842] 3 QB 222.

R v Camplin [1987] 2 All ER 168.

R v Cory Brothers & Co. Ltd [1927] 1 KB 810.

R v Daily Mirror Ltd [1922] 2 KB 530.

R v Donachie (1982) 4 Cr App R (Sentencing) 378.

R v Duffy [1949] 1 All ER 932.

R v Great North of England Railway Co. (1846) 9 QB 316.

R v H.M. Coroner for East Kent, ex parte Spooner and Others, R v H.M. Coroner for East Kent, ex parte De Rohan and another (1989) 88 Cr App R 10.

R v Hancock & Shankland [1986] 1 All ER 641; [1986] AC 455; [1986] 2 WLR 357.

R v Ibrams (1981) 74 Cr App R 154.

R v The Mayor, Alderman and Burgess of the Borough of Stratford-upon-Avon (1811) 14 East 348.

R v The Mayor etc of Liverpool (1802) 3 East 86.

R v Mawgridge (1707) Kelyng 119.

R v Medley (1834) 6 Car. & P. 292.

R v Moloney [1985] AC 905; [1985] 1 All ER 1025.

R v Nedrick [1986] 1 WLR 1025.

R v Newell (1980) 71 Cr App R 331.

R v Steane [1947] KB 997.

R v Thornton [1992] 1 All ER 306.

R v Thornton (No. 2) [1996] 2 All ER 1023.

R v Whitfield (1976) 63 Cr App R 39.

Regulating the Qualifications of Pharmaceutical Chemists Act (1852) 15 & 16 Vict. c.56.

Scott v Scott [1913] AC 417.

Sheriffs Courts (S.) Act (1825) 6 Geo. IV c. 23.

Sheriffs Courts (S.) Act (1838) 1 & 2 Vict. c. 119.

Smith v Birmingham & Staffordshire Gas Light Co. (1834) 1 AD & E 527.

Stamp Act (1815) 55 Geo. III c. 184.

Stevens v Midland Railway Co. & Lander (1854) 10 Ex. 352.

Summary Jurisdiction Act (1879) 42 & 43 Vict. c. 49.

Summary Jurisdiction (S.) Act (1881) 44 & 45 Vict. c. 33.

Summary Jurisdiction (S.) Act (1908) 8 Edw. VII c. 65.

Summary Procedure (S.) Act (1864) 27 & 28 Vict. c. 53.

Summary Prosecutions Appeals (S.) Act (1875) 38 & 39 Vict. c. 62.

Tesco Supermarkets Ltd v Nattrass [1972] AC 153.

Thabo Meli & Ors v R [1954] 1 All ER 373.

Tilson v Town of Warwick Gas Light Co. (1825) 4 B. & C. 962.

Whitfield v South Eastern Railway Co. (1858) EL BL and EL 115.
Yarborough v Bank of England (1812) 16 East 6.

Other Jurisidictions
<u>**Australia**</u>
Runjanjic and Kontinnen (1991) 53 A Crim R 362.

<u>**Canada**</u>
R v Lavallee (1990) 55 CCC (3d).

<u>**New Zealand**</u>
R v McGregor [1962] NZLR 1069.

<u>**United States**</u>
McKay v Gratz 260 US 127 (1922).

Newspapers
Blom-Cooper, L. (1990) 'Corporate Persons and the Law', *Financial Times*, 20 October.
'Cleared but Insane — Wife with the Knife', *The Guardian*, 22 January 1994.
The Gazette, 31 March 1992.
The Guardian, 12 March 1993.
The Guardian, 25 November 1993.
The Guardian, 23 March 1994.
The Guardian, 17 December 1994.
The Independent, 10 September 1991.
Miami Herald, 11–14 September 1994.
The Observer, 28 November 1993.
'Woman Who Knifed to Death Jeering Husband Released', *The Guardian*, 28 November 1992.
'Your Penis or Your Life', *The Guardian*, 21 January 1994.

Other Sources
'Murder They Said' (1991) The Heart of the Matter programme, BBC1, broadcast 3 November.
'Women Who Kill' (1994) Network First programme, broadcast 11 January.